METEOR EJECT!

First edition, published in 2000 by

WOODFIELD PUBLISHING
Woodfield House, Babsham Lane, Bognor Regis
West Sussex PO21 5EL, England.

ISBN 1-873203-65-9

Meteor
EJECT!

Nick Carter

Woodfield Publishing
BOGNOR REGIS · WEST SUSSEX · ENGLAND

Author returning to RAF Strubby after intercepting a 'target' over the North Sea during Exercise Dividend.

Contents

A 257 Squadron Gloster Meteor F8 on the pan at RAF Wattisham, 1953.

Photo courtesy of R. Smith.

Acknowledgements

I doubt if I would have persevered with the book had it not been for the help and encouragement given to me by Bill Gunston. I am also indebted to Wing Commander Beamont, CBE, DSO, DFC, FRAeS for allowing me to quote from his book *Testing Early Jets* in which he so accurately describes the problems we experienced when flying the Gloster Meteor in its Day Fighter role.

To the archives department at the RAF Museum and the Public Records Office. To John Robertson for checking my list of Meteor crashes against his own records.

Also my thanks to Air Commodore 'Mac' McEwen, AFC, FIMgt, for letting me quote verbatim from his historical record of No.257 (Burma) Squadron which he and Allan Keys produced when we were on our first tour with the Squadron in 1954.

My son Lance, and my daughter Nicky, for proof reading the early chapters but above all my appreciation to my wife Gladys who spent many lonely hours while I beavered away on my Amstrad PC, recalling events which happened fifty years ago.

*This book is dedicated to the
434 RAF pilots and 10 navigators
who lost their lives flying the Gloster Meteor*

Introduction

Many books have been written depicting the exploits of pilots in the Second World War, but very little is known about the chaps who took over from them – flying the new jet fighters at the height of the Cold War in the early 1950s.

Although I had a close connection with flying and the aviation industry after leaving school, it never entered my head that one day I might finish up actually flying these aircraft. This opportunity literally came out of the blue and I grabbed it with both hands. Although commissioned I had no desire to be a career officer, just simply to enjoy my flying - and the social life that went with it!

I happened to be one of hundreds of pilots who were trained during the rapid expansion of the Royal Air Force at the time the Korean War. Most of us went into Fighter Command – we all wanted to be jet fighter pilots. Despite its shortcomings, we loved the 'Meatbox' – the thought that we might have to go to war in it did not enter our heads!

The book is heavily dependant on personal memories, of events which occurred nearly half a century ago. Others may remember them differently but every effort has been made to substantiate contentious issues from other sources.

As a young man I was not aware how fortunate I was. It was not until many years later that I realised that of all the mistakes I made in my life, leaving the Royal Air Force was the biggest!

LESLIE L. IRVIN
F.R.AE.S., F.R.S.A.
HONORARY SEC.
EUROPEAN BRANCH

c/o IRVING AIR CHUTE
OF GREAT BRITAIN LTD.
ICKNIELD WAY
LETCHWORTH, HERTS
ENGLAND

CATERPILLAR CLUB

30th June, 1955.

F/O J. G. Carter,
17, Courthouse Road,
MAIDENHEAD,
Berks.

Dear F/O Carter,

I have received a letter from your
Commanding Officer, Major H. N. Tanner,
confirming and giving details of your forced
Parachute descent on the 21st December, 1954.

It is indeed a pleasure to welcome
you as a Member of the Caterpillar Club, and
the official insignia is being made and
engraved for you; this, together with your
Membership Card will be forwarded as soon
as possible, but I regret to state that
delivery takes anything from two to three
months.

Major Tanner's details did not
include the destination of your descent,
and it will be appreciated if you will kindly
forward this information at your convenience
in order to complete our records.

Yours sincerely,

Sec. to L. Irvin.

HMA.

CHAPTER 1

Eject!

Tuesday 21st December 1954 was a cold, bright, clear day. I was a pilot with No.257 (Burma) Squadron, a crack RAF Battle of Britain Squadron that at one time had been commanded by the legendary Sqn Ldr Bob Stanford-Tuck, one of the RAF's top-scoring fighter ace's of the second world war.

It was the first sortie of the day, and I was to fly my Meteor jet as No.2 in a four-ship formation on a training flight over East Anglia. Little did I know that my Christmas was about to change in quite a dramatic fashion. We were 'Bendix Blue', and we had been authorised to practice battle formation at 35,000 ft, followed by a cine' tail chase, and finally low flying in the 'Uxbridge One' low-flying area.

Leading the formation was Flt Lt 'Cherry' Kearton, who said during the briefing that the tail chase would be gentle to start with but would progressively become more difficult. How right he was, but not quite in the way he meant! Kearton was the 'A' Flight Commander, a recent graduate from the Day Fighter Leaders School (DFLS), a unit at the Central Fighter Establishment (CFE) at RAF West Raynham. They were considered to be a 'Top Gun' outfit with a reputation for operating to limits somewhat beyond what was expected on the front-line squadrons. So much so that in later years they had the unique distinction of crashing four Hunters over the Norfolk countryside after the formation ran out of fuel!

I signed the Form 700, did a quick external pre- flight inspection and clambered into the cockpit of WH299. First, I strapped on the parachute harness, making sure that the release wheel was in the locked position, and then fastened the seat harness. One of the ground crew plugged in my headset and finally, after checking all was OK, he removed the safety pin from the ejection seat. After start up we checked in with the leader, and the formation was then cleared to taxi to runway 23. Take-off checks were completed, we turned onto the runway, air traffic cleared us for take-off, and away we went.

As we both hurtled along the runway at RAF Wattisham with wing tips less than 5 ft apart my eyes were glued on the leader. When his nose wheel lifted off the runway, I gently eased back on the stick to follow him. Just as he got airborne, he went into a steep climbing turn to port as he raised his undercarriage. I followed, hanging on to his wing tip and copying his every move. The pair behind, staying low, cut the corner in the turn and formed up with us in a left-hand finger four formation.

Eventually we levelled off at 35,000 ft, and after practising battle formation for some twenty minutes, I heard the leader call, "Bendix Blue, long line astern go". Flying at No.3 was F/O Phil Philip, and F/O Phil Pickford was in the No.4 slot. Responding to the command, I slotted my jet into position some 300 yards behind and slightly below the lead aircraft. The two Phils moved into position behind me, and the tail chase began.

The leader started with a turn to the right followed by a fast barrel roll and then a wing over. I then followed him into a fast descending turn, whilst at the same time using my gun sight to range and track on his aircraft as part of our cine' exercise. Whilst pulling back on the control column to hold my position the aircraft suddenly flicked inverted and started a high- speed spiral dive earthwards.

I took normal recovery action by extending the airbrakes and closing the throttles, as well as trying to ease the aircraft out of the dive, but there was no response to any of these actions. It seemed as if the jet was spinning, but spin recovery was also ineffective. Clearly, I had a problem - the Meteor had become eight tons of useless metal, hell bent on self-destruction.

Glancing at my flight instruments, I saw that I had already lost 15,000 ft with the altimeter still unwinding fast. The indicated airspeed was over 400 knots and the whole cockpit was rattling and banging with the effect of compressibility on the airframe.

The controls were now locked solid, and, conscious of the ground getting closer with every second, I thought perhaps it was time to 'bang out' - I had less than a minute.

With my left hand, I pulled the yellow and black handle to jettison the hood. As it departed, my head was suddenly subjected to severe buffeting from the slipstream, coupled with a deafening noise. Remembering my ejection drill, I took both feet off the rudder pedals and placed them firmly into the foot-rests. I then put both hands over my 'bone-dome' to pull the blind and fire the seat. To my horror I could not reach it - I was clutching thin air.

I tried again by pushing my right hand over my head with my left hand, but the slip stream caught my hand and smashed my wrist against the back of the seat. I was aware that this hand was now useless and resting in my lap but I did not know the reason.

By now the ground was getting closer as the stricken aircraft spiralled headlong towards the USAF airfield at Bentwaters. It was no comfort seeing their runway getting closer and closer by the second. Yet again, I tried to grasp the blind without success. I thought 'Well this is it - what's my Mum going to say', as I calmly resigned myself to the inevitable!

Making one last desperate attempt with my 'good' hand, I clawed my fingers over my oxygen mask, over my sun visor and over my 'bone-dome' and suddenly I touched the elusive firing handle. I closed my hand quickly around it; did I have enough height left to make it? The ground appeared to be only inches beyond the nose of the aircraft. With a desperate heave, I pulled the handle one-handed and hoped for the best. With a loud double bang the seat shot out of the stricken aircraft and I blacked out. My survival was now completely dependant on ejection-seat technology, and the need for having sufficient height for it to work.

Once clear of the aircraft, another explosive device attached to the seat deployed a small 2 ft drogue parachute. The purpose of this was to quickly reduce the forward speed of the seat, and to stabilize it in an upright position ready for separation. A time-delayed barometric unit then released my harness and the seat and I parted company. As I fell away, the drogue automatically deployed my main parachute.

Seconds later I came round with a jolt as the parachute opened, I then discovered that I wasn't waiting at the pearly gates but gently floating earthwards - I had made it, I was alive! Almost immediately, this enormous sense of relief changed to one of despair. I appeared to be about 500ft above a forest. Even worse, I could see blood streaming down my right leg and my right flying boot was missing. I then saw that my right hand was almost severed just above the wrist. Whilst pondering this turn of events, and thinking what bad luck it would be to lose my hand in the top of a tree, I hit the ground with a thump.

Unfortunately, RAF aircrew, unlike the Red Devils and others, don't have the luxury of big parachutes. Ours were smaller, only 24 ft in diameter, so you came down faster, at 21 ft per second, and consequently you hit the ground harder. My descent was no different, but after getting over the initial shock of hitting the ground, I found I had missed the trees and was lying flat on my back in a clearing – being admired by a group of farmers.

It was a relief to find my hand still attached, albeit only by the slenderest piece of flesh. I really didn't feel much pain, at least not until one of my admirers attempted to put the parachute under my arm - rather ungratefully I told him to bugger off.

It was impossible for the Americans not to notice that my Meteor had crashed - it was a smouldering heap in a copse only 900 feet from their main runway, and adjacent to their ammunition store! They contacted my squadron with the news that I had 'bought it'. This report was quickly changed after one of their chaps told the tower he had seen me eject shortly before impact. My landing was close to the village of Butley, 8 miles east of Woodbridge in Suffolk. The farm workers had raised the alarm, and according to a report in the local paper, a Dr Ander came out from his surgery at Orford to attend to my injuries and to give me a morphine jab.

Eventually I was picked up by the Americans and taken by ambulance back to their base at Bentwaters. On arrival, I was placed on the floor in sick quarters as they attempted to set up a drip. A smile quickly came to my face when a rather dishy nurse with a film-star body inadvertently gave me a flash of stocking tops and black lace panties, whilst attending to my more pressing needs, far better than anything seen at the Windmill Theatre! All of a sudden, my luck seemed to be changing.

Next was a Hollywood-style ride by ambulance to the Borough General Hospital in Ipswich with sirens blaring, unheard of in those days. On arrival I was rushed through to casualty by my cigar-chewing 'posse.' The sister in charge was not impressed by this invasion, "Jet pilot or no jet pilot, I refuse to treat this young man until you all leave" she bellowed.

A preliminary examination by Mr Bell-Jones, the consultant orthopaedic surgeon, confirmed that the damage to my arm was serious, both bones were shattered just above the wrist and my hand was all but lost. He was also concerned that extensive bruising along my back might indicate some spinal damage. An Australian and a big man with a commanding presence, he was highly experienced in the field of orthopaedic surgery despite having only four fingers on his right hand. He was well known for having treated a large number of aircrew after they crash-landed on the emergency runway at RAF Woodbridge during the war.

Saving my hand was uppermost in his mind. An operation would be a long ordeal, I was in a state of shock, and I had lost a considerable amount of blood. He had two options. He could amputate my hand, which would take all of five minutes, or he could try and save it, but at some risk. By now I was unconscious, so my mother was contacted by telephone. She told him to do whatever was necessary to try and save it.

The next morning I woke to find myself in the tender care of Sister Joslyn, the sister in charge of the ward. I was in the first bed inside the door next to her office, always a sure sign that the patient is either of some importance, or about to die. I hoped it was not the latter! Later that morning the house doctor came to see me and in the course of our chat, he casually mentioned that I no longer had a little toe on my right foot. "Why did you take it off" I enquired. "Sorry old chap, it wasn't on when you came in" he replied with a grin.

Eventually the hospital confirmed the extent of my injuries; compound fractures of the radius and ulna in my right arm, broken fingers on my right hand, a double fracture of the tibia bone in my right leg, traumatic amputation of my fifth right toe with considerable loss of skin, and a fractured right ankle. Thankfully, there was no damage to my spine, despite the multiple bruising. As I lay in hospital I had time to reflect on my predicament, how on earth had I managed to get myself so close to death and, more importantly, would I now ever fly again?

'PLANE CRASHES AT BENTWATERS

R.A.F. Pilot Saved by Ejector Seat

The pilot of a Meteor jet aircraft used his ejector seat to bale out just before the 'plane crashed into a wood near Bentwaters U.S.A.F. station. yesterday morning and burst into flames. He sustained a broken arm, fractured wrist, crushed foot and other injuries.

Wreckage was scattered over a quarter-mile area of the wood, and the crash occurred only 300 yards south of the main Bentwaters runway.

Air crash firemen from the aerodrome with several fire engines rushed to the scene and the blaze was soon under control.

The pilot. Flying-Officer J. G. Carter, of Maidenhead, stationed at Wattisham. landed at Butley, over two miles away, and was attended immediately by Dr. G. R. Ander. of Orford.

ON TRAINING FLIGHT

He was then taken by a U.S.A.F. ambulance to Bentwaters, and after treatment, to Wattisham base hospital. While at Bentwaters his condition was stated to be "fairly comfortable."

F.-O. Carter was on a training flight from Wattisham and it is understood that his injuries were sustained on landing.

P.-c Randle. of Orford. who visited the scene of the crash, told our reporter that the aircraft had apparently "crashed into the wood, disintegrated, and burst into flames."

CHAPTER 2

Early Years

The crash of a Lockheed Hudson close to Maidenhead Bridge was set to change the course of my life. I had left Gordon County Secondary School in Maidenhead, in 1944 without achieving much in the way of an education. Not the fault of the school which had a good record pre-1940, but because we had to share our school premises with some kids from London who had been evacuated to Maidenhead. Consequently, we only attended class for half a day, alternating between mornings and afternoons.

As youngsters, we thought this was great for developing football skills and periodically getting into mischief collecting shrapnel, tormenting the Italian prisoners of war billeted in the town and playing war games in the black-out.

On one occasion a group of us had boarded a bus in the bus terminal to go to school for the afternoon 'shift'. For a bit of fun we had taken a long branch from a tree with us onto the top deck. As the bus made its way through the town we had the branch suspended out of the window and were hooking old ladies' hats off as they disembarked! We then made two fatal mistakes. First, getting caught by taking the branch back down the stairs when we got off and second, when the conductor asked us which school we came from telling him 'St Lukes', which was a bit dumb because the bus was stopped right outside our school and St Lukes was miles away. That same afternoon we were summoned before Mr Adderson, the Headmaster, to explain our behaviour. We pleaded guilty and he said that he would let us off with a caution. We thought we had got away with it, but in the same breath he continued,

"But I expect all of my pupils to be proud of their school - you obviously are not, otherwise you would not have lied that you went to St Lukes. Two strokes on each hand"! It was an early piece of character building that I was to benefit from in later years. After leaving school I was sent by the local labour exchange to work in Hewens Garages, who had a contract to repair military vehicles in addition to their normal work. I didn't like it and didn't want to be a motor mechanic, but under the wartime regulations I had little or no choice. Even school leavers had to do their bit for the war effort.

We were a family of three, my mother, brother and myself, my father having died from a heart attack when I was only a year old. Our holidays were mostly taken in South Wales where we had uncles, aunts and grandparents. Uncle Norman was a bus conductor but, with money earned playing a trumpet in a dance band, he took flying lessons at a flying club on Pengam Moors airfield close to his home in Cardiff. Sadly, a few years later whilst serving as an airman he was run over and killed by an RAF vehicle whilst stationed at Pembroke Dock. During the war my mother was a housekeeper to a number of households, and as a result we moved around a bit, but always within close proximity to Maidenhead. Our only holiday during that period was to stay with friends in Brighton, but on arrival we appeared to be among thousands of troops and equipment. We had arrived during the build up to the D-Day landings at Normandy, and the whole of the south coast had become a restricted area. It was only after my mother had convinced the local army commander that we were not a security risk that we were allowed to leave. I had joined No.155 (Maidenhead) Squadron of the Air Training Corps (ATC) a year earlier by putting up my age by three months. Like most boys I was thrilled by the thought of flying, but until then the nearest I had been to an aircraft was when one happened to crash in the vicinity of White Waltham airfield. We then descended in hordes to pinch bits and pieces before the Home Guard or the police got there. Later I was fortunate enough to be taught gliding at the ATC gliding school which operated from what was for a while in the 1930s the Maidenhead Aerodrome. We only did short hops solo, a tow up to about 300 ft and then land straight ahead, but it was good fun. I also learned to drive, towing the gliders back to the take-off point in a Land-Rover. The school was available to all ATC squadrons within the local area, including some from well-known local public schools such as Eton and Wellington College, some of whom were known to pick up the bill after we had all consumed egg and chips in the cafe across the road.   The Air Transport Auxiliary (ATA) had its headquarters at White Waltham, and throughout the war we saw a steady stream of aircraft, all shapes and sizes, being ferried in and out of this large grass airfield. They also had a flying training school for converting pilots on to medium-size twins, using Hudson and Albemarle aircraft. Rather unusually, this school employed ATC cadets to fly as pilots' assistants, mainly to operate the flaps and undercarriage for student pilots when they were flying solo in the circuit.

With the agreement of the RAF, the cadets were allowed to wear their ATC uniforms at work. The down side of the job was that they also had other duties, such as post room runners and sometimes as couriers taking urgent documents and parcels to other ATA airfields. When not required by the school or the post room, they could bid to go on ferry trips if spare seats were available.

Needless to say, these chaps were the envy of all other ATC cadets in the area. Very few vacancies ever came up but when they did they were quickly filled, usually by word of mouth. There was never any need to advertise.

I had been sweating away in the garage for nearly a year when the Hudson crashed behind the Dumb Bell Hotel on the A4 near Maidenhead Bridge. Within hours the whole town knew that the lady pilot and an ATC cadet had been killed. I was sorry that Cadet Regan had lost his life but, sensing this great opportunity, I cycled over to the airfield the next morning, presented myself before Flying Officer 'Hutch' Hutchinson RAFVR, Officer I/C Cadets, and applied for the vacancy. I got the job and started the following Monday. My first trip was 30 minutes in an Avro Anson which flew up to Heathrow, did two circuits round the new airport which was under construction and back. Within three weeks of starting, I had been checked out by Captain Imes on a Hudson, and I became operational! It was March 1945 and I had just passed my 15th birthday.

Although the ATA was disbanded eight months later, I accumulated nearly 100 hrs flying time, mostly on Hudsons, Albemarles and Ansons. But the main attraction for us was getting a place on a ferry flight.

Ferry pilots were taken to a pick up point by a taxi aircraft, either an Anson or a Fairchild Argus. They would then deliver an aircraft to its destination before being picked up by the same Anson or Argus, and brought back to White Waltham.

To get on a ferry flight you first had to check to see if there was a spare seat in the taxi aircraft, both out and back. If there was, you then asked the pilot scheduled for the ferry flight if he or she would take you along. If the answer was yes, and after getting clearance from the duty operations officer, off you went!

In quick succession I flew in a Mosquito B.25 (KA951) from Henlow to Middle Wallop, another Mosquito NF.36 (RL157) from Leavesden to Hullavington and a dual Mosquito T3 (RR316) from Leavesden to Harwell flown by Third Officer Mackenzie who gave me 20 minutes dual instruction. A Wellington B.X (HF729) from White Waltham to Little Rissington where it was placed alongside thousands of others awaiting disposal. A Halifax VII (PP362) from Radlett to High Ercall - and then seeing it broken up on arrival! Other cadets said that some pilots swapped seats with them whilst flying in aircraft without dual controls, in order for them to have a go, but I never flew with anyone silly enough to do the same for me!

At the other end of the scale I flew with First Officer Greenside delivering a brand new Tiger Moth II from the Morris factory at Cowley, Oxford, to a storage unit at Whitchurch, south of Bristol. Its serial number was EM774 - I wonder if it is still flying?

Trips in Ansons were easy to come by, as long as you had a good left arm to wind the undercarriage up and down, sometimes as many as four or five times on short sector trips. On a few occasions I flew with women pilots, one being a trip in a Hudson doing twin conversion training with Joy Ferguson at Aldermaston. We stopped the aircraft and went across the road picking strawberries before returning to White Waltham. Also a trip in a Martinet from Woodley to Colerne with Captain Rosemary Rees. For some reason the taxi aircraft failed to pick us up, forcing us to return from Bath by train complete with parachutes, an unusual sight on the railways even in wartime.

In May there were celebrations in the town as the war in Europe came to an end, and in August the strange new atomic bombs were dropped on Japan. I had taken some holiday entitlement and was at an ATC summer camp at RAF Shillingford near Faringdon when news came through that the Japanese had surrendered. We got a lift back to Maidenhead to join in the celebrations anticipating hitchhiking back to camp afterwards. Sadly, lifts were not so easy after midnight and, after walking a fair amount of the way, we only just managed to get back in time for the early morning parade.

Many of the airfields which I flew into with the ATA have long since disappeared, or are no longer operational; Aston Down, Henlow, Langley, Heston, Hanworth, Culham, Harwell, Whitchurch, Woodley, Cowley, Radlett, Hatfield, Hullavington, Leavesden, Hawarden, Shrewsbury, Wisley, Portsmouth, Little Rissington, Litchfield, Henstridge and Cosford are some that feature in my log book. Sadly it all came to an end when the ATA was disbanded in November 1945. For a final fling they organised what was probably the first air display to be held in the UK since before the war. We sold display programmes to the public for 6d each, and at the same time I remember we made a few bob from people offering us a shilling and telling us to keep the change.

The ground display included a Spitfire, Firefly, Mosquito, Barracuda, Tempest, Wellington, Stirling, Warwick, Halifax and Lancaster. Also on display were a FW190, Messerschmitt 110 and a Feiseler Storch, but the enemy aircraft which were of most interest were the jet engined Heinkel 162 and the rocket propelled Messerschmitt 163. There was one particular item in the display which I have never forgotten, neither should I imagine have the thousands of spectators who were present on the day. An RAF pilot in a Mosquito did a fast beat-up at no more than 50 ft, as the aircraft crossed the perimeter fence he feathered both propellers and flew the whole length of the airfield with both engines stopped! As he crossed the far end - and rapidly running out of airspeed - he pointed the Mossy skywards, unfeathered both, and climbed away!

But now I had the problem of what to do next. My mother had long felt that I should stop mucking about and get myself a proper job. At the time she was working for Sir Richard Fairey's secretary, who happened to mentioned my name to her boss with a view to me joining the Fairy Aviation Technical School at Heston. He was sympathetic but rightly thought that Heston might perhaps be a long way to travel each day, so he arranged for me to have an interview with R Malcolm Ltd at White Waltham (later ML Aviation Ltd) who were carrying out aeronautical research and development projects for the Ministry of Supply.

They accepted me as an apprentice draughtsman, not quite as exciting as flying with the ATA, but nevertheless an interesting and secure job with prospects. They had their own technical training school and it was anticipated that, after spending 5 years in all the different departments I would finish in the drawing office with a Higher National Certificate (HNC) in Mechanical Engineering.

The company was situated in a large purpose built hanger on the Southern side of White Waltham airfield. There was strict security, and all staff were subject to the Official Secrets Act. After landing, aircraft would taxi up to the factory and then disappear behind big heavy gates which opened and closed along a railway track.

The Chief Designer was Marcel Lobelle, an extrovert Belgian who had previously been with the Fairey Aviation Company and who had designed the Fairey Swordfish. Eric Mobbs, whose family owned the Slough Trading Estate, was the Managing Director. The White Waltham plant was purely research and development, all production being undertaken by a sister company, ML Engineering Ltd, on the Slough Estate. When I joined, work had already started on the development of aircraft ejector seats, the prototype having been installed in the gunner's position of a Boulton Paul Defiant ready for flight tests. But trials with the Defiant were later to be abandoned after the Ministry of Supply decided it would be better to use a Meteor F.3 jet. One of my first jobs was to remove its forward fuel tank, together with the ammunition bay to make room for the installation of the ejector seat, behind the cockpit. There were also four Spitfires in the hanger being converted into pilotless drones. This was one of the many contracts cancelled at the end of the war and they subsequently disappeared on an RAF Queen Mary, a 60 ft low loader used for transporting aircraft by road.

ML were also working on an autopilot to be installed in a Horsa glider. Input into the autopilot being achieved by extending an arm 10 ft beyond the nose of the glider which then rested on the top of the tow rope. As the tug turned, climbed or descended the Horsa would follow - hopefully.

There was work on a Target Towing Winch which was shaped like a long drop tank with a short stubby prop on the front providing power to play out or draw in a drogue target. Quite a neat job which could be slung on a wing pylon. It went into production but was used mainly by the Fleet Air Arm, the RAF preferring to snatch their larger banner targets off the runway using a variety of aircraft including Mosquitos and later Meteors. Even a design for a complete aircraft to replace the Varsity was worked on at one stage.

Probably the most successful project to come out of ML at that time was the Retractable Gyro Gun Sight (GGS) Mounting. This installation enabled the gun sight to be retracted down behind the instrument panel when not needed, thereby not only improving the pilot's forward vision but ensuring that his knee caps remained intact should he need to eject! It went into production and was subsequently installed in nearly all fighter aircraft of the period.

Shortly after I arrived ML became involved in attempts to snatch gliders off the ground with a hook trailing below a Dakota. It is unlikely the troops on board the glider would be amused, and fortunately for them nothing came of it! However later trials did include snatching stores and even personnel off the ground from a standing start!

The number of apprentices at ML Aviation probably didn't exceed ten at any given time so we received training virtually on a one-to-one basis. Studies up to Ordinary National Certificate (ONC) standard were completed at the company's own technical school, with practical training being carried out in the workshops at White Waltham. Before moving on to the next department we were required to pass a practical examination, and it was customary for the MD, Mr Eric Mobbs, to add comments. For Lathe Work I received a mark of 83% and 'Quite good', for 'Tool Grinding' 82% and Fairly Good!', for 'Fitting & Erecting in the Hanger' 82% and 'Fairly good', for 'Milling' 79% and a comment from the examiner, 'Carter stated he left his answers to questions 34 and 35 at home,' to which Mr Mobbs noted 'very foolish of him! 'Finally for 'Joining of Metals' (Welding) 81% with the examiner stating that "Carter has done quite well, but needs more instruction in economy of time and materials – he goes on feeding costly solder into a joint after it is properly filled."

I had by now passed my ONC exams and much to my surprise gained a distinction in engineering drawing. For the final two years to the Higher National Certificate (HNC) I attended Southall Technical College on day release whilst working full time in the drawing office. What was unusual about ML apprentices was that none were ever called up for National Service! It was normal for students to be deferred from military service up until their 21st birthday in order that they could complete their studies, but even after qualifying the ML lads were still not called to the colours. Perhaps this was a left over from the war years when people in jobs which were important to the war effort were classed as being in a reserved occupation and excused military service. Whatever the reason, it seemed OK by me. Mr Mobbs was also the President of the Slough Boys Boxing Club and he regularly attended the training sessions in the Slough Community Centre. The club was enormously successful with two members, Peter Brander and 'Tot' Glanville, being selected for the 1948 British Olympic Team. They were also employed by ML Aviation.

I thought this might be a stepping stone to better things, especially as I had previously boxed with the ATC, so I joined. "Glad to see you, Carter" said Mr Mobbs, as I danced intelligently around a punch bag. I then had a number of easy fights, all of which I won. Then I was matched against a chap called the Killer of Kilburn who gave me such a good hiding that I packed it in there and then. Mr Mobbs was not impressed by this sudden change of heart and I quickly lost my status of being 'one of Mr Mobbs' boxers.' My first holiday on my own was to the St Athan Miners' Centre at Llantwit Major with the Maidenhead Youth Centre. At the same time my brother, Norman, went with his school to Holland, staying with a Dutch family. This gave me the desire to go further afield, so a year later I went to Jersey with a friend, John Sharman. Having grown up during wartime it was of great interest to visit the island so soon after it had been liberated. To see the fortifications, the underground 'hospital' built by slave labour and the graves of German soldiers most of whom had died not in conflict but from sickness. But the holiday I remember most was in 1951 when along with a group of friends we went to Butlins at Skegness. When we arrived at the holiday camp on the Saturday afternoon, we saw the chalet's opposite were empty and they were still empty at nightfall. We were baffled as to why this should be until Sunday afternoon when in came 12 Sherman Fisher Girls, who were the dancers in a variety show opening at the Butlins Theatre the following day. Needless to say, we were quite pleased by our good fortune, and it was not long before we were getting to know them. I particularly liked Colleen who had dark hair, a lovely figure with long shapely legs. I was sharing a chalet with my friend Dave Hessey, so when he struck up a friendship with the other girl in Colleen's chalet we were set up for the week. Sadly it ended much too quickly, I was going back to Maidenhead and she was going on to the Winter Gardens at Weston Super Mare.

I said I would go and see her in Weston the following weekend, without really having any idea how I could manage it. I mentioned my predicament to my brother who said I could borrow his scramble motor bike if I was desperate! Whether I took him up on this offer I do not remember, but somehow I did get there and we had the afternoon together before she had to get back to the theatre for the evening performance. I had no money and seaside landladies were positively hostile to any men being brought back to their boarding houses, so I spent the night in a 'house' made of deck chairs under Weston pier. I was besotted, so much so that a couple of months later I took the overnight bus from London to Edinburgh, spent the day with Colleen before returning the same way!

During that Christmas and New Year the show was at the Chiswick Empire, and she took me to meet her parents who lived close to Heathrow Airport at Bedfont. Like most other lads of my age I had no car and we had to depend entirely upon public transport. I realised she was something special when we were waiting for a bus outside the Magpie pub on the A4 at Heathrow. A Rolls-Royce pulled up and asked if we wanted a lift! The driver probably thinking I was not with her, so I jumped in first just in case!

Work on the ML ejector seat was continuing at a fast pace. It had already been fitted into the Hawker P.1052, the Hawker P.1081 and the Westland Wyvern. But then disaster struck. Sqn Ldr 'Wimpey' Wade, the Hawker Chief Test Pilot, ran into problems when test flying the P.1081. Unable to recover from what had become a high- speed dive he decided to eject. He fired the seat but was still strapped in it when he hit the ground and was killed. It was subsequently discovered that there had been a malfunction of the hood jettison system which suggested that he might have ejected through the hood and possibly rendered unconscious.

This was a setback for ML Aviation at a very critical stage. The seat was unjustly blamed for Wade's death. Pointed questions as to the 'reliability' of the ML seat were raised in the House of Commons, and from then on it was finished – the contract for the supply of ejector seats for the RAF going to the Martin-Baker Aircraft Co at Denham.

Even so ML still had a valuable contribution to make. The ML barometric unit, which released the seat harness after ejection, and which had been a very important component on their automatic seat, was subsequently fitted to the early Martin-Baker seats. This reduced the minimum height that a pilot could safely eject from 2,000 ft to 1,000 ft, an improvement which pilots flying Meteors, Venoms, and Canberras in the early 1950s found most comforting.

CHAPTER 3

Joining Up

Approaching my 21st birthday a brown envelope arrived in the post marked 'On Her Majesty's Service'. In it was a letter instructing me to report for a medical prior to being called up for National Service. This was a shock, as I was due to sit my final exams for the HNC in three months' time, and I was reluctant to see five years of study go down the pan. I took the letter into my boss, Bob Parsons, the Chief Draughtsman.

"Don't worry, leave it with me - you won't have to go" He said confidently.

But a week later I was back in the office to be told that things had changed, there was nothing he could do - I was about to become the first person from the ML Technical School to do two years military service. This did not appeal to me at all. I was happy, a full-blown draughtsman now working full time on the retractable gun sight mounting design. What further bothered me was the thought that I might end up being drafted into the infantry, or worse still, being one of the really unlucky ones (one in ten of those called up) who were sent to work in the coal mines. These poor buggers were know as Bevin Boys, aptly named after the then Minister of Labour who was responsible for the scheme.

I gave this predicament very careful thought, especially with regard to what such rough treatment might do to my delicate draughtsman hands, and came to the conclusion that my best (and safest) course of action was to volunteer to be a regular in the Royal Air Force by signing on for the minimum period of four years.

Author's ATA pass.

ATA Flight Authorisation card.

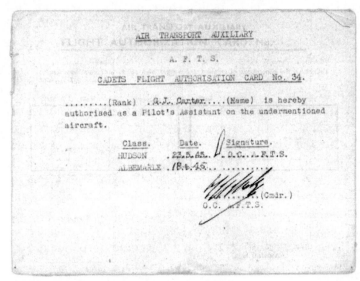

Now this was not as daft as it might seem. I had been tipped off that anyone who subsequently failed their trade training with the RAF would be discharged from the Service and that their National Service commitment would be considered complete. A good deal I thought - I might even be out in a year!

I went initially to the RAF recruiting office in Reading to see what was on offer and, much to my surprise, I discovered that my ONC and a nearly completed HNC was an acceptable qualification for aircrew. However, in view of my technical background the Flight Sergeant conducting the interview kept pushing me to go for a ground trade as an aircraft technician. I told him I would think about it and the next day I took the train to London and walked into the main RAF Recruiting Centre in Kingsway and announced,

"I've come to join up."

"What trade?" Enquired the burly Warrant Officer.

"Pilot" said I, going straight for the jugular!

I left the recruiting centre two hours later having convinced them that I was at least a suitable candidate to attend the Aircrew Selection Centre at RAF Hornchurch. I was on 'cloud nine' all the way back to Maidenhead, but not daring to tell anyone in case I failed to make the grade.

Even so there was a more important hurdle to overcome. I had been told to take with me a reference from the Headmaster of my school, as well as evidence of my technical qualifications. I already had the certificates from the technical college but a letter from my Headmaster was a worry, what with the escapade on the bus and other silly pranks which had brought us together from time to time. Go and see him in person I thought, better than writing.

"Hello Carter, nice to see you again after eight years. What have you been up to?"

I gave him a quick rundown on my technical training and mentioned that I was a draughtsman with ML Aviation, and now I had volunteered to join the RAF.

"What as?"

"A pilot Sir, and they need a reference!"

He paced across his study deep in thought.

"Tell me Carter, are you proud to have been a pupil at this school?

"Yes Sir, very much so" I replied, grovelling.

"In that case if you care to wait I will get my secretary to type the appropriate letter, and we all wish you the best of luck in your new career".

Not long after I received instructions to report to RAF Hornchurch to undergo a three-day selection process. On arrival I joined about 50 other hopefuls and was shown a bed in a grotty old barrack block. The selection criteria had recently changed and now all future pilots and navigators would be commissioned. This meant we were to be assessed not only on our ability to be aircrew, but whether or not we were officer material. You could not be one without the other. The time was mostly taken up with aptitude tests, interviews, medicals and a fair amount of individual scrutiny. You really had no idea how well you were doing, many of the questions and tests seemed to have no logical explanation, for example being told that you were on the run after baling out over enemy territory and you were hungry. You saw a duck in the middle of a pond and you had a gun. Would you shoot it (1) where it was, (2) wait for it to come nearer the edge, (3) wait for it to get airborne or (4) not shoot it at all. The answer you gave could depend on number of factors; if shot in the middle how would you get it; waiting for it come to the edge might be long wait; you might miss if you let it get airborne first and by shooting it you might attract those searching for you. I learnt subsequently that to think about it for more than three seconds was a fail. They were not interested in which option you went for; all they were looking for was to see how quickly you could make a decision. They didn't want ditherers.

It came as a shock to be asked at my final interview if I would accept an offer of another trade should I not be selected as a pilot.

"Would you consider a career as a flight engineer?" Asked the President of the Board after studying my file in front of him.

Did this mean I had failed or was there another reason for the question? I realised flight engineers were NCOs. Were they checking to see if I was in just for the commission?

"Yes I would" I replied without any hesitation.

On the afternoon of the third day we were all assembled to hear the worst. A squadron leader started by thanking us all for coming and then read the names of the nine candidates who had been selected for pilot training. One of the names on his list was Carter J G.

Not a bad achievement for a young man whose junior school teacher told him he was wasting his time taking the 11 plus. Perhaps he was being practical, it was at the time that the Luftwaffe was bombing the hell out us, and with the German invasion barges massing on the French coast the future was uncertain for everyone.

In due course I received a railway warrant with instructions to report to RAF Cardington near Bedford. At that time all volunteers for the regular Air Force, whatever trade, went to Cardington for kitting out. Consequently it was a mixed bunch of lads who got off the train at Bedford station to be shipped in three ton trucks to the old R101 airship base. The camp consisted of row upon row of wooden huts, much like a prisoner of war camp but without the watchtowers! Within hours of arrival we had been paraded at the clothing store and issued with a standard airman's uniform, basic kit and a kit-bag. At the same time we were instructed to put all our civilian clothes into cardboard boxes which were then sealed and mailed back to our next of kin. An unnerving experience for those of us who had just left mum and the comforts of home.

The only topic of conversation between the inmates seemed to be where we had come from, and what our future trade was going to be. It was clear that potential pilots were in a very small minority, and were destined to come in for a fair amount of good natured (I think!) stick, especially from the corporal in charge of the hut.

Along with our kit we were issued with a personal set of 'irons' (knife, fork and spoon) which enabled us to join the queue for a meal in the airmen's mess. An interesting experience. On reaching the end of the line, food was dolloped on your plate quite without ceremony, with no second helpings, if you were still hungry you could fill up with bread and butter. This initial introduction to service catering took a comic turn when a chap sitting opposite me on the bench table had a fit and promptly took a headlong dive into his soup. Needless to say, he disappeared and wasn't seen again.

The following day we were given numbers, which in true service tradition you had to memorise and be able to recite at the drop of a hat, especially on pay parades.

I recently attended a presentation given by Brian Blessed, the well known Shakespearian actor and mountaineer. During his talk he mentioned that he had done his National Service in the RAF and recited his number to the audience. Afterwards, when signing a copy of his book, *Nothing's Impossible*, he asked my name,

"3512884 Carter" I replied.

"You weren't National Service - you were a bloody regular" he boomed. He had remembered how it was possible to tell a serviceman's origins by his service number.

In the book he wrote 'To 3512884 Carter from 2744376 LAC Blessed.'

We were issued with our 1250s (identity cards) and mustered for an attestation parade, a solemn occasion to swear allegiance to the Queen. The date was 1st April 1952 - who was the biggest fool we had yet to find out!

Chaps left Cardington for the various training establishments as and when courses became available, but not before each hut had been minutely inspected by the corporal in charge for possible damage or inventory losses. It had been rumoured that on the day of departure it wasn't uncommon for huts to be suddenly deficient of light bulbs. Ours was no exception,

"But the light bulbs were all there this morning Corp." we all chorused.

"Must have been those buggers from the other hut then - pinching 'em - anyway it's going to cost you all a tanner each before I sign you off" he said with a smile. A nice little earner we thought, as we dropped our sixpences into the palm of his hand as we walked out of the door.

The potential pilots and navigators were put on a train to RAF Cranwell, not the grandeur of the RAF College but a motley hutted encampment on the opposite side of the Sleaford to Newark road, called No.3 Initial Training School (ITS). We were to be No.6 Course which consisted of 92 pilots and 59 navigators. Rumour had it that nearly half would get the chop somewhere along the line.

Nevertheless a new intake arrived every two or three weeks, which was indicative of the speed at which the RAF was expanding, mainly due to the intensification of the Cold War and the war in Korea. Being the first all-officer intake, we wore a white disk behind the RAF badge on our berets signifying our new rank of officer cadet. In his speech of welcome the Station Commander, Group Captain L G Levis, told us in blunt terms what was to be expected of us during the three months we would be at the Training School.

"Some of you won't make it to the end, but all of you can take pride in the fact that we only select the very best for aircrew training, an achievement you can all be proud of - whatever the outcome."

Was he preparing us for something? The first couple of weeks were devoted to square bashing and yet more square bashing, rifle drill and yet more rifle drill, bullshit and more bullshit all became the order of the day. The old military saying, 'If it's stationary paint it, if it moves salute it', could not have been more appropriate. Our hut became a shrine, the coke stove in the middle was black-leaded every day, its concrete base was redleaded and the brick edging was painted white. The brown lino floor had a mirror image and you only walked on it by shuffling about on felt pads. Discipline was everywhere - the only concession to our officer cadet status was that the drill instructors called you Mister. There were kit inspections every morning. We leapt to attention as the Station Warrant Officer (SWO) shouted ""Stand by your beds"" as he and the Orderly Officer entered the hut at 0700 hrs. By this time you had already been up over an hour to wash, shave (some doing it for the first time), get dressed, fold your sheets and blankets and ensure they were placed in the approved manner at the bottom of your bed.

The output of the boiler house had difficulty keeping pace with the increasing number of chaps going through the ITS, which meant that on most mornings you needed to be into the wash-house by 0615 hrs if you wanted to attend to your ablutions while the water was still hot. Occasionally the Station Medical Officer (SMO) would also be present. When ordered by the SWO we would all rather bashfully drop our trousers and underpants. The SMO then, armed with a short stick, would walk along the line giving us an FFI (free from infection) inspection. There hardly seemed much chance of that as we were all exhausted most of the time, but it did cause a bit of a laugh.

Evenings would be spent sipping a few beers in the NAAFI before returning to the hut to clean buttons, blanco webbing belts, press uniforms and polish boots until you could see your face in the toe caps. Once they had managed to knock us into some sort of shape we began a classroom routine, being taught basic navigation, meteorology, aircraft instruments, and the principles of flight. At the same time we were being assessed on our personal qualities. We were left in no doubt as to what was expected of us as potential officers, with much time being devoted to leadership exercises and customs of the Service. One or two chaps learnt to their horror that you never referred to the RAF as 'The Raf' although 'The Mob' was considered to be not so bad! Chaps dropped out at regular intervals either to be offered other jobs in the RAF or to return to civilian life. Compulsory church parades were held every Sunday, until halfway through the course when they became optional, as a result the Padre lost half his flock over night. Although the RAF College was just across the road there was absolutely no contact between them and us. In fact ITS cadets got bawled out if we were even seen walking on the college side of the road - they could have been in a different air force for all we knew. At one stage we were 'invited' to beat for the college beagles which I thought was bit of a cheek, but a couple of the lads had a go thinking it might improve their 'personal qualities' assessment.

Whilst there we had our first escape and evasion exercise, code name Squadron Jaunt, to give us experience of escaping and evading should we ever have the misfortune to get shot down over enemy territory. This involved being dropped at some inhospitable location late at night, and being told to make it on foot to a point some 10 miles away without being caught. Sadly most of us were captured within the last mile due to fatigue, and a heavy concentration of the 'enemy' from RAF Kirton-in-Lindsey close to the target point. The clever (and fit) ones made it by skirting around the pick up point and coming in from the opposite direction.

Dinghy drill in the camp pool was another trauma, each one of us having to pass the 'swimming proficiency test' by jumping off the top board, inflating our Mae West's, then swimming the length of the pool to get in a dinghy. Easy for some, but not so clever for those of us who were non-swimmers.

Half way through the course we were given ten days leave - to go home and bring back our civilian clothes. Not any old clothes but the regulatory black blazer (with RAF buttons but no badge), grey or cavalry twill trousers, suede shoes and of course a ratting cap - officers did not go about bareheaded! We were warned early on that we would each have to give a 15-minute talk to the rest of the course on a subject of our choice. Having never given a presentation before I decided that it had to be a topic which I knew a bit about, where I would not be put off by awkward questions, and preferably a subject with an aviation slant which would impress my instructor. I settled for the ML Retractable Gun Sight Mounting which was now coming into service. I wrote to my old boss Bob Parsons at ML Aviation, and the company sent me a complete presentation with charts, diagrams and photographs. Of course it went like a dream, there were no questions and I achieved top marks.

With the end of the course in sight disaster struck. I suddenly became covered in spots and was rushed in to the doc, who diagnosed German Measles. I was put in isolation in sick quarters, with my food being passed through a hatch in the wall. As a result of this I missed the end of course party at the Clinton Arms Hotel, in Newark, but worse still I missed going with the rest of the course to Southern Rhodesia for flying training. Three weeks later I was pronounced fit and joined 7 course to complete my training.

Even before we knew whether we had passed out or not we were each given an allowance of £110 to purchase our officer's uniform, shoes, shirts, overcoat, mac and other pieces of kit and a tin trunk to carry it all. I thought this was tempting fate a bit as we would have to hand it all back if we failed the final exams. However a representative from Gieves, the Bond Street tailors, came to the camp and measured us for our uniforms. But their peaked caps were not stylish enough for us, a bit like those worn in the Navy, so most of us opted for a hat made by Johnsons which although more expensive had a nice 'panzer' shape.

When the final examination results were posted up I saw to my horror that I had failed navigation and that I was down to be interviewed by the Chief Instructor. Was I up for the chop?

"Well Carter, you made a bit of cock of it didn't you?"

"Yes Sir" I replied rather sheepishly.

"Bloody good job you weren't hoping to be a navigator" he joked!

"Yes, it is Sir" I said attempting a smile.

"Well, in view of your overall marks, and taking into account that you only missed a pass mark in navigation by 5% I'm happy to let you go on - good luck."

I felt that having been a member of the ITS cricket team, and the fact that he was the team captain might have also helped a bit!

We were then sent on leave for three weeks. But the RAF must have had second thoughts about giving us all this free time at home because, after one week, I received a railway warrant in the post with instructions to report to RAF Merryfield in Somerset, to take part in yet another escape and evasion exercise. But this one was to be different.

Within hours of arrival I once again 'baled out' from the back of a three ton truck with a small map and a button compass. All I knew was that I had 'landed' somewhere on the Black Down Hills with instructions to rendezvous with the 'underground' at a prearranged location some 5 miles distant. I was on my own. I needed to get a fix and it seemed right at the time to set off in the same direction in which the lorry departed. Of course, sod's law, it was the wrong way and after an hour or more I was back roughly in the same place - and it was getting dark.

Setting off in the opposite direction I soon came across a road sign and was then able to pinpoint my position and the direction I needed to go. I still had about 4 miles to walk to reach my contacts who, I had been told, would be holed up in a derelict farm cottage. Just before midnight and thoroughly exhausted and hungry I staggered into the farm building. A figure with a

ITS Cricket Team, RAF Cranwell. (Author, front row 3rd from left).

blackened face slowly emerged from the shadows dressed in combat clothing. He asked me a few questions and then his mate came in from another room. They had very little to say after that but it was clear they were military, they knew what they were about and they were taking this exercise for real. We left the building together and travelled across country to avoid the police and various army units who were now out looking for us. Dawn was breaking when we arrived at an isolated barn and within seconds I was fast asleep on a damp muddy floor. I slept like a log whilst my 'friends' took it in turn to be on guard. When I woke it was midday and they fed me some rations which they had with them.

They carried a small radio which suddenly crackled into life with instructions to take me to another location, and we had to be there by 1600 hrs. As it meant travelling by daylight they said most of the journey would be along ditches and hedgerows to avoid being seen. It was freezing cold and for a lot of the time we were up to our ankles in mud and water. Completely exhausted and absolutely sure I was going to die of pneumonia we reached a small copse close by a field and took cover. My 'friends' said an Auster aircraft was on its way to pick me up and as soon as it landed I was to break cover and run like hell and get on board. 'If you get caught you're in real trouble' - what trouble they did not say. Sure enough spot on time the Army Air Corps aircraft appeared over the trees and even before it had stopped I was on my way. The pilot leaned across and opened the door and I fell into the cockpit. He opened the throttle and was airborne before I had time to strap in. Fifteen minutes later we landed at Merryfield and after a hot bath and a good meal the bar opened. "Who were those chaps?" I asked, "Special Air Service" was the reply.

CHAPTER 4

Flying Training

I now had a posting to No.7 Flying Training School (FTS) at RAF Cottesmore near Oakham but, pending the start of the course, we were given another week's leave. The *London Gazette* listed me as being an acting pilot officer on probation, which meant my commission would be retained only if I graduated at the end of the course with a pair of wings on my chest. The leave went slowly, I was impatient to get cracking. Eventually in early September I arrived at Oakham Station in my blazer, ratting cap, suede shoes and carrying the large tin trunk with all my other kit. Officers or not, we were still met by the customary three tonner and told to get in the back by the AC2 driver!

Arriving at the airfield we were taken to No.2 Officers' Mess which had been erected just inside the main entrance. It was a group of prefabricated Secco huts joined together to provide an anti-room, dining room, bar, TV and games room, as well as single bedroom accommodation. No.1 Officers' Mess, a proper pre-war building, was some distance away and was exclusively the home of the permanent staff who were of course proper officers!

Some 40 years later I had the pleasure of staying in No.1 Mess when attending a Fighter Command reunion, it was like treading on hallowed ground after all those years.

RAF Cottesmore was a bomber base during Second World War, but in the late 1940s it was taken over by Flying Training Command, and in March 1948 No.7 Flying Training School moved there from RAF Kirton-in-Lindsey. The base was commanded by Group Captain R Sorel-Cameron, CBE, AFC, the Wing

Commander Flying was Wing Commander G McKenzie DFC, and the Chief Ground Instructor (CGI) was Squadron Leader Don Hannah, DFC. The school was equipped with Percival Prentices and Harvards, although brand new Boulton Paul Balliols had just arrived to replace the ageing Harvards, and we were destined to be the first course to be fully trained on this aircraft.

The first two weeks were devoted entirely to classroom work and further officer training in the form of leadership exercises, but no more polishing boots, making beds or dobying - we had batmen! At the end of the first week I was summoned to the CGI's office and told that I was to be the Course Leader and Bert Fraser, an ex Halton apprentice, was to be my deputy. Sadly Bert was later killed while flying a Whirlwind helicopter off the Malayan coast in 1965.

In addition Dan Hicks and Bob Fisher had been nominated as flight commanders. There were only 17 of us on the course, so it did seem that perhaps we had a lot of Chiefs and not so many Indians, but that was the way it was.

The other chaps on the course who had to put up with my 'leadership' were Andy Anderson, Dennis Baxter, Dave Blackford, Keith Bretherton, Alan Brew, Johnny Collins, Mike de Courcy, Malcolm de Garis, Brian Golder, Bob Greenhow, Keith Guscott, Tony Coward and one other whose name I cannot remember, probably he was scrubbed off the course at an early stage.

I was uncertain what to make of this responsibility especially as I was likely to have my work cut out coping with the flying and the ground school studies let alone anything else. However, when Don Hannah told me that it was customary for the Course Leader to pass out top of the course I didn't give it a second thought!

The Prentice was an ugly machine, grossly under powered, and not an aircraft one could look back on with fond memories. But it got off the ground and got back again, which was about all one could say. Why the RAF bought them God only knows, probably because 'side by side' seating had become the 'in-thing' for dual instruction, even though large numbers of Meteor T.7s were entering service in a tandem format.

My instructors were Flying Officer Ken Bowden and Sgt Hudd, both likeable chaps with whom I got on well. Most of my early circuit work was carried out at RAF Spitalgate, a First World War airfield just off the A1 south of Grantham, and it was there after only 5.10 hrs dual, that Sgt Hudd clambered out of the aircraft and said

"There you go laddo – see if you can get round the circuit without bending it".

The first-solo party was held in the local pub, and on the way back Dave Blackford discovered it was no fun being legless in the back of a three tonner.

One of the first upper-air exercises was spinning, an unpleasant experience in any aircraft but in the Prentice it was awful. Recovery action had to be taken after two turns, otherwise it went into a flat spin and the subsequent recovery became difficult if not near impossible. Spinning was a piece of cake when you had an instructor in the aircraft telling you what to do - he of course had a vested interest in ensuring that you recovered - but the syllabus called for students to also spin the aircraft when flying solo.

It goes without saying that the only reason why some of us failed to write ourselves off when spinning on our own was because not many of us did it!

After returning from a solo spinning detail one's instructor would enquire during the debrief:

'How'd the spinning go?'

'Fine, two turns and it came out a treat'.

You could tell by his face that he didn't believe a word of it! Other than that, I found the Prentice pretty easy to fly. I was of course helped by having 100 hrs of flying already clocked up with the Air Transport Auxiliary, as well as gliding experience with the ATC. I did just one hour of night flying before passing the basic flying test with Wing Commander Mackenzie. I had completed a total of 62 hrs flying in 38 days.

Before moving up the road to the Balliols we were told we could have a Private Pilot's Licence (PPL) if we wanted one, but the Board of Trade (predecessor to the CAA) insisted that we sit the Aviation Law exam. This we did – in the bar that same evening – and in due course each of us received a shiny new civil licence.

It was also time for another escape and evasion, this time a major exercise in Leicestershire. All the students at Cottesmore were to be escapees, and we were again dropped off from the back of a lorry on a freezing cold night in November. We were despatched in pairs and, although I do not remember who my companion was, it soon became obvious after studying our maps that the most direct route to the rendezvous point would take us through the centre of Leicester. This seemed to be a bit risky, so we opted to go through the suburbs of the city as best we could. We did quite well initially by walking along a railway line, managing to avoid the odd train as it came hurtling out of the darkness. By midnight we had reached the built-up area ... then we were spotted. Someone shouted asking what we were doing, so we slid down the opposite embankment and ran across some waste land. Eventually we came to a fence over which we climbed to find ourselves in a large cemetery where we hid among the gravestones. We rested until the panic had died down before moving off again. Now we were a bit unsure of our position so somehow we needed to find a road junction with direction signs.

We stood out like sore thumbs dressed in green overalls which were now covered in mud. In this condition we were not only avoiding the police and others who were looking for us but the public as well. They would immediately telephone the police if we were seen lurking about in such a dishevelled state. We followed unlit roads (a lot of them in those days) until we came to a park. We climbed the fence and could see what looked like a major road junction on the far side. Our progress was now slower, we were tired and it started to rain. After checking which direction to go we set off again. Then disaster struck! As we turned a corner we came face to face with a special constable, 'you're under arrest' he said grabbing me by the collar. My buddy saw the opportunity and staggered off in the other direction and got away. The constable dragged me to a phone box and within minutes a police patrol car arrived and took me to Leicester Jail. I was given a cup of coffee and thrown in a cell. After an hour a chap in civies came to ask me a few questions.

"3512884 Pilot Officer Carter".

"It's OK old chap the exercise is over, we've been instructed to give you a meal and then take you back to your unit in one of our patrol cars - which base are you from?"

I nearly fell for it.

"If they want me they will come for me" I replied,

Whereupon the civvy left and I languished in the cell for a further two hours before being driven back to Cottesmore in the customary three tonner. How many more of these exercises would there be?

During this break between the Prentice and the Balliol stage the station decided to put on a boxing tournament with the student pilots being invited to take part. Needless to say there were no volunteers. The CGI then looked at our records and discovered that on joining both Carter and Hicks had previously claimed to having 'done some.' There was no wriggling out, especially as I was now expected to set an example as the Course Leader, and Dan being a Flight Commander. Foolishly we assumed that as we had not trained or boxed for a couple of years that we would be matched against someone of similar standing. Imagine my surprise then to discover on the night that my welterweight opponent was a Corporal Stocks from RAF Swanton Morley - a physical training instructor no less. I survived until mid-way through the second round, when I received a pile driver of a punch to the side of the head and woke up next morning in sick quarters with a cut eye, a split lip and a headache. The Wingco was not impressed, and banned all student pilots from participating in future tournaments.

We started flying the Balliol three days later, and soon discovered that this was a real aircraft, similar in performance to a Spitfire, but with a very wide undercarriage, a steerable tailwheel and airbrakes. It was powered by a huge Merlin 35 engine developing 1,100 BHP at sea level, with a four-bladed, constant-speed propeller. It had a maximum permissible all-up weight of over 9,000 lbs, which made it heavier than a Spitfire. It also had the luxury of windscreen wipers and an electrically operated hood. For storage and maintenance purposes the wings could be folded.

I was introduced to my new instructor Flying Officer Pat Salter, an extrovert with a big handlebar moustache and a great love for draught Guinness. Before we had even looked inside the cockpit he told me and Johnny Collins, his other student, that one of us would win the aerobatic competition which was always held at the end of the course. Some hope we thought!

When Pat got out of the aircraft and sent me off solo after three hours I knew he must be mad, it normally took up to eight hours on Harvards. On my very next dual trip I discovered that in addition to the Guinness, Pat's other great love was low flying. The low-flying area for Cottesmore was encircled by a railway line which extended from Melton Mowbray in the north to Corby in the south. On odd-numbered days he would fly around the track in a clockwise direction at 250 ft. Even-numbered days it was my turn to fly anti-clockwise at 250 ft. It was great fun especially when beating up the odd train, passengers would wave out of the windows and we would wave back. We were lucky that low flying was still an acceptable part of life in the UK so soon after the war. There was no likelihood of ever being reported.

Being the first course to fly the aircraft, we soon reached the unusual situation where we had more hours on type than the instructors, so we probably got away with a lot more than we would have done in normal circumstances.

The relief landing ground for the Balliol Squadron was Woolfox Lodge just across the A1 from Cottesmore. It was mainly used to practice circuits and forced landings when the Cottesmore circuit was busy. It was a derelict wartime airfield, but when needed air traffic would send a 'bod' over in a jeep to check the runway for obstructions and to keep a lookout. Dual details at the Lodge with Pat were experiences not to be forgotten - as you walked out to the aircraft at Cottesmore it would be noticeable that he was walking a bit stiff-legged. Then once inside the cockpit and away from prying eyes he would produce a 12-bore shot gun from inside his flying suit.

"When we get there you're going to do half an hour on your own, local flying, some circuits, then practice a couple of forced landings whilst I go off shooting - any questions?"

On arrival he would get out and disappear into the woods, saying "Pick me up in thirty minutes."

After swanning around Lincolnshire for half an hour I would go back and he would unceremoniously dump a load of dead birds and rabbits on my lap and fly us back to base.

This was all great fun until, one morning at met briefing, the Wingco Flying announced that the 'Trappers' (examiners) from the Central Flying School (CFS) were on the base and would be flying with a few selected students to check their progress. Johnny and I looked at each other in complete horror, but Pat leaned across and said "They won't be flying with either of you 'cos I've fixed it."

After the briefing we walked into the crew room and came face to face with no less than the senior trapper, a Squadron Leader Forth.

"Pilot Officer Carter get your gear on, I'll fly with you first!"

My legs went to jelly as I walked across the hanger to the locker room, closely followed by Pat who was desperately attempting to brief me on all the exercises that we should have completed to date. The Squadron Leader briefed me on what he wanted me to do, and off we went. Thirty five minutes later we were back on the ground, and as we walked back to the crewroom, he said

"Generally Carter not a bad effort, but who the hell taught you to low fly like that?"

Wednesday afternoon was sports afternoon, and we soon learnt how to manipulate this to our advantage by opting to go ice skating in Nottingham, but in practice spending the afternoon at the pictures followed by a night out on the town. We also got to know all the local pubs within a 15-mile radius of the base, *The George* at Stamford and *The Ram Jam Inn* on the A1 being particularly popular. Our main source of female company was

Kesteven Teachers Training College at Grantham, although all contact with the girls came to an abrupt end when the 'queen bee' at the college complained to the Station Commander that his pilots had stolen the balls guarding their main gate!

Further enquiries by the Station Adjutant revealed that two enormous concrete balls which once topped the pillars at the entrance to the college were now proudly on display outside No.2 Officers' Mess. Our course had nothing to do with this, but in true military fashion we were all held responsible. The 'Station Master' was not amused, especially as the works dept had to reinstate them with the bill being paid by the RAF.

No one claimed responsibility, so we were all confined to base on the following Saturday which actually meant an evening in the Astra (station cinema) followed by a few beers in the mess bar.

On another occasion at a dining-in night one chap on another course was seen to commit an horrendous sin by sloping off to bed early. Later as a prank, and whilst he was fast asleep, he was taken outside in his bed and carefully hoisted onto the flat roof of the building. In the early hours of the morning he got out of bed to have a pee and fell off the roof breaking his ankle.

The punishment for some misdemeanours was more severe, especially if they involved the safety of personnel or aircraft. Walk away from an aircraft leaving the magneto switches on, and you were in serious trouble. Offenders were usually made to run round the airfield perimeter whilst wearing a parachute – very difficult and physically exhausting.

Early in the new year we had a fatality. Mike de Courcy was doing unauthorised low level aerobatics near Stamford when he misjudged a loop and crashed on the Bourne road. His room was immediately sealed and myself and Dan Hicks started the delicate job of producing a statement of personal effects. Whilst doing this we discovered that Mike was in fact married. This was a surprise to us, as it was a condition of our acceptance for aircrew training that we should be of single status. Anticipating a problem, we quickly contacted the Station Adjutant. It was not a moment too soon, within the hour reporters from the national press were either at the main gate or telephoning the duty officer at the Air Ministry. It transpired that Mike was the grandson of Baron de Courcy, and there had been some controversy in the newspapers a year previously about his marriage in a Scottish registry office. To make matters worse, there was also speculation that his wife was in fact living in the Stamford area close to the site of the crash.

Everyone went a bit quiet for a few days whilst the tragedy sank in. It was probably the first death that many of us had experienced, and it brought home the dangers of this flying business. Mike was given a full military funeral, which we all attended, and he was laid to rest in the village churchyard at Cottesmore. Afterwards we said our final farewell, by tradition in the mess bar, and it was back to work.

There was a humorous sequel to Mike's untimely death. We still had our highly 'bulled' boots which we had brought with us from Cranwell and which for some strange reason were all stored together in a cupboard. Mike, being an old Etonian, was not much good at keeping boots shiny so he tended to 'borrow' others when the need arose. When Mike's effects were collected from his room

Mike's crash as reported in the national press.

Crash ends romance of baron's heir

THE typist who married a baron's heir less than two years ago is now a widow.

For yesterday the Air Ministry announced that Acting Pilot-Officer Michael Charles Cameron Claremont Constantine de Courcy was the pilot of a training plane which crashed on Wednesday.

The 22-year-old grandson and heir of the 34th Baron Kingsale, premier Baron of Ireland, died when his single-seater crashed near Stamford, Lincs.

In September, 1950, the 6ft. 3in. tall Michael planned to marry 21-year-old Anne Grey Barrett.

HE VANISHED

She worked in the office of his cousin and former guardian, Mr. Kenneth de Courcy.

The wedding was postponed two days before the date set. Michael vanished. He was made a ward in Chancery for three weeks.

He was persuaded to return to his cousin's home at Alderbourne Manor, Gerrards Cross, but "vanished" again the next day for two months to stay with friends at Faversham, Kent.

Early in 1951 he married Miss Barrett at a register office at Annan, Dumfriesshire.

The new heir to the title is his 12-year-old step-brother, John.

the highly polished boots belonging to Alan Brew were taken by mistake. By the time this was discovered Mike's effects and Alan's boots had left the station. But Alan was not allowed to use Mike's (not very bulled up) boots as they were not his, forcing him to borrow boots for the duration of the course!

We were now into the second half of the course, with much time being devoted to instrument flying, both actual and simulated in preparation for our Instrument Rating Test. To simulate being in cloud, the instructor would raise a pneumatically operated screen blanking off the student's forward vision and another screen was placed manually into position to stop sly glances out of the side. Finally, to ensure no cheating, the student was made to wear a pair of tinted goggles. The instructor had no screens on his side as he had to keep a look-out for other aircraft, consequently if you had good eyeball movement you could get a glimpse of the natural horizon through his side window should you get disorientated.

A popular trick was to tell your instructor that the goggles were misting up and then he would allow you to take them off. Unlike some of the others, I absolutely loved instrument flying, it really gave me a buzz to get everything spot on and within limits.

What I did not enjoy was Standard Beam Approaches (SBA), an approach procedure left over from the war, and hardly appropriate for budding jet fighter pilots, but if you could hack it you could master anything. The main beacon of the system was situated at the upwind end of the instrument approach runway and it transmitted a beam within a 2 degree arc along the runway. Overhead the transmitter there was no signal. This was known as the cone of silence. If you were to the left of the beam on the approach you heard a letter 'A' (dit dah in Morse code) and if you were to the right of the beam you heard the letter 'N' (dah dit). When on the beam you heard a continuous note (dah). Two marker beacons completed the system, one at 3 nautical miles from touchdown which transmitted dashes and another 150 yards from touchdown transmitting dots.

To commence the procedure you first had to fly the aircraft to a position overhead the main transmitter. This was not easy so to save time the instructor would do it for you. You then flew outbound along the beam at 1,500 ft. On this leg you had a problem, because you were flying in the opposite direction to which the system had been calibrated. To get back onto the beam you had to turn in the opposite direction because the 'A' and 'N' signal were now on the wrong side. After leaving the inner marker outbound you had 90 seconds to assess the drift and get settled comfortably on the beam before reaching the outer marker. One minute after passing the outer marker you did a left-hand procedure turn, at the same time descending to intercept the beam inbound at 1,100 ft. Once established inbound you descended to cross the outer marker at 600 ft and then the inner marker at 100 ft AGL. Then to finish off you had to follow the overshoot procedure, climbing back to 1,500 ft until you heard those magic words, "I have control. You can take your windscreen blinds down, and if it's OK with you I'll just do a few aerobatics before we go back."

After successfully completing the Instrument Rating Test we were given a 'White Card' Rating, which gave us operating limits of 500 ft cloud base and 1,000 yards visibility for take off, and 500 ft and 2,000 yards for landing. It is interesting to note that the RAF always did approach and landings with the airfield QNH (which gives height above sea level) set, whereas civil operators used QFE (giving a height above the airfield) settings. From the military point of view it did avoid the need to reset the altimeter pressure setting at a critical stage on the approach, and you did have an instant comparison to any high ground in the vicinity. On the down side, you did need to make a mental note of the airfield elevation and to subtract it from the altimeter reading in order to check your height above touchdown. This was no problem as you were nearly always landing back at the same airfield from which you departed but landing away needed more care.

Apart from two VHF radio sets, the only other piece of radio equipment carried on the Balliol was IFF (Identification Friend or

Foe) which was of course never used. It had no radio navigation aids so we were completely dependant upon VHF Direction Finding (VHFDF). You could call any airfield on the R/T, pass your callsign and rabbit on for a few seconds whilst an airman sitting in a little hut swung his aerial around until he had a bearing on your transmission, much the same as the TV detector van! He would then pass the bearing to Air Traffic and the controller would tell you what your magnetic bearing was to or from the airfield. Sadly, there was a reluctance to use this service whilst under training, as you got no brownie points for advertising the fact that you were uncertain of your position!

The VHFDF service really came into its own following a call from an aircraft on the emergency frequency 121.5 Mc/s. On hearing the call, a number of airfields would take a bearing on the transmission and pass it to the rescue co-ordination centre. Within seconds the information would be plotted to provide an instant fix on the aircraft's position. The pilot would then be given a heading and distance to the nearest airfield.

In due course VHFDF was superseded by Cathode Ray DF (CRDF), the 'bod' in the hut having been made redundant by new equipment in the tower. As you requested a bearing, the air traffic controller was able to read off your bearing from the CRDF screen and pass it to you. Probably the least used 'aid' was the Voice Rotating Beacon, which thankfully soon went out of business. When tuned to the transmitter frequency you would hear a recorded voice (much like a well-scratched 78 record) telling you your QDM to that beacon every 72 seconds. As a pilot-interpreted aid it was pretty useless and at times confusing, for example it only broadcast bearings every ten degrees and it only relayed the first two digits of the bearing, consequently 'one zero' was 100 degrees but could be confused with 010 degrees. After a while it became obvious to us all why there was so much emphasis on map reading at flying training schools.

One afternoon we were delighted to see a two-seat Meteor T.7 jet join the circuit and land. It taxied to our dispersal, and we were told that each of us were to be given a 20-minute ride in it. If the intention was to stimulate our enthusiasm it was a success. The Meteor was different altogether, with none of the noise and vibration associated with piston engines. We could not wait to get our hands on it. The sensation was exhilarating. Who cared if they seemed to be crashing every other day, 'it only ever happened to the other chap' was how we thought about it! Towards the end of the course we did some night flying, which was successfully completed except for a slight incident involving our Squadron Commander, Squadron Leader James, and Bert Fraser. They managed to plough their way through the approach lights after touching down 300 yards short of the runway whilst looking for the landing-light switch. Both escaped uninjured, but the Balliol was a write-off.

*Graduation of No.7 Course at No.7 FTS RAF Cottesmore July 1953.
Author seated centre front row.*

Eventually the day came for the aerobatic competition. Although the rules were that each instructor could only put one name forward, Pat in his usual way, had somehow contrived that both Johnny Collins and I would take part. It was to be low-level aerobatics over the airfield, with each competitor carrying a neutral instructor on board as a safety pilot. He would give no help or assistance, unless of course you tried to kill yourself, and him. In the end Johnny Collins won it hands down, and Pat was pleased. I felt I might have done better if it had been a low-flying competition! But in the end I did get a suitably high mark for personal qualities, which, just as Don Hannah had prophesied, meant I passed out top of the course!

On 1 July 1954, of the original 17 trainee pilots, 14 of us were presented with our wings by Air Marshal Sir John Baldwin, KBE, CB, DSO. A typical summer's day, pouring with rain, which meant the graduation parade was hastily moved into a hanger and our wings presentation took place in the mess. Later that day we packed our bags and said goodbye to a very happy flying school. We had worked hard, and at the same time enjoyed ourselves. One had the feeling that life at an advanced flying school and jet conversion would be very different.

CHAPTER 5

Jet Conversion

In the early 1950s a large number of Meteors were crashing, not only at the Advanced Flying Schools in Flying Training Command but also with the front-line fighter squadrons. It was no coincidence then that the aircraft became affectionately known among fighter pilots as the 'Meatbox.' Affectionately because, despite its shortcomings, there was a certain pleasure in flying the RAF's first jet fighter.

Of the Advanced Flying Schools (AFS), No.203 at RAF Driffield had a particularly bad record. The station had really hit the headlines in October 1951. Flight Sergeant d'Avoine, an instructor, was leading a formation of three Meteors after having been briefed to practise close formation flying. The two other Meteors were flown by Pilot Officer Quinton and Lieutenant Prast of the Royal Netherlands Air Force, both were students at the base. The exercise was carried out above cloud just off the East Yorkshire coast near Scarborough. On completion d'Avoine led the formation back down through cloud off the North Yorkshire coast for a visual run-in back to Driffield. When they levelled out below cloud on a westerly heading they were at 300 ft above the water in poor visibility. In the gloom the instructor failed to see towering cliffs until the very last moment. With a desperate heave he cleared them by inches, but Quinton and Prast formating on either side of him were not so lucky - both flew straight into the 400 ft high cliffs at Flamborough Head and were killed instantly.

Despite this and other accidents we were keen to be trained on Meteors, and eventually to be posted to one of the crack day fighter squadrons in Fighter Command.

The Meteor AFS at RAF Worksop was a popular choice (if we had one!). Firstly because they seemed to have fewer accidents, and secondly they were flying the later Meteor F.8s fitted with ejector seats.

It was not to be, we received our posting notices just prior to leaving Cottesmore and discovered that if you can't stand a joke you shouldn't have joined - six of us were posted to Driffield!

When we arrived we found ourselves on No.78 Meteor Course, which was due to pass out at the end of October. The first two weeks were spent in the ground school studying the fuel, hydraulic, pneumatic, electrical and vacuum systems. Special emphasis was made of the fact that you only had one hydraulic pump and that was on the starboard engine. If that engine failed in flight, and the hydraulic accumulator was fully charged, you could use the airbrake only once before lowering the under-carriage and flaps. Should the accumulator become exhausted you had to pump the gear and flaps down with a hand pump on the starboard side of the cockpit floor, whilst at the same time flying the aircraft left-handed. For this reason it was drummed into us that, when shutting down an engine for practice or for endurance, it should always be the port engine.

Then the big day came, and we presented ourselves to 'F' Flight of No.3 Sqn. Captain Ben Ruys introduced himself as my instructor, a Dutchman on exchange posting from the Royal Netherlands Air Force. He seemed a nice enough chap who as a teenager was in Holland during the German occupation. Rumour had it that at one stage he had been deported to a labour camp but he never talked about that side of his life to us. What did cross my mind was whether it might be hard enough coping with the Meteor without having a possible language problem to overcome.

The first thing he did was to put me into the front seat of the T.7 cockpit to see if I could lock my leg straight at the knee when applying full rudder. The reason for this was soon to become obvious as the first instructional flight in the T.7 would not be circuits and landings, as was normal on the Prentice and Balliol, but a rapid climb to altitude to practise stalling and single-engine flying. We soon appreciated the reason for this, a stall was very different in a jet, the recovery took longer, and the aircraft lost more height in the process. Because of this you needed to be much more speed conscious on final approach. But the main difficulty converting to the Meteor was going to be handling the beast on one engine. With less than 200 hrs flying experience, all on single-engine piston aircraft, this was not going to be easy.

Starting the Derwent engines was simple; press the starter button, wait for the undercarriage lights to dim and then open the HP fuel cock, initially halfway and then fully open whilst checking that the jetpipe temperature was stabilising at about 500 deg C. The speed at which you opened the HP cock could be critical, if too quick, resonance and overheating would occur, and the engine had to be fully shut down before attempting a restart. Another problem was failure of the engine to light up, which meant you had to do a dry run to remove as much of the surplus fuel in the engine as you could. Even after having done that, the second attempt at starting was always spectacular with a long orange flame extending back to the tail as the remaining fuel was ignited.

The mnemonic for the take-off checks was TAFFIOHH, Trim, Airbrakes, Fuel, Flaps, Instruments, Oxygen, Hood and Harness. For landing BAUFFH, Brakes, Airbrakes, Undercarriage, Fuel, Flaps and Harness.

Many Meteor accidents, especially those during flying training, were the result of the syllabus calling for the 'dead' engine to be completely shut down when practising single-engine circuits and landings. This was unfortunate, as on many occasions pilots lost rudder control at low speed and then were unable to recover by opening up the 'dead' engine with fatal consequences. Fortunately for us, a number of changes had taken place prior to our arrival at Driffield, the most significant being that flying on one engine now had to be simulated by simply throttling back the 'dead' engine. Then if things got out of hand, full power could be restored on that engine.

Even with that safeguard, we soon realised why the introduction to single-engine flying was done at height. The foot load when applying full opposite rudder was so great that it was impossible to hold, unless you were able to lock your leg straight at the knee.

Before demonstrating single-engine flying, the instructor would need to establish what your single-engine critical speed was. To find out, you would be told to 'fail' the engine of your choice and trim out. This was not difficult at 250kt, but your instructor would then ask you to put full power on the good engine and slowly raise the nose. As the speed dropped off, the foot load counteracting the asymmetric thrust of the good engine became heavier and heavier until you lost control and the aircraft started to roll inverted towards the 'dead' engine. The speed at which this happened was your critical speed - in my case 160 kt, which was about average.

Some students found it difficult to hold their leg in the locked position especially if they were a bit short in the leg, and as a result they lost control at a much higher speed. These chaps were allowed to fly with a hard piece of sorbo rubber behind their backside to get a firmer lock at the knee, but if that failed they were posted off the course.

As it happened Ben Ruys turned out to be an excellent instructor with a down to earth manner. If he sensed that things were not going well and I was getting tense he would shout over the intercom

"Carter, part the cheeks of your arse and try again."

There was another problem that we had to be very aware of when flying the Meteor T.7. If it yawed at speeds below 170 knots with the airbrakes out, as might happen when lowering the undercarriage in the circuit, the elevators became ineffective and the aircraft took a dive earthwards. It was called the 'phantom dive' and was the cause of numerous accidents.

Despite these potential problems we heard on the student grapevine that if you failed to go solo within five hours you were considered borderline, and at seven hours you were up for the 'chop' (meaning taken off the course alive, as opposed to being killed which was the 'big chop'). True or not, as you reached the five-hour mark you became increasingly twitchy. But all was well, on the morning of 24 August 1953, after 5 hours and 50 minutes dual, Ben Rys sent me off solo in the T.7. That same afternoon I went off on my own in Meteor F.4 serial number RA397. I had made it, I was a jet pilot!

There was no time for celebrations, the exercise the following day was high-speed runs at 35,000 ft. Full poke straight and level until the aircraft hit the compressibility barrier. At this point the controls became very heavy due to the formation of pressure waves as the aircraft approached the speed of sound, this was accompanied by a fair amount of buffeting, vibration and noise in the cockpit. Not a comfortable experience, but recovery was quickly achieved by selecting airbrakes out and throttling back.

Next we were introduced to the Controlled Descent Through Cloud (QGH) which, because of the short endurance of the Meteor, was vital in getting back to base quickly and safely. After being homed to overhead by the approach controller you were directed out on a safety lane, from which you were then turned inbound after a timed interval and continued letting down until visual with the airfield for a normal run-in break and landing.

The need to watch your fuel carefully was brought home to us early on the course. One of the lads found himself running short of fuel and as a precaution decided to land at Carnaby, a relief airfield for Driffield but which was unmanned at the time. A sensible move he thought. Then he found a bowser beside a hangar and on the spur of the moment he refuelled the aircraft using a hand pump and took off again for Driffield. In the mean time his instructor was hot-footing it to Carnaby by road – on arrival he was not amused to discover our gallant aviator had used his initiative and had long since departed.

On the lighter side word got round that there was a nudist colony on the coast up from Bridlington and, after some searching, it was eventually located just south of Scarborough. Eventually it became such a popular attraction that we had to agree an unofficial left-hand circuit over the naturists to avoid colliding with each other.

In spite of everything else we were fortunate to be at Driffield during the summer months. As well as good weather making the flying just that bit easier, we were able to take in the delights of Bridlington's seaside attractions at weekends and on Wednesday sports afternoons. Many a young Yorkshire lass was to fall under the spell of this new young breed of jet pilot.

Our social activities got a considerable boost when Johnny Collins was given a car by his parents after getting his wings. Johnny's approach to car management was, if you can get in you can come, consequently it always carried many more 'bods' (some female) than it had seats. It was inevitable that whilst on our way to Scarborough one Saturday afternoon with seven up the clutch burnt out, and we were back on public transport until it was repaired.

We had been at Driffield for three months (it seemed like three years!) When we were told that the airfield was closing for the runway to be resurfaced, and that those of us who had not yet completed the course would be sent to another AFS to finish our Meteor conversion.

I had flown with fourteen different instructors during my short stay, which was probably due to the demands of the station aerobatic team which seemed to take preference over our training. Students in the average civil flying school complain bitterly if they have two changes of instructor.

I have no lasting memories of Driffield other than, to everyone's surprise and relief, we got through without having a fatality.

Johnny Collins and I were sent to No.207 AFS at RAF Full Sutton, in the Vale of York. We arrived in his car (complete with new clutch) in pouring rain on the evening of 1st November 1953, to discover that it was a wartime base, with accommodation to suit. The airfield and the runway had been built in the valley, with Nissen-hut accommodation dispersed over a wide area. If you stepped off the cinder path you were up to your ankles in mud, reminiscent of scenes from M.A.S.H. We found the Officers Mess and checked in.

"Don't take your coats off" said the steward "you've got a long walk."

He eventually ushered us into a corrugated tin hut furnished with three iron beds with horsehair mattresses, three wardrobes, and lino on the concrete floor. In the centre of the room was a coke fire, but unlit since there was no coke in the bucket. It was freezing cold. This was now an ideal opportunity to put all our leadership and escape and evasion exercises to good use. Little thought was needed: in very quick time we set about breaking up the third wardrobe, and along with the inside of a spare horse-hair mattress, we got the stove going like a 'good un.' Red hot in no time at all.

Next morning we presented ourselves to the Flying Wing Adjutant.

"Settled in OK?"

"Yes, thanks" we replied.

"Good, you're going to 'B' flight, shouldn't be too much of a problem."

We could sense a totally different relaxed atmosphere at the base, although they did have their moments just like all the other AFSs.

Probably the most widely publicised was when an instructor and student doing a single-engine approach in a T.7 managed to collide with the Hull to York fish train as it crossed the end of the duty runway. The aircraft was a write-off, but both occupants survived after being buried in 20 tons of prime cod.

We were told we had four weeks to complete because, like Driffield, they were also closing down at the end of the month. This seemed ample time, but we had not bargained for the appalling weather in the Vale of York at that time of year. A lack of aircraft was also a problem, as the school had their own courses going through at the same time. Nevertheless, we made steady progress for the first two weeks; then the weather clamped and we were grounded for the next fortnight!

The last day of the month, a Friday, was bright and sunny at last. I flew two dual trips in the morning and two solo trips in the afternoon. My log book was made up and signed, and by 1930 hrs I was on York station waiting for the London train, having completed my Meteor conversion and at last heading home on leave.

I had only been at Full Sutton for a month but remember it with affection. I also remember that it was there that I flew the oldest Meteor in the RAF. It was EE517, the first Mk 4 to be manufactured. Six months later it was scrapped!

It was no surprise to discover that, despite the rush to get our jet conversion finished, we had nowhere to go at the end of it. The Operational Conversion Unit (OCU) was unable to accept us for another three months, so Flying Training Command in their wisdom decided to send us on a Meteor refresher course! This was to be at another AFS, No.215 at RAF Finningley near Doncaster. Would we ever get out of the clutches of Flying Training Command?

In fact we remained on leave for a month before presenting ourselves at Finningley in the first week in January 1954. During the two months I was there I did a paltry 15 hrs flying, mostly refreshing what I had only completed at Full Sutton a few weeks previously. I suppose it was all good stuff, better than being stuck in an office, but there was always the fear that whilst you were still on a training establishment that you might still get scrubbed for doing something silly.

It also crossed my mind that so far I had not done any night flying in the Meteor. I am not sure whether this was intentional, or whether it was missed as a result of being shunted around different AFS's, but it nearly led to a disaster a few months later.

CHAPTER 6

No.226 Meteor OCU

On the 1st March 1954 I arrived at RAF Stradishall near New-market, the home of No.226 Operational Conversion Unit (OCU). I had at last left Flying Training Command, and was now on the posted strength of Fighter Command. 'Strad' was the Day Fighter OCU, and its task was to introduce 'sprog' pilots to the art of air fighting. To successfully take four guns to 35,000 ft, shoot down the enemy and return to base.

It was a happy station and, although the course would not be easy, we could sense that we were at last on a real operational base. The high morale on the base being due in no uncertain manner to the charisma of the previous Wingco Flying, Wing Commander 'Stutter' Mackenzie. He was legendary, and stories about him were still being told while we were there. Probably the most dramatic was the day he was supposed to be watching a staff pilot practising for an aerobatic display. The Meteor screamed across the airfield at 100 feet and pulled up into a loop, but with insufficient height for the pull-through went straight in. Everyone looked at the pall of smoke in horror but 'Stutter', watching from a distance, said 'Ssssshit hot!' and casually walked back to his office. Whether the story was true is not known but it was indicative of the laid-back attitude to danger that was prevalent amongst fighter pilots at that time.

We were introduced to the F8, the latest version of Meteor which was now operational with all the front-line day fighter squadrons. It looked more functional than the all-silver, yellow striped, Meteors in Training Command, plus it had an ejector seat, a bubble canopy giving improved all-round vision, a modified fin and rudder, wide engine intakes and the 'stick' had been changed from the old Spitfire 'spade handle' to a modern upright hand grip. But the most notable difference was of course the 'bang seat' - from now on we would have a lump of dynamite under our bums, hopefully making it easier to bale out should the occasion arise. To prepare us for that possibility we were each fired up a ramp in a dummy seat, but with only half the charge in the gun. Even so it seemed to go a hell of a long way up before being lowered back on to terra firma. Next we had our inside leg checked, not for new trousers but to ensure that our kneecaps were not amputated by the windscreen should we need to eject. Unfortunately, our flying clothing had not kept up with technology. Flying suits looked more like overalls worn in a factory, and we still wore the old wartime leather helmets. Aircrew shirts had not yet been introduced so we had to remove our tie, collar, studs and cuff links. For some inexplicable reason we were issued with hideous string vests made with 1/8th-inch thick rough twine and strips of canvas. Our fur-lined flying boots were eventually replaced with leather boots with a loose upper into which you tucked the bottom of your trousers, much like a Cossack. Needless to say we looked at our American counterparts and their equipment with some envy.

Formation flying played a very important part in fighter tactics, and this figured prominently in our training. We were trained to 'snake climb' four aircraft to altitude, sometimes through as much as 35,000 ft of cloud before getting 'on top,' then to fly in battle formation whilst being vectored on to a target, and finally for the formation to be 'recovered' to base, either in battle or close formation depending upon the weather.

A battle formation consisted of two pairs of aircraft, each pair covering the tail of the other, a formation flown by the Luftwaffe during the last war and later adopted by the RAF. Once in combat the two pairs became independent of each other, and carried out their own target interception. The leader of the pair carried home the attack with the wingman guarding his leader's tail.

The two pairs would be, say, Red 1 and 2 and Red 3 and 4, with Red 1 being the overall formation leader. For take-off, all four aircraft would line up on the runway. Red 1 on the left side and Red 2 on his right just over the runway centre-line, Red 3 would then tuck in behind and between Red 1 and 2. Finally Red 4 would take up position between Red 2 and the right-hand edge of the runway. This was well rehearsed and quite easy, in fact for ceremonial flypasts it was often necessary to have stream take-off's with six or more pairs lined up on the runway at the same time.

Once in position all four aircraft would run up to 12,000 rpm on the brakes, the first pair would roll followed 5 seconds later by the second pair. Once airborne the leading pair would pull high, allowing the second pair to pass through their slipstream whilst still on the runway. It became progressively more hairy with more than two pairs taking off together, especially if the runway was a bit on the short side! When airborne the lead pair would turn on to a pre- determined heading, and five seconds later the second pair would do the same. Passing through 2,000 ft the leader would instruct the formation to change to the Sector Control frequency. After the formation had checked in the Controller would pass target information and vectors to steer. The leader of the second pair would comply with these instructions after a five second interval. Whilst this was happening the two wingmen were hanging on in close formation to their respective leaders, all fat dumb and happy! For tactical reasons and to avoid unnecessary chatter on the R/T all instructions from the leader to his wingman whilst in close formation would be by hand signals.

In theory if both leaders flew accurate speeds and headings, the second pair would see the leading pair just ahead of them as they popped out of the cloud tops. In practice this very rarely happened! The second pair would invariably find themselves further behind, or to the left or right, possibly above or below of the lead pair, but hopefully never in front!

Once contact with the lead pair was established they would turn towards you. This might not be the direction they wanted to go, but it was the only way the second pair could catch up and get into position.

On days when there was little or no cloud, both pairs would join up immediately after take-off and climb in a loose finger-four formation. Finger four could be either left or right hand. If the leader called left hand, each one of us knew exactly what he meant by looking at the finger tips on the back of our left hand! The tip of the middle finger would be the overall leader (No.1), the index finger would be his wingman (No.2). The leader of the second pair (No.3) was the ring finger, which left the little finger for his wingman (No.4). If a right-hand finger four was called for, then of course the reverse would apply. Simple really!

As the formation reached its assigned altitude the number three moved out to a position about 1500 yds abeam and slightly behind the leader. The two wingmen then moved to an outside position, and slightly behind their respective leaders looking into the formation. When everyone was in position the formation had complete look-out coverage throughout 360 degrees.

So far so good, but a problem arose when the leader needed to turn the formation on to another heading - if only to come home! If the leader turned away from the Nos.3 and 4, they immediately had to cut across to the inside of the turn, passing below and behind the lead pair. The two wingmen then had to move to the other side of their leaders so as to maintain the cross cover. Geometrically of course it was only possible to execute this manoeuvre and finish up in formation if the change of heading was about 90 degrees. Anything more or less left the poor No.3 and his wingman miles out of position and with the cross cover in tatters.

The Meteor was particularly vulnerable when flown operationally at 40,000 ft. This was because the difference between the stall and the onset of compressibility at that altitude was only 60 knots, this naturally called for some very careful handling when flying in formation and during target interceptions.

For a while Fighter Command continued with the practice of flying standing patrols (called Loiter), a wartime tactic when the

Luftwaffe had fighter and bomber bases along the occupied coast of Europe. But in the 1950s the situation changed as the NATO radar network in western Europe gave the UK a far earlier plot of approaching bombers from the Eastern Bloc.

Once having reached altitude, and been vectored on to a target, you had to intercept it and shoot it down. Practice Interceptions (PIs) were good fun, if a bit hairy during the final stages. Occasionally, we did PIs on bombers but generally worked as a pair with one acting as the 'target' flying straight and level in much the same way as a bomber might. The other taking up a position abeam and about 2,000 ft above. The the attacker would then turn 90 degrees towards target which was quickly reversed so as to commence a curved approach for the attack. The maximum range to open fire was 600 yds, and at 200 yds the attacker would break away below the target.

By repeatedly attacking another Meteor you instantly knew when your range was 200 yds, but later when attacking a Victor or B-47 we found we were breaking off far too early, the size of the bomber gave the impression that you were much closer than you were. Generally bomber pilots were not at all happy about gung-ho fighter chaps doing dummy attacks on them, which is probably why attacking large bombers was not part of the OCU course.

Ranging and tracking on a target is of course the most important element of being a fighter pilot. Its no use getting four guns up behind a target and then missing it. We were lucky in that the aircraft was fitted with a Gyro Gun Sight which automatically compensated for deflection, but it did completely fill the windscreen when in use. Fortunately it could be retracted down behind the instrument panel as previously described.

In technical terms the GGS measured the angular velocity of the line of sight to the target by reference to a centre dot in the centre of a gyroscopically controlled graticule. By twisting the starboard throttle lever the pilot was able to increase or decrease the diameter of the graticule until it encompassed the targets'

A frame fron the author's Gunsight Recorder film of a practice interception on another Meteor.

wingspan, if then you had the centre dot on the cockpit you couldn't miss!

It was not easy - as you closed on the target you had to progressively increase the size of the graticule as the wing-span of the target got bigger. Each time you did this, the dot would be displaced to correct for the changing deflection. By the time you got the dot back on the cockpit the range setting would again need correcting, and so it went on. If at any time during the few seconds at your disposal you happened to get them both right, you pulled the trigger quick!

For training purposes, instead of pulling the trigger you 'fired' a camera by pressing a button on top of the control column. The camera was installed above the GGS and it filmed exactly what you saw in the gun sight. There was no getting away with flannel or bullshit, it was all there for everyone to see when the film was developed after landing.

The most exciting part of the course was being let loose with live ammunition for the first time. For target practice a Mosquito would tow a banner (flag) which was 60 ft long and attached to a 10 ft high post. In the centre of the flag would be a large yellow circle. The whole thing was towed some distance behind the Mossy to allow the crew some degree of safety. The attack procedure was similar to PI's but you had to stop firing if you found yourself getting into a line astern position. If you failed to stop, all you saw in your gun sight was the Mosquito, which was why the Mosquito pilots got a bit nervous from time to time. If on your return to base there was a nice big picture of a Mossy on your film you were on the next bus to civvy street. The other hazard was leaving the break too late. A number of chaps did, and then discovered that a Meteor with a large metal bar embedded in the wing had very different flying characteristics.

The position of the four 20 mm cannons meant there was much noise in the cockpit when they were being fired. This was because two were located on top of each other on either side of the cockpit. This installation also meant that when fired, unlike wartime fighters, there was little or no bullet spread to assist the pilot.

Air-to-air firing was carried out in a danger area about 25 miles off the Norfolk coast, the whole thing being under radar control, which not only enabled us to find the tug towing the banner but also alerted us to any other aircraft or ships which might have strayed into the area.

Although a bit hairy, success on air-to-air sorties did the old ego a bit of good, and there was always a sense of hushed expectation as the tug arrived back over the airfield and jettisoned the banner. In order to determine whose hole was whose, the armourers put a blob of wet paint on the tip of each bullet which then left a coloured mark around the holes in the banner. Any holes with no colour markings were rather gratuitously given to those who had no other hits. On my first flight I got a massive 1%, then three consecutive zeros!

It called for drastic action so, despite the aforementioned risks, I decided the answer was to get closer before opening fire - it worked, my last three scores being 6%, 14% and 10%. I had made it, and eagerly awaited my posting to a squadron.

We had been asked if we had any preferences, Johnny Collins opted for No. 41 Sqn at Biggin Hill and I thought it would be nice to be posted to one of the squadrons based at RAF Tangmere near Chichester. When the posting notices went up Johnny had got 41 Sqn, and four of us were posted to the Wattisham Wing near Ipswich. Hedley Molland and Alan Watkinson going to No.263 Sqn, and Geoff Sanger and myself being posted to No.257 Sqn.

CHAPTER 7

No. 257 (Burma) Squadron

My posting to 257 Squadron was not a disappointment, even though RAF Wattisham happened to be in the sticks and away from the night life. The Station Commander was Group Captain Hughie Edwards VC, DFC, who as a Wing Commander with No.105 Sqn led the low-level Blenheim raid on Bremen in 1941. Later he was ADC to the Queen, was knighted, and eventually became Governor of Western Australia.

So it was that on the morning of 24th April 1954 Geoff Sanger and I presented ourselves to the Squadron CO, Major Howard Nelson Tanner, an American Officer on exchange from the USAF, an ace who had flown F-86 Sabres on active service in Korea.

Although the Second World War was long over, pilots on fighter squadrons still retained a lot of their war time flair. The top button on the uniform was always undone, and peaked hats were still worn with working uniform in preference to the sloppy beret that had recently been introduced. Sadly the white silk scarves much favoured by our predecessors had been banished, and handlebar moustaches no longer seemed to be popular in the new jet age.

The boss took me into the crew room to meet my Flight Commander, Flight Lieutenant 'Chalky' White and the other pilots on 'B' Flight.

"What's your name, son?" asked Sergeant Pilot 'Sim' Eastman, in a successful attempt to deflate any ego I might have had in my officer's uniform.

"Graham" I replied nervously.

"We don't want any Grahams on Two Five Seven - from now on you're 'Nick' - get it" I did.

Early in 1940 No.257 Sqn had been adopted by the Burmese people who donated the sum of £150,000, a massive amount of money, to equip the squadron with Hawker Hurricanes, and in recognition of this the squadron took up the title No.257 (Burma) Sqn. The squadron crest was changed to incorporate the figure of a Chinthe, symbolising royalty. In ancient Burmese mythology the Chinthe was the king of all the beasts and creatures on this earth, and represented strength, leadership and all that is royal and majestic. Several Burmese pilots went on to serve with the squadron with distinction.

During the Battle of Britain the squadron was in 11 Group and operated mainly from Northolt and Martlesham Heath; it was whilst the Squadron was at Martlesham that Bob Stanford-Tuck became its new CO. He was to command the squadron with great success, and his outstanding leadership, courage and skill brought with it high morale and efficiency. He has been described as probably the best fighter pilot of the second World War. His total of 28 enemy aircraft destroyed would have certainly been much higher had he not been captured by the Germans after baling out in 1941.

On the 11 November 1940 the cream of the Italian Air Force thought they would get into the action by bombing the port of Harwich. They had been led to believe there would be little or no resistance from the RAF. As a result a very large formation of Fiat B.R.20 bombers escorted by 40 Fiat C.R.42 fighters appeared over the Thames estuary. No.257 Sqn was scrambled, but the pilots were somewhat surprised when they encounter these strange looking aircraft, but after checking with the sector controller they were recognised as being Mussolini's much vaunted 'Regia Aeronautica'. The pilots from the Burma Squadron had a field day, destroying 12 aircraft and damaging a further nine. One Italian even landed his undamaged C.R.42 fighter on the beach at Orford Ness and gave himself up. This was the first and last time that Italian bombers attempted to take on Fighter Command.

In 1942 the squadron re-equipped with Typhoons, and adopted a ground-attack role against railway marshalling yards, trains, airfields and troop concentrations in Northern France. This role continued until 'D' day when dive bombing was added to the Typhoon's repertoire. The squadron followed the advancing armies as far as Lille, where it was disbanded on 3rd August 1945.

Exactly a year later the squadron was reformed at RAF Church Fenton flying Spitfires, and nine months after that the Squadron moved to Horsham St Faith and was re-equipped with the Meteor F.3. In due course these were swapped for the F.4s, and before moving to Wattisham in 1950 the squadron took delivery of their F.8s.

What struck me on walking into the squadron offices for the first time was the complete lack of any historical ambience or visual pride in the squadron's illustrious past. There was nothing on display to depict the historic achievements of the squadron, not even a photo. It seemed very strange to me, and could only reflect a general lack of interest by post-war squadron commanders.

The squadron had been flying its F.8s for only a few months when Sgt Edwards had a very unpleasant surprise. Whilst practising aerobatics, the first-stage cartridge in the ejector seat fired, wedging his head at a twisted angle up against the inside of the canopy. In this most uncomfortable position, and with a cockpit full of acrid smoke, he successfully returned to base and probably did the smoothest landing of his life. It was fortunate for him that the secondary cartridge failed to fire. The next day Mr James Martin, Managing Director and Chief Designer of the Martin-Baker Aircraft Company visited Wattisham personally to investigate the problem. About the same time Flying Officer Stoney was flying his Royal Australian Air Force Meteor when suddenly the seat ejected him from the aircraft for no apparent reason. He was the first pilot to eject safely from a Meteor, a distinction no doubt he could have done without.

Stories about ejector-seat mishaps spread like wildfire, and they became even more sensational in the telling. So much so that some chaps became decidedly uncomfortable sitting on top of a 'load of dynamite'.

The original seat in the Meteor was the Mk 1E, which only banged you out of the aircraft. Once clear, you needed to release yourself from the seat and deploy the parachute by pulling the rip cord in the usual way. Subsequently the seat was improved when it was fitted with the ML automatic seat-harness release mechanism. In 1954 the fully automatic Mk 2E seat was installed in the Meteor Another potential hazard was that the Meteor had no external ladder to gain access to the cockpit. After strapping you in an airman would remove the seat safety pin, show it to you, and then stow it away. Whilst doing this he was clutching the side of the cockpit, and simultaneously balancing his toes in two small footholds in the side of the fuselage. Until he got down you were in a state of nervous tension, should he slip and inadvertently grab the firing handle.

Whilst working on ejector seats with ML Aviation in the 1940s I well remember hearing the story of a fitter who had installed a seat in a trials Meteor in preparation for a airborne test firing. Whilst getting down he slipped and accidentally fired the seat by grabbing the firing handle. Fortunately, nobody was sitting in it at the time, but it make a big hole in the hangar roof at Farnborough.

On my first day on the squadron I did two dual sorties in the two-seat Meteor T.7, one with the Squadron Instrument Rating Examiner (IRE) to see what my instrument flying was like, and the other being a general handling check with Flight Lieutenant 'Cherry' Kearton 'A' Flight Commander. Then I was let loose on my own, a big moment. The squadron was doing air-to-air gunnery on the flag, and much to my surprise I was given a go, achieving 1% and 4%. Anything better than a duck! I often wonder if as a new boy I had been credited with an unmarked hole to get on the score sheet!

It soon became obvious that although I had finished my training there was still a lot to learn before I was considered a fully operational fighter pilot. I also needed to know that 'Angels' was your height in thousands of feet, 'Bandits' were the enemy, 'Buster' was full power, 'Tally Ho' meant I was in contact with the target, 'Bogies' were unknown targets, 'Bingo' said my fuel state was such that we should be heading for home, 'Pigeons' was a heading and distance to base. Hand signals were also important especially when doing a formation take-off or landing. The leader moving his hand in a circular motion to indicate he was increasing power for take -off, nodding his head forward meant he was releasing the brakes. On the approach, a continuous movement bringing his thumb and fingers together indicated he was lowering his flaps, and an action similar to pulling an old-fashioned lavatory chain meant he was about to lower his undercarriage.

My first two weeks were spent entirely flying in close formation as a wingman, doing takeoffs, let-downs, circuits, GCAs and landings with all instructions from the leader by means of hand signals.

Fighters are at their most vulnerable when returning to base, especially in good weather, when they are low on fuel and flying at slow speed for the approach and landing. Pilots were heavily dependant upon sector controllers and their radar. In most cases you had no idea where you were after being vectored around the sky chasing 'bandits', so on completion you would be given 'pigeons' to get you home. The airfield would be approached at high speed, letting down to run in for a break and landing at 500 ft. If the circuit pattern was left-hand the formation would fly echelon starboard. Crossing the airfield boundary, the leader would break hard left, throttle back, airbrakes out and climb in the turn to circuit height. This bled the speed off, enabling the gear to go down at 175 knots, quickly followed by one-third flap at 150 knots and full flap halfway round the final turn, rolling out as you crossed the runway threshold at 105 knots. The rest of the formation would break at two-second intervals, each watching the chap ahead like a hawk. Aircraft would then be landed on alternate sides of the runway and if you were all very clever the last one would be touching down just as the leader turned off at the far end.

Bad weather was different; in cloud you were not so vulnerable but recovery took longer. The formation would be given vectors to steer so as to get overhead the airfield at altitude for a QGH. Once you were inbound at 6 nm and 1,500 ft you were be handed over to 'talkdown' for a poor man's GCA. With this particular equipment (EKCO), which had only been installed the previous November, you were given a radar approach but with no glide-slope guidance. The operator had no height information, so at regular intervals he would tell you your distance from touch down and the height you should be passing through. It was then up to you to adjust your rate of descent accordingly, so that a 3-degree glide path was maintained until you were visual with the runway. Full GCA was a luxury which was not available to us at Wattisham.

The patter on an EKCO type talkdown might be 'Red 3 you're slightly left of the centre-line, come right onto 245, you're 3 miles from touchdown and your height should be 1,200 ft'. This was OK if you were on your own, but if you had a buddy hanging on your wing tip he sometimes had a rough ride whilst you juggled to get it right. The limits for an EKCO approach was cloud base 300 ft and 2,000 yards visibility.

We were indebted to the United States Air Force for allowing us to practise proper GCAs at their bases in East Anglia. On my seventh trip I was sent off on a whole detail just practising GCAs with the USAF at Wethersfield in Essex.

Next I was introduced to Distance Measuring Equipment (DME). DME was a new radio aid which had recently been installed in the Meteor F.8s, so new in fact that there was no mention of it in the Pilot's Notes. Basically, when the airborne equipment was tuned to an ground transmitter it would indicate a heading and distance to that beacon. The heading indicator was very basic, it only told you if the DME was to your left or right. As with much new equipment at the time it was also unreliable, but CFE devised a system whereby Fighter Command pilots would use it as a pilot interpreted navigation aid in the event of radio and radar jamming. The idea was that you carried in the cockpit a map of south-east England which had been mounted on a board with a Perspex covering. On the map you had previously marked the position of two DMEs with circles radiating from them every 10 nm. The GCI station would blast out a continuous broadcast through the jamming, giving the position, height and heading of known bandits. All the formation leader had to do was to make a note of the target position, then establish where he was by getting a fix from the DME circles on his map and setting up an interception.

The problem was that the Meteor had only one DME set, so it was necessary to tune in the first, get a range and mark it on your map. Then tune the other and mark that range on your map. Now, as every schoolboy knows, the circles in question will cross in two places. You could probably guess as to which fix was the correct one, but if you were unsure you needed to tune in a third to be absolutely accurate. By the time you had worked all this out the target would be miles away from its original position. Who was kidding who!

It was a hopeless tactic, and needless to say it died a quick death - at least on the Burma Squadron it did. Later in the more stable world of commercial aviation DME was to became a very successful navigation aid, but its early use in single-seat jet fighters was a failure.

One of the more enjoyable sorties was 'Rat and Terrier' which was training to intercept low-flying intruders. Four aircraft flew in a finger-four battle formation at 500 ft, which was great fun and exhilarating but not without some risk.

The Wattisham Wing consisted of Nos.257, 263 and 152 squadrons, but each squadron was truly independent - the 'big wing' having died a death long before the end of the war. No.152 Sqn was a night-fighter unit flying Meteor NF.11s. Needless to say, they flew at night so we saw very little of them except at weekends. The Wing was in 11 Group, which was responsible for the fighter defence of south-east England much as it was during the war. The

Group consisted of a number of sectors. Wattisham was in the Eastern Sector, which extended from north-east London out to beyond Ipswich, and the GCI station for our area was in a hole in the ground strategically located on the coast at Bawdsey near Felixstowe. The success of any fighter interception was dependent upon the skills of the fighter controllers, and at Bawdsey they were the best. They would pick us up on their screen shortly after take-off, and put us into a position to attack a target over 100 miles away at a height of say 30,000ft. After the interception, they then had the responsibility of getting you back to base, or to a diversionary airfield if you were short of fuel or the weather was bad. Sadly, we had little or no personal contact with them, which to most of us was a disappointment because we were frequently controlled by a lady with a very confident but sexy voice.

Rather disrespectfully she was known to the chaps on the squadron as 'Golden Tits', but as a fighter controller she was ace. Even when not working under GCI control it was customary to check in with them and 'listen out' - you never knew when you might need their help in a hurry. Radar coverage was pretty poor below 1,000 ft, which meant the GCI's were heavily dependent on the Royal Observer Corps (ROC) for reporting and plotting low-flying targets. Working with the ROC involved a lot of low flying, either to simulate incoming raiders or chasing after others. It was great fun, but at the speed the enemy would be flying it is doubtful if many would have been shot down.

Even with better communications, and improved radar coverage extending well into eastern Europe, it was still imperative that we should get airborne within one minute of being scrambled. During an exercise the procedure was to bring us to readiness in pairs. This entailed each pair taxiing to a pan at the end of the runway. A new innovation was the introduction of telescramble, whereby once on the readiness pan the ground crew plugged in a GPO cable to the rear of the aircraft which put you in direct contact with the sector controller. After checking in with him (or her!) you would be updated on the situation. You would then shut down engines and get stuck into a good book, or sit and marvel at the beauty of the countryside and the twittering birds. This tranquillity might suddenly be interrupted by 'Wattisham, Wattisham, Bendix Blue scramble, heading 120, contact Bender on 128.5.' 'Roger', press the tit and away you went. During my second month on the squadron I did 18 hrs 50 minutes which, when one considered that the average sortie was about 45 minutes, was a good effort. The flying consisted of battle formation, practice interceptions, ranging and tracking, individual aerobatics, low flying, QGHs and GCAs and even two simulated single-engine landings. We did some 'dusk rollers' which entailed circuits after sunset but before it became dark, thus being credited with night flying but actually doing it in daylight! My firing on the banner improved to 17% and 10%, and in my mind I was an ace in the making, that is until the afternoon of 18th June 1954!

Perhaps there had been a late party in the mess the night before, I cannot remember, but it was my third trip of the day. I had earlier completed two details of formation QGHs and GCAs when I was authorised for cine' attacks on the flag off Lowestoft, with 'Sim' Eastman leading. On our return to base we broke for a circuit and landing, but half-way round finals Slim decided to overshoot. Why was that, I thought? Was he in a bad position for landing, crosswind? Will it affect me. No its OK, I'll land. I rounded out and then for a split second I knew that all was not well! There was a scrapping noise as the ventral fuel tank scratched its way along the runway, the fuel vapour in the tank ignited and the aircraft was enveloped in a ball of fire for a couple of seconds. As the Meteor slid to a sudden halt I shut down the engines and leapt out like a scalded cat. The boss arrived on the scene the same time as the 'blood waggon.'

"Wassa matta, Carter - the gear collapse?"

"No Boss, I didn't put it down" I said with some embarrassment.

There were mitigating circumstances. On all RAF airfields a man sat in a chequered caravan near the touchdown point of the active runway. His main task was to alert aircraft to any danger whilst on final approach by firing a red verey cartridge which told the pilot to overshoot. Needless to say I saw no red stars. The chap in the caravan later admitted that he failed to notice that my wheels were not down. It made no difference, the charge sheet read:

> *The accused Flying Officer John Graham Carter (3512884) of No.257 Sqn, Royal Air Force Station, Wattisham, an officer of the regular air force, is charged with NEGLIGENTLY DAMAGING AN AIRCRAFT BELONGING TO HER MAJESTY in that he at Wattisham, on 18 June 1954, when pilot of Her Majesty's aircraft Meteor 8 WH291, so negligently flew the said aircraft as to cause it to crash land with wheels up.*

I was summoned to 11 Group Headquarters at RAF Uxbridge and duly marched in front of the Air Officer Commanding (AOC), Air Vice-Marshal 'Sam' Patch to answer the charge. He studied my file whilst I stood to attention with my hat under my arm. Then he raised his head.

"Do you wish to say anything Carter"

It crossed my mind to mention that it might not have happened if the chap in the caravan had been on the ball but then thought better of it.

"No Sir"

"Hum - well you can't go about bending Her Majesty's aircraft like this, see that it doesn't happen again, do you understand?"

"Yes Sir"

"Very well - a reprimand"

"Thank you, Sir"

"Well that's got the formal bit over, now sit down and tell me how you're getting on at Wattisham."

We then had a very pleasant chat and at the end he suggested that as I had to go back through London I should take advantage of the situation and have a night on the town, which I did.

Many years later I discovered that WH291 was eventually repaired, and continued to fly for a number of years with various

Photo courtesy of J. Robertson.

Gloster Meteor WH291 taking off. This is the same aircraft that the author landed 'wheels up' in 1954.

squadrons before being retired from military service. It is now owned and displayed by the Second World War Aircraft Preservation Society on the north side of Lasham Airfield in Hampshire.

Within days it was all forgotten. I achieved the squadron's highest air-to-air score on the flag with 25%, and my average was also the highest at 20.3%. With the squadron average being only 9.9% I was quite chuffed, especially as there were some real aces on the Burma Squadron and I was still considered 'non-operational'. I also managed to get some practice interceptions on a Lincoln, a rare treat indeed.

The real excitement during July was taking part in the annual defence exercise, code-named 'Dividend'. Three days of intense activity defending the country against hordes of aircraft from 2nd TAF and other NATO Air Forces attempting to bomb targets in the UK. Late on the first day of the exercise I was scrambled as No.2 in a battle four led by 'Chalky' White. There was a warm front across East Anglia and we entered cloud at 500 ft, eventually breaking out of the top at 35,000 ft. We intercepted our target well out over the North Sea, but by the time we got back overhead Wattisham the cloud was on the deck and after some discussion it was decided that we should divert to RAF Duxford. They were our best bet, but were giving a cloud base of 300 ft in continuous heavy rain with a surface wind of 290/20. It was dark when we arrived overhead, with all four of us low on fuel. On top of that I told 'Chalky' on the R/T that I had not flown a Meteor at night before, which just about made his day!

As we started letting down through 30,000 ft of cloud I tucked in close, just two feet off his wing tip. All I hoped was that I had enough fuel to make it first time round, the alternative being to eject, not an attractive option in those conditions. Five miles out we completed our landing checks as the turbulence became more severe. As we proceeded on the approach the radar controller said the base was now 200 ft, still with heavy rain. With his next breath he said the surface wind was now 340/25 and we were clear to land. A crosswind from starboard, must be careful not to drift into the leader as we touched down I thought. Then suddenly I caught a glimpse of some lights out of the corner of my eye just as 'Chalky' called "Cut". I chopped the power and kicked off the drift, keeping one eye on the leader and the other on the runway lights. The aircraft seemed to hang in the air for ages but just when I was getting concerned there was a mighty thump and I was down. As we turned off the runway the pair behind were touching down. We all sank a few pints in the Duxford Mess that night, and wondered who it was who said 'only birds and fools fly, and birds don't fly at night!

Exercise 'Dividend' was one of the largest air defence exercises to be held since the war. The C-in-C Fighter Command, Air Marshal Sir Dermot Boyle in his post-exercise debriefing said the UK air defences had shown themselves to be effective, with interceptions taking place between 40,000 and 50,000 ft some 100 miles out over the sea. As a final assessment he said that we were rather ahead of the threat as it existed at present. This might have been the case with the two squadrons flying Canadian-built F-86 Sabres, on temporary loan with American funding, but it certainly was not the case as far as the other 26 squadrons in Fighter Command flying Meteor F.8s were concerned. The only 'bandits' that we intercepted were either other Meteors from Training Command or Canberras and USAF B-47s which by arrangement were flying at a height and speed that the Meteors could cope with. An arrangement we could not expect from the Soviets.

I was still seeing Colleen as often as possible, but she was on tour and our meetings depended upon which town the show happened to be in at any given time. I made full use of periodic free travel warrants, saving them for the longest distances, and at other times taking advantage of the cheap fares on the railways which were still available to service personnel. On one such occasion, I was pleased to be best man when her sister Beryl married Derek Nicholson. Later Colleen became a Tiller Girl at the Adelphi Theatre in London and we became engaged. Some of the lads on the squadron, keen to get in on the act, suggested that I invite the whole troupe to the mess for a Sunday night 'whooly' but before it could be arranged I had 'banged out' and had taken up residence in the Borough General Hospital in Ipswich.

Social life in the Mess was great, so there was little need to go off base. Needham Market and Stowmarket were not a ball of fire, and neither was Ipswich for that matter. Another factor was that only a few of us had cars, making us heavily dependent on buses or service transport.

Station duties cropped up from time to time, the most tedious being Orderly Officer of the day. This entailed being present when the RAF Ensign was raised outside Station Headquarters in the early morning and again at dusk when it was lowered, visiting the Airmen's Mess and checking any deliveries for shortages, inspecting the kitchens and seeing if there were any complaints - always a bit hazardous!

In the evening you were expected to do the same in the Sergeant's Mess - it was not easy, especially as some of the NCOs were senior pilots on the squadron. You were either 'set up' for a laugh and made to look a right berk or, more than likely, invited into their bar for a 'laced' drink, finishing up legless! Finally, if sober, you were expected to tour the airfield boundary by Land-Rover to check that nobody had broken in. This was a problem for most of us, because we had no idea where the boundary was or where to go, so we would drive around the hangars for a while then return to the comfort of the mess bar. You slept in the Orderly Officer's Room in the mess, and during the night it was inevitable that the telephone would ring about some fracas or another. Fortunately with about 100 officers on the base this onerous task came round rather infrequently.

Late in the summer of 1954 it was decided that bus loads of Police, Firemen, members of the Observer Corps, the Red Cross and St John's Ambulance and others should be shown how to rescue a pilot from a crashed Meteor whilst still strapped in his ejector seat. Geoff Wright and myself landed this job one Sunday morning, when we would have much preferred to be in bed. I sat in an aircraft in the hangar whilst they each peered over my shoulder and Geoff told them where all the important knobs and tits were. Of course the seat-firing handle was high on the list of things not to touch - it was not there as a handle to grab! Unbelievably, I was told to wear my best blue with my flying helmet, and not the flying suit I would be wearing if I crashed. The RAF in those days insisted that the proper dress if you were on duty with the public present was your 'best blue'.

Another unexpected duty cropped up when I was summoned to the Station Adjutant's Office and told that I was to conduct a one-man Board of Enquiry, to establish how a boat belonging to the Station Sailing Club happened to sink in the River Orwell. The RAF wanted to know how it came to sink, and whether anyone in the Sailing Club had been negligent. My report said that it had been securely moored by club members when they left the mooring, and that the only explanation was that vandals must have untied the craft during the night. The Sailing Club were pleased with this finding, and I was back in the bar by lunchtime. A clear case of not wishing to rock the boat!

There was much rivalry in the mess between us and the chaps on No.263 especially at dining-in-nights. On the top table would be the Station Commander, along with other senior officers on the base. Members of the two day fighter squadrons would be seated separately down either side of the long dining room, and once the Padre had said grace there might be some throwing of bread rolls. These high spirits were accepted by those in authority but should any civilian guests be present the Station Commander would take a very dim view of it, with the offender being told to leave the room! Mess games in the ante-room after dinner were legendary, and although a fair amount of beer was consumed it was a black mark to be drunk. If you felt a bit under the weather you quietly slopped off to your room, before you 'put up a black'.

The squadron's main watering hole off the base was *The Swan* at Lavenham, where parties and darts matches were held from time to time. The locals took our antics in good part. The squadron party piece was well known. On the call of 'dead ants' all the chaps, including the boss, would drop their backsides onto the floor and waive their arms and legs in the air - like dead or dying ants! There were competitions for drinking the fastest pint of beer, for the fastest yard of ale, and all new chaps to the squadron had to drink, in one go, a liqueur mix of green chartreuse topped up with crème de menthe, which also happened to be the squadron colours of green and yellow.

I had been on the squadron for about three months when I suddenly noticed that my name on the operations board was now permanently printed in black instead of being handwritten in green Chinagraph. This meant that I was now a fully operational fighter pilot, ready to be chucked at the enemy should the need arise - and I could now wear the coveted squadron badge on my flying suit and have a squadron tie.

As it was, I knew not a great deal more about fighter tactics than when I arrived, which was mainly due to a seemingly casual approach to the on-going training of new squadron pilots. This stemmed from pre-war days, when it was not considered proper to talk about flying other than at flight briefings. At any other time it was not on, and you would be told to 'close the hangar doors.' This bred a degree of uncertainty, until you managed to work it out for yourself. You never admitted to not knowing by asking questions, if your leader said you had flown a good sortie you left it at that.

The practice of having your own aircraft, with your name painted on the fuselage, had been discontinued, but the new status of being operational did open the door to a little-known perk, the use of a squadron aircraft to go away for the odd weekend. The extent to which this was done depended upon individual squadron commanders. Some units did it quite often, others never.

It was a standing joke that the Russians could not start a war at a weekend, because the RAF always shut down on a Friday night! I quickly took advantage of this perk when going home to Maidenhead for a weekend, by flying a Meteor into RAF Benson. With tongue in cheek I once asked if I could take one into White Waltham. I had seen all sorts of aircraft landing there during the war, and in recent times the odd Meteor had been in and out of this 1,000 yards grass airfield for ejector-seat trials. But the boss would have none of it, which probably was quite sensible because there was no operational reason for a squadron aircraft to land there and awkward questions might have been asked about front-line fighter aircraft being deployed in this way.

Fighter Command had both a day and night fighter squadron permanently on 24 hr standby to scramble and intercept any unknown aircraft entering UK airspace. This was known as exercise 'Fabulous', which squadrons did by rotation from RAF Horsham St Faith, Norwich. At other times a pair on a normal training flight might be asked to check out an unidentified blip on the radar. These always turned out to be a Viscount or some other airliner flying off-airways without having filed a flight plan. We enjoyed it - it was good fun, especially as the GCI controller would invariably ask you to get the registration of the offending aircraft. It was surprising how short-sighted some fighter pilots became when given the opportunity to formate close enough to wave to the passengers, who were looking back at you with some apprehension. It was a different story for the many interceptions carried out from bases in Scotland, which often turned out to be real Russian aircraft on eavesdropping flights.

Battle of Britain Day meant that Wattisham, along with many other stations, would be open to the public with the three resident squadrons putting on flying displays. The best part for me was the day before, when the whole squadron, dressed in flying gear and complete with our new 'Bone-dome' helmets went to Sudbury, Hadleigh and Lavenham advertising our open day and rattling tins for the RAF Benevolent Fund. As a relative newcomer to the squadron I missed out on the flying, and instead was delegated to 'fly' a coconut-shy stand, but the party that night made up for it. The station had 20,000 visitors and we took £1,000.

With the nights getting longer, the boss said we were to do some real night flying - whether this was as a result of my close shave at Duxford or an additional training task from 11 Group Headquarters was not clear, but we were programmed for night flying on three consecutive nights. On the first night I flew a simple navigation exercise from Wattisham to Bournemouth to Brighton and back to base. The following night I went up to Blackpool, twice round the tower and back home! On the third night the boss gave me the shock of my life.

"You can come as my No.2 Nick, in a four-ship formation, we'll do battle formation at 35,000 ft then a tail chase followed by a QGH and a pairs landing"

"What, at night!!" I blurted.

"Not to worry, It'll be nice and gentle"

It was an experience not to be forgotten. A month later we repeated the exercise with a night cross-country from Wattisham to Linton-on-Ouse to Norwich and back to base in loose finger four-formation. According to Howard Tanner the USAF often flew their F-86s in formation at night.

With the Americans across the road at Bentwaters it was inevitable that we would encounter their jets over East Anglia, and often dogfights would develop. In nearly every encounter we came off second-best due to the F-86's superiority over the Meteor. Nevertheless we plodded on with what we had, encouraged by the news that No.257 was earmarked to be the first squadron in the RAF to re-equip with the Hawker Hunter F.2. The first aircraft was due to be delivered to Wattisham in September 1954. Unlike the Hunter F.1 the F.2 was powered by an Armstrong Siddeley Sapphire engine, and was being built, not by the Hawker Aircraft Co but by the Sir Armstrong Whitworth Aircraft Co at Baginton, Coventry.

The Squadron was invited to visit the company to see the aircraft being assembled. We were given a conducted tour through the factory, followed by a sumptuous lunch in a country club, and then in the afternoon Air Commodore Winter-Morgan accompanied us to the flight test centre at Bitteswell. It was very exciting seeing these brand-new fighters which would shortly to be ours to fly. The following week test pilots from RAF Boscombe Down came to Wattisham to brief us on the handling and performance of the Hunter. We could hardly wait to get our hands on them. In a blaze of excitement the first two arrived at Wattisham late afternoon on 29th September, and on 22nd October the boss did the first flight.

In the meantime I increased my gunnery score on the flag to 26%, and I started to lead four-ship battle formations. I had now achieved a senior pilot status on the squadron but, by a twist of circumstances, Geoff and I were still the most junior simply because no new pilots were posted in whilst we were re-equipping with the Hunter.

The Meteors were being taken away quicker than the Hunters were arriving, which left us a bit short of aircraft, so a number of us were sent off on two-day liaison visits to various GCI stations. I was sent to Wartling near Bexhill, an interesting place set deep underground and accessed by a lift in what seemed to be an old farmhouse.

As soon as we had four Hunters serviceable on the line a full conversion programme got underway, and I looked forward to my turn to fly this beautiful aircraft. Then morale took a dive. We were told that six of the ten pilots who had not yet converted were being posted to other squadrons - flying Meteor night fighters of all things. It would seem that it had been decided, rather belatedly, that Hunter squadrons would have a complement of 16 aircraft and 20 pilots. Rather less than was the case with the Meteors. By good fortune I was not one of the unlucky ones, but we did feel sorry for them especially when, shortly after their departure, two ex-cadets from the RAF College at Cranwell were posted to the Squadron.

As it was, the conversion programme suffered a set-back when on 20th December with darkness approaching Sgt Garthwaite pressed the starter button to do a ground run on Hunter WN896. Much to his surprise, both starter cartridges fired and the engine caught fire. This caused a bit of a panic as the aircraft was only just outside the hangar, but prompt action by the fire crew had a spectacular blaze quickly under control. Sadly the aircraft was completely burnt out with less than 5 hrs in its log book.

The very next day, on what I imagined would be one of my last trips in a Meteor, I took off from Wattisham on a pretty routine sortie, but within 30 minutes I was as close to death as one could possibly be. Three Meteors crashed on that day, but the other two pilots were not so lucky. One from the Central Gunnery School at Leconfield spun in near Hull, and another from RAF Worksop flew into high ground in bad weather. Both pilots were killed.

CHAPTER 8

Court of Enquiry

Meteor F.8 WH299 was only three years old, and had flown a mere 685 hrs when it crashed, but it already had a history as they say. It was first allocated to No.263 Sqn, but they managed to bend it when the leading edge of the wing broke off as one of their pilots was pulling out of a high-speed dive at low level. After making an emergency landing at RAF Marham, it was returned to Gloster Aircraft for repair. Five months later it was delivered to No.257 Sqn.

As with all aircraft accidents, a Court of Enquiry was hastily convened by Fighter Command, and by late afternoon on the same day members of the Court had assembled at RAF Wattisham. The President was Sqn Ldr Clause from No. 500 Sqn at RAF West Malling, assisted by Sqn Ldr Kotlarz from HQ Fighter Command and Flt Lt Plowman from No. 63 Sqn based at RAF Waterbeach. After reporting to the Station Commander, they got to work.

For some time there had been concern about the high accident rate being experienced with the RAF's first jet fighter, and members of the Court had this very much in mind when they visited me in hospital the following day. I was still pretty weak, having lost a lot of blood, plus the after effects of a three-hour operation the previous afternoon. However I made a statement as best I could. I was particularly concerned about the struggle I had in reaching the blind to eject. I felt there should be an alternative, more accessible, firing handle, possibly between the legs or on the thigh guards similar to the early American seats. I felt that most pilots would prefer the option of using a secondary firing mechanism, even at the risk of spinal injury.

The Court took statements from the other two members of the formation, Phil Philip and Phil Pickford. They had also encountered problems similar to mine and were forced to abandon the tail chase. My Flight Commander 'Chalky' White in his statement spoke highly of my ability, and said that I had above average potential as a fighter pilot.

This was in stark contrast to the evidence of the formation leader. He told the Court that throughout the flight my flying had been poor and that my position in the tail chase was so close that it was affecting his elevator control! This conflicted with the evidence of Phil Philip who was immediately behind me in the tail chase; he said that in his opinion I was in the correct position - about 300 yards behind the leader.

Apart from allocating any blame, the Court was looking to see if this accident could throw any light on previously unexplained Meteor crashes. Why did the aircraft not respond to the normal recovery action? Recovery action was regularly practised on training exercises, but only in straight and level flight, but I was attempting to recover whilst in a spiral dive, and at a high Mach number. Was there any connection?

The purpose of the Machmeter was to provide the pilot with a continuous indication of the relationship of the speed of the aircraft to the speed of sound. The scale on the instrument covered the range 0.5M to 1.0M and it was graduated so that 1.0M was the speed of sound although the Meteor could not get anywhere near that!

In fact at 0.7M (70% the speed of sound) shock waves formed on the wing and tail surfaces, disrupting the normal airflow and causing turbulence and stiffening of the controls. As the speed was further increased to 0.8M the turbulence became severe with the controls nearly solid. When the speed was reduced back to below 0.7M by extending the airbrakes and closing the throttles normal control was regained. Consequently the Machmeter became a very important instrument to the jet pilot.

As the Court was taking evidence, another pilot on the squadron told how he found himself in a similar situation some three months previously - in the same aircraft! Whilst in a diving tail chase at 30,000 ft at a speed of 0.8M the aircraft flicked and went into an uncontrolled downward spiral. He lost 23,000 ft before managing to recover!

It was becoming obvious to the Court that serious handling problems with the Meteor were coming to light. On the evening of the following day the President of the Court sent the following priority signal to HQ Fighter Command.

INVESTIGATION INTO ACCIDENT TO METEOR 8 WH 299 HAS REVEALED SIMILAR CIRCUMSTANCES TO ACCIDENT OF 604 SQN on 5 DEC 54. FURTHER EVIDENCE OF SIMILAR OCCURRENCE AT THIS UNIT HAS COME OUT AT THESE PROCEEDINGS. THIS INDICATES THAT IF THE METEOR 8 FLOWN AT 0.8M HAS APPLIED TO IT AILERON AND POSITIVE 'G' THROUGH THE ELEVATORS THE AIRCRAFT MAY ENTER A STEEP SPIRAL AT HIGH MACH NUMBER. PILOTS DESCRIBE THE SENSATION AS SPINNING. OPENING AIRBRAKES, CLOSING THROTTLES AND APPLYING STANDARD SPIN RECOVERY APPEARS TO BE INEFFECTIVE. AIRCRAFT RECOVERY APPEARS TO BE DEPENDANT UPON AIR TEMPERATURE AND BECOMES EFFECTIVE BETWEEN ONE AND NINE THOUSAND FEET.

The following day the Court presented its findings to the Station Commander. It recommended that all units flying Meteors be notified that if elevator and aileron are applied together giving a positive 'G' loading when the aircraft is flying at or near 0.8M it may enter a spiral at a high Mach number. It would appear that controls are ineffective in this spiral, and the aircraft recovers on its own when it enters warmer air. Evidence shows that this may vary between 1,000 and 9,000 ft

The court also recommended that an alternative firing handle be placed on the seat in such a position that it is easy for the pilot to reach when experiencing high 'G' loading and turbulence.

The Court found that the formation leader was indirectly responsible for the loss of control of Meteor WH299 in that he made an error of judgement in flying too close to the limiting Mach number whilst his No.2 was ranging and tracking during the tail chase.

The Station Commander in his remarks agreed with the reasoning and recommendation of the court. With regard to the allocation of responsibility he said that no blame should be attached to me for deciding to abandon the aircraft after what appeared to be normal recovery action had failed to produce the desired effect. He did not agree with the statement of the formation leader, and considered he made an error of judgement in not allowing a sufficient margin of safety for the other aircraft in the formation.

In due course alternative firing handles were fitted to Martin-Baker ejection seats, and the Meteor F.8 was restricted to a maximum speed of 0.8M at all altitudes. Furthermore the High Speed Flying section in Pilots Notes was completely rewritten (AL.3 Apr 56) to read:

> 'Severe vibration may be experienced on some aircraft below the Mach number limitation of .8M. Should this happen, no attempt is to be made to fly at a higher Mach number. If the Mach number limitation of .8M is inadvertently exceeded in a diving turn, violent wing drop and complete loss of control may occur, particularly if high positive G is applied. The ensuing dive or spiral is likely to be very steep; buffeting and high stick loads will be experienced and a great loss of height is inevitable. When manoeuvrering at high Mach numbers at or just above 20,000 ft particular care is needed.

> When out of control in a dive the controls will become effective as height is lost. It is particularly important to avoid high positive G until the Mach number is reduced, because its application will nullify the beneficial effects of a reducing Mach number and prolong the uncontrollable dive'.

The following months in the Borough General Hospital were pretty uneventful, until one day they had the rare distinction of having not one but two ejectees in their care. I was just taking afternoon tea, as they say, when one of the nurses wheeled a trolley into the ward;

"Here's a friend come to join you".

It was dear old Hedley Molland from 263 Sqn. He was an even bigger attraction, in that he had just ejected from a Hunter whilst supersonic! He finished up in the drink off Felixstowe; just as his parachute was about to pull him under for a third time he was hooked out of the water by the crew of a passing dredger. In the circumstances he looked pretty good, a few bruises but nothing else. He attracted visits from a great many medics. Although an American pilot had already ejected whilst supersonic, Hedley was the first RAF pilot to do so. He very soon left the hospital and returned to his squadron.

Later two RAF specialists came to see me. After looking me over, they asked a simple question. Did I want to fly again? Before I had time to reply they said that, if my answer was no, they would simply assess me as being medically unfit for aircrew duties. This was a kind thought, as it removed any possibility of being categorised as Lacking in Moral Fibre (LMF) at a later date.

"No question about it" I said, "I'll fly again and next time it will be in a Hunter, but what about this useless bloody arm I've got?"

The plasters had been removed a few days previous and, whereas my leg and foot were mending quite well, my right arm was a mess. The radius and ulna bones had fused together, which meant I had no wrist movement whatsoever.

The RAF medics discussed the situation at length with Mr Bell-Jones.

"For him to fly again we need to see at least half wrist movement from the elbow, and some strengthening of his grip. Is there any chance of that being achieved?"

"Yes."

"OK, in that case you can keep him at the Borough General for as long as it takes."

I was lucky in that I had ejected near a hospital which had one of the most distinguished orthopaedic surgeons in the country. The next day I was back in the operating theatre, where he broke my arm and started again! This time he sawed a piece of bone 4 inches long from my left shin, then he opened up my right arm, from my wrist to my elbow and screwed the bone to the radius. It was held in place - and still is - by four silver round-headed screws. The weak grip was due to the thumb muscle being damaged beyond repair. He overcame this by joining my thumb to the muscle of my index finger. It did mean that at first they both moved together, which was a novelty.

As time went by I became a bit of a celebrity, with a constant stream of visitors. A pilot being blasted from an aircraft was a bit unusual in those days. Some visitors were welcome, others perhaps not quite so much. A favourite trick, with some help from the nursing staff was to appear to be asleep. The nurse would then say 'Its probably best if you let him sleep, he's had a restless night!' This was in some instances quite true, as I was now able to get myself out of bed and into the night nurse's rest room unaided! In addition to my family and fellow pilots from Wattisham, I was visited by the Mayor of Ipswich, numerous vicars, even a 'trick cyclist' who was sure I needed his services. The most welcome of all was Colleen, who travelled up to Ipswich every Sunday, her only day off from the theatre. I was the 41st RAF pilot to have ejected at that time. Forty years, on over 6,500 aircrew from many Air Forces world-wide have become members of the Martin-Baker Tie Club. Having also used an Irvin parachute, I also became a member of the exclusive Caterpillar Club, and in due course I received an engraved gold caterpillar from the company. I missed qualifying for the 'Goldfish Club' (landing in the sea) by five miles, for which I was extremely grateful. Three months later the plaster was removed from my arm for a second time. Preliminary indications were that the bone graft had been successful, and that I would get the wrist movement demanded by the RAF medics.

A short but happy time was then spent in a convalescent home near Ipswich before being taken to the RAF Officers' Rehabilitation Centre at Headley Court, near Epsom. This was a large old mansion which had been given to the RAF by the Chartered Institute of Accountants for the rehabilitation of aircrew during the war. It was like a large officers' mess, but with extensive physiotherapy and therapeutic facilities. Most of my time was spent either exercising limbs in the heated pool or constantly plunging my broken bits into a vat of hot wax.

Although an RAF establishment, the patients included a few chaps from the Army and even a BOAC pilot who was suffering from polio. Spirits were high, and there was a fair amount of inter-service rivalry, especially in the bar after dinner. One particular 'brown job' was in the habit of skiving off to his room, and not joining the rest of us in the bar. The RAF chaps, led by a nameless wing commander, thought this was bit anti-social, especially from a guest on an RAF establishment!

Now the fire escape from the top floor of the building was very interesting; only the military could get away with such a contraption. It consisted of a noose on the end of a rope. To escape the flames, the noose was put over your head and under your arms, you then opened the window and jumped out. The rope, because it passed through a series of cogs and pulleys, gently lowered you to the ground. Surprise, surprise! The workings of this system were not known to the 'brown job' who, after having the noose fitted round his waist, let out a piecing scream as he was chucked head-first out of the window into what seemed to be a bottomless pit of darkness!

This unofficial testing of the escape system failed to impress the staff, and the following morning we were summoned before the Commanding Officer. He was a wing commander in the medical branch, who seemed a bit ill at ease with a bunch of crocks standing before him accused of conduct unbecoming of officers. Our wingco (a wartime bomber pilot with three rows of campaign ribbons) had obviously had a previous word with the CO, because we escaped with a mild bollocking, but he threatened that we would be returned to our units in disgrace should it happen again.

After two months of this high life I was sent to the RAF Hospital at Ely in Cambridgeshire for a full medical examination and assessment. On arrival I was put to bed - clearly this medical was going to take some time! In fact it lasted two days. The specialists marvelled at the excellent bone graft that Bell-Jones had done on my arm. They did have one reservation, however, and that was the lack of flesh around the outside of my foot where my toe was missing.

The Group Captain medic suggested that I might have trouble in later years, and perhaps it might be better if at this stage they did a flesh graft on to the foot.

"What does that entail?" I asked in panic.

"Stitching your right foot to your left thigh for three months"

"Not bloody likely, I've just spent eight months in hospital and had umpteen operations – enough is enough – Sir"

"OK, Carter, we'll leave it at that then, you are now AI GI ZI, and you can return to you squadron." It had been a long sortie!

CHAPTER 9

The 'Meatbox'

In 1946 the new Chief of Air Staff, Air Chief Marshal Sir Arthur Tedder said,

> *"Now the war is over we shall have fewer aircraft and most certainly none to waste. The accident rate must be drastically cut; we cannot afford accidents. The days of taking extreme risks and of hazarding lives to achieve vital wartime purposes are over".*

It would seem that not a great deal of notice was taken, because by 1952 Meteors were crashing at a rate of 150 a year, nearly one every other day.

With some justification, Members of Parliament were becoming increasingly concerned about the rising number of crashes, but in reply to question Mr George Ward, Under Secretary of State for Air, told the House that the fatality rate in 1953 was roughly half the lowest fatality rate for the Spitfire. A pretty ambiguous comparison, one would think.

The Meteor was easy to fly, every Tom, Dick and Harry flew them, even Air Rank officers flew them, my mum could have flown one, so why did so many crash? Its worst day was 9th September 1952, when five crashed in different parts of the country. On numerous occasions the RAF lost three in a day.

From the start there were problems. Even experienced fighter pilots converting from piston-engined aircraft needed a careful understanding of the different techniques in flying a jet.

In his book *Fighter Command*, Norman Franks quotes Steve Stephen, a wartime fighter pilot as saying 'Often pilots got the idea they could fly anything having survived the war, but it was not always true'. He recalled that one of Bader's former flight commanders was posted as CO of No. 222 Squadron following his Meteor conversion. Within a week he was dead; crashed doing a beat-up of the airfield. 'You couldn't treat a Meteor jet as you could a Hurricane or Spitfire in low-level aerobatics. As you manipulated the throttles of a Spit or Meteor to slow down the acceleration, the reactions were totally different. Throttle back a propeller-driven aircraft and it acts as a brake, not so in a jet. Open up the throttle on a prop aircraft and it reacts immediately, not so a jet'.

As a fighter the Meteor was hardly an improvement on the aircraft it replaced, and by 1949 it was completely outclassed by both the MiG-15 and the F-86 Sabre. Some of the problems with the Meteor were already known, but post war they were either overlooked or deemed to be acceptable. 'We were after all the first Allied Air Force to have a jet fighter in operational service, and it did hold the World Air Speed Record' was the attitude in Government circles, and to some extent within the Royal Air Force as well.

Sir Ben Lockspeiser, Director-General of Scientific Research at the Ministry of Supply also said at a press conference at the time that manned UK supersonic research had been ruled out as being too dangerous.

As a result of this decision, Fighter Command was left for nearly a decade with a front-line fighter that was useless in high-level aerial combat.

Its main problem was the airframe, an old-fashioned out of date design. 'Not to worry chaps the jet engines will make it go fast' was the thinking, but all they did was to push the aircraft into a high-subsonic environment which was way beyond its capability.

The shortcomings of the Meteor have been well documented by a succession of test pilots, most notably by Michael Daunt, Chief Test Pilot of the Gloster Aircraft Co, Wing Commander Roland Beamont, Chief Test Pilot of English Electric Aviation, and the RAF Test Pilots at the Aeroplane & Armament Experimental Establishment, Boscombe Down.

Beamont first flew the Meteor on a visit to No. 616 Sqn in 1944, and as an experienced fighter pilot he was ideally suited to test the capabilities of this new aircraft. His impressions are fully described in his book *Testing Early Jets*:

> ...*it ought to have been an impressive experience, but somehow it was not...*

> ...*the stiffening controls confirmed that we were not only going fast but we had no operational manoeuvrability worth mentioning...*

> ...*despite praiseworthy efforts by the squadron (616) the operations carried out with the Meteor from Manston were in the nature of window dressing...*

> ...*later marks of Meteor gave good peacetime service in the RAF while remaining heavy, relatively unmanoeuvrable and curiously unsuitable for their intended role as front-line fighters. With stable and docile general handling qualities, however, they gave good service for hack duties such as target towing, instrument-rating training and weekend transport...*

Three years later, after Beamont became Chief Test Pilot with English Electric, he conducted a programme to determine the effects of compressibility on high-altitude intercept manoeuvrability using a Meteor F.4. These tests are reported in detail in his book *Fighter Test Pilot*. It confirms his earlier assessment that the Meteor had serious handling problems as a fighter aircraft.

No.77 Squadron, Royal Australian Air Force, had re-equipped with Meteor F.8s, a disappointment as they thought they were going to get F-86 Sabres. Shortly after they were sent to help fight the war in Korea. Their task was to provide fighter cover for USAF bombers, but it was immediately apparent that they were out of their depth as day fighters - within weeks they had been relegated to a ground-attack role. If proof was needed this was it, but for the next four years until the arrival of the Hunter, Fighter Command had to persevere with this obsolete aircraft.

Flying Training Command had a horrid time with the Meteor. With the Korean War and a gradual deterioration in East/West relations, after the Soviets blockade of Berlin, the Command had to cope with a massive expansion in pilot training in the early 1950s. This put an enormous strain on the twin-jet conversion programme, the number of Meteor AFSs increased from one to ten in little over a year, and the accident rate shot up accordingly.

The RAF had not felt it necessary to have training versions of fighter aircraft. There were no two-seat, dual control, Hurricanes, Spitfires, Tempests or Typhoons, so why have one for the Meteor. Read up the notes, strap yourself in and off you go, was the thinking. Fortunately for the RAF the Gloster Aircraft Co had already developed a two-seat training version for the Argentinian Air Force, and in due course the Government were persuaded to place an initial order for seventy T.7 aircraft. The first one was delivered to 203 AFS at Driffield in late 1949. But it had a vice, which if it failed to kill, was certainly enough to give the odd chap a terrible fright.

A short note in Pilot's Notes stated;

'If the aircraft is yawed at speeds below 170 knots with the airbrakes out, the nose may drop suddenly and the elevators become ineffective until the yaw is removed'

What it meant was that, if you were downwind for landing with the airbrakes out to reduce speed, then, by lowering the undercarriage the aircraft yawed, you stood a pretty good chance of making a very large hole in the ground! The Notes also said that by removing the yaw you regained elevator control - but as you would only be at 1,000 ft or less, there was little chance of recovering before hitting the deck. This interesting handling characteristic was know to all Meteor pilots as the 'phantom dive'.

The problem was that it was necessary to leave the airbrakes out to reduce speed below 175 knots in order to lower the undercarriage. But you then had to get the airbrakes in before the speed fell to 170 knots, to avoid the possibility of a 'dive' developing.

Flying any mark of Meteor on one engine in the cruise was no problem, but in the circuit it could be a handful, especially for those pilots straight out of basic training with less than 200 hrs and with no previous experience on twins. Some were given a short twin conversion on Oxfords, but for some reason this was discontinued.

Single-engine flying required considerable strength in the leg, so much so that your critical speed on one engine was determined during your first dual instruction flight in the T.7. As already mentioned, your instructor would flame one engine out. Then, selecting full power on the live engine, trimming out, and with your leg locked holding full rudder, he would tell you to ease back on the stick to reduce speed until you were no longer able to hold the aircraft in level flight. The speed at which you 'lost it' was your critical speed. It is easy to confuse this with the manufacturer's safety speed of 165 knots. Basically they are the same thing, but safety speed is a generalisation, whereas critical speed is the speed applicable to individual pilots and was the one you paid attention to.

The aircraft was flown off the runway at about 115 knots but, should you have an engine failure before reaching your critical speed you had a problem. However, Pilot's Notes stated:

'Should an engine cut immediately after take-off, the aircraft may be controlled at lower speeds, provided that prompt corrective action is taken'.

In other words you might make it if, in a split second, you established which was the failed engine, got on a boot-full of rudder, locked your leg to hold it, wound on full rudder trim, and put on 10 degrees of bank towards the live engine. Add to that you might be at 200 ft and just entering cloud in formation, and it was a fair bet that in reality you would finish up a smouldering heap. We were to learn later that Fighter Command were a bit more aware of the problem, and their instruction was to crash land straight ahead should you have an engine failure before reaching your critical speed.

Single-engine landings required some skill, and again there were different approaches to the problem, which was again not helped by Pilot's Notes stating:

> *A single-engine landing presents no difficulty. Maintain a speed of 140 knots until a decision to land has been made.*

But if you have a critical speed of say 165 knots there is no way you are going to maintain control when attempting an overshoot at 140 knots. The aircraft will just roll over and go in with a bang.

Pilots in Fighter Command had specific instructions to maintain their critical speed to 600 ft whilst on final approach when a decision to either land or overshoot had to be made. Once below 600 ft you were committed to land whatever the circumstances.

Until 1952 the 'dead' engine was completely shut down when practising single-engine circuits. This left no escape when pilots got into difficulties and lost directional control, resulting in many pilots being killed; until it was decided to simulate the 'dead' engine by just throttling it back. The irony of it was that Derwent engines were very reliable and there were few real engine failures. It is sad therefore that as late as 1975 two pilots, one an Air Rank Officer, should needlessly die attempting, of all things, a single-engine roller at a speed of 100 knots! All told, of the 641 Meteor T.7s built, no fewer than 204 crashed.

It is interesting to compare the losses between various units. For example, the RAF Flying College at Manby had a relatively high accident rate. The College often writing off aircraft as 'Rogue Cat 4.' No.203 AFS at RAF Driffield was also high on the list, with 45 crashes over five years - and possibly the worst reputation. But 205 AFS at Middleton St George had the highest accident rate of all, with 42 crashes over a four-year period - the most notable of which was a student losing control and crashing into the officers' mess while attempting a single-engine roller, demolishing his own room in the process!

No.209 AFS at Weston Zoyland also had an epic in February 1954 when night flying, a student blocked the runway after landing with his wheels up. Two other aircraft in the circuit were then diverted, but whilst en route to the alternate airfield both pilots flew into high ground and were killed. It is not surprising, therefore, that the number of crashes in Flying Training Command were up to three times greater than on the squadrons.

On the plus side, the Fighter Command Instrument Rating Squadron at West Raynham appears to have had no accidents. The reason behind their clean sheet no doubt was the fact that their task was purely and simply instrument flying.

There is no doubt that most crashes on the squadrons were a direct result of attempting to meet an operational task that was beyond the capability of the aircraft. That was to intercept and shoot down a target flying at a speed in excess of 0.8M at 40,000ft. We flew day in and day out, flying in battle formation and practising interceptions in aircraft that were either close to the stall or about to become uncontrollable due to compressibility.

Mid-air collisions accounted for 110 crashes, mainly caused by inexperience. However there is no logical explanation for the number of aircraft which crashed simply after running out of fuel! Not just the odd one but sometimes whole formations! In December 1947 No.245 Sqn based at RAF Horsham St Faith lost a pair which ran out of fuel, and later a four-ship battle formation from No.56 Sqn ran out fuel and all four aircraft were lost, three of the pilots ejecting. In 1954 a pair of Meteors from No.208 Sqn crash-landed after running out of fuel, and in 1957 this was repeated when a further three aircraft from the same squadron had to crash-land in the Iraqi desert with no fuel. In all 68 Meteors crashed after running out off fuel!

Other accidents were caused by aircraft crashing whilst on approach to landing (59), flying into high ground (45), crashing during take-off (34), undercarriage collapsing after heavy landings, often after hitting slipstream of the aircraft ahead (33), aircraft breaking up in the air (25) and crashing whilst performing low-level aerobatic displays (23). 890 Meteors crashed in service with the RAF, over a quarter of the total delivered.

These crashes are easily attributable, but when an apparently serviceable aircraft spins in from height, killing the pilot, it is difficult to be precise about the cause of the accident. Some pilots became disorientated whilst in cloud, like the pilot of Meteor WF760 of 615 Sqn who spun in on 29th March 1953 - the accident record stating that the pilot had never flown solo in cloud before!

In the early days unexplained accidents were put down to a lack of oxygen. One accident report went so far as to say that 'Evidence shows that the pilot was unconscious (anoxia) prior to impact, since no attempt was made to recover from the dive'! It was not until the mid 1950s that it was acknowledged that many of these crashes were due to pilots losing control of their aircraft because of compressibility, and a lack of oxygen had nothing to do with it. 109 pilots were killed in Meteors after 'losing control' and spinning in.

How was control lost in the first place? Early Pilot's Notes stated that above 20,000 ft there was no speed limitation. In the day fighter role we were expected to fly the Meteor to its limits, and most of us at the time felt confident that we could chuck the aircraft about the sky much as we wished when above 20,000 ft - but we were wrong.

The average squadron pilot did not know until much later that by putting the Meteor into a descending turn at a high Mach number, much like a target interception, the aircraft could enter an uncontrolled spiral from which he might not recover.

We all knew that the controls became heavy and ineffective at high Mach numbers, but what was not known was that any attempt to recover from a dive by pulling back on the control column (a natural thing to do!) at a high Mach number only prolonged the out-of-control condition. It was not until the speed was reduced to below 0.7M that normal control was possible. This could be as low as 1,000 ft, by which time of course a lot of pilots were resigned to the inevitable.

Further to the recommendations of the Court of Enquiry into my accident, a Special Flying Instruction was issued to all units flying Meteors, limiting the speed to 0.8M and warning pilots of the handling difficulties that might be encountered. Subsequently the High Speed section of Pilot's Notes was completely rewritten in 1956.

However the limiting speed at sea level of 515 knots (590 mph) remained unchanged; but this is only 20 knots less than the speed attained in the World Record attempt of 1946. It was therefore natural for squadron pilots to fly the aircraft up to this speed, but the experience would not be pleasant. The High Speed Flight aircraft were specially strengthened and modified but, even so, they suffered with airframe buckling and structural damage aft of the wing trailing edge. Roland Beamont recalls in his book *Fighter Test Pilot* being involved in a series of flight tests in preparation for the World Record attempt. Diving the aircraft to 500 ft along the Severn Estuary and approaching 0.79M, with buffeting, wind roar, heavy vibration and near solid controls, he attempted to level out but, at that moment, the Meteor suddenly changed trim, pitching nose-down with the Machmeter touching 0.8. (530 knots) There was a brief moment when he thought he was going to 'bounce off the water' but he was lucky enough to get enough response to a two-handed heave to level out at 100 ft. It is no wonder that aircraft broke up or flew into the ground whilst doing low-level beat-ups.

Pilots are the same the world over, reluctant to admit they have had a near squeak or made a cock of it, especially if it puts their professional ability into question. The civilian transport pilot might lose his job or the fighter pilot might be posted to a desk. Because of this reluctance, we failed to learn from the mistakes of others, which was unfortunate.

Line-shooting on squadrons was the norm, one heard the odd chap talking about rolling the Meteor onto its back at 30,000 ft and pulling through with full power, but in retrospect a lot of that was bullshit. Most of us tried it, but chickened out long before reaching the vertical.

The tragedy was that, although the problems with the aircraft seems to have been well recorded, it was not passed down the line for the benefit of others.

The cost to the taxpayer was astronomical. Each aircraft costing £25,000 represented a total loss of £25 million over a ten-year period, equivalent to £450 million by today's reckoning. But the real loss was the lives of 434 Meteor pilots and 10 navigators.

The only Meteors fitted with an ejector seat were the Mks 8, 9 and 10. Of these 312 crashed, killing 125 pilots, strangely only 39 successfully ejected. What was the reason for this? Did they leave it too late and have insufficient height, or were they unable to reach the blind after jettisoning the canopy? Of course those who crashed on take-off, into hills or in the circuit had no chance, but what about the many who spun in from altitude?

The first Martin-Baker seat to be installed had a minimum safe altitude for ejection when straight and level of 2,000 ft, but very few would be straight and level at the time. Later, when fitted with the ML Automatic Seat Release Unit - the minimum height was reduced to 1,000 ft, although the ejectee still needed to deploy his parachute manually. In due course the early seats were replaced with the Mk 2E, which were fully automatic and had a minimum height for safe operation of 500 ft.

There is no doubt that the location of the seat firing handle above and behind the pilot's head was not ideal. There had been resistance to suggestions that an alternative 'dead man's' handle be fitted on the seat pan or thigh guard. Certainly Martin-Baker were not keen on the idea, and this view was supported to some extent by the Ministry of Supply. The Ministry went so far as to tell ML Aviation, the other seat manufacturer at the time, that they should think about using the blind principle on their seats, much to the annoyance of James Martin who pointed out that it was his patent.

In many ways this reasoning was understandable. Early test ejections had been conducted whilst flying straight and level and at a low Mach number, with no reported problems. Strangely, the

Ministry of Supply and the RAE had not called for live test ejections, so although those conducted by Martin-Baker might not have been extensive, they were over and above what was called for. During these tests Bernard Lynch, the company test ejectee, was not encumbered by a Mae West or a 'bonedome', neither was he subjected to a high 'G' loading or the effect of shockwave turbulence. Consequently, firing the seat with a handle above and behind his head seemed easy - and it did ensure that the ejectee had his back straight and it protected his face.

What was overlooked was that the only time a pilot is going to eject is if the aircraft is out of control and about to crash. Rarely is the aircraft going to be flying straight level at 5,000 ft at a speed of 250 knots.

Under pressure from the RAF, the Ministry finally instructed Martin-Baker to develop and install an alternative firing handle on the front of the seat pan, and this was subsequently incorporated on the Mk 4 seat.

Another drawback for Meteor pilots was the need to jettison the canopy before reaching for the blind. The turbulence and buffeting at high Mach number made this very difficult, so much so that Fighter Command issued an Special Flying Instruction suggesting that pilots should consider ejecting through the canopy! In later years the same problem existed with the early Hunters.

It would have been infinitely better for the canopy to have been jettisoned automatically when pulling the face blind. Such an arrangement had already been adopted by other ejector-seat manufacturers.

The research and development of ejector seats for the RAF and RN was not made any easier by the constant hostility and mistrust that existed between James Martin (as he was then) and the Ministry of Aircraft Production and in later years with its successor the Ministry of Supply. There was also animosity between Martin Baker and ML Aviation, and this came to a head when Benny Lynch left Martin-Baker to work for ML Aviation on their automatic seat programme. This unhappy state of affairs was partly because the Ministry of Supply had contracted ML Aviation to develop a seat in collaboration with the Royal Aircraft Establishment at Farnborough, on a cost-plus basis, but Martin-Baker was financing their own research as a private venture at that time and naturally guarded any patent rights which belonged to them.

Once the seat arrived in service there were some pilots who were not at all happy having to sit in it!. The odd chap was even known to leave the safety pin in during flight, while others were careful not to apply negative 'g' for fear that the seat might rise and bang out on its own accord! It did happen, the most sensational occasion, late in 1956 was when Flt Lt Roy Watson was involuntary ejected from a Hunter at 43,000 ft whilst carrying out a quarter attack on a Canberra bomber. He survived with a broken ankle.

We were also told that, when ejecting, the speed of the aircraft should be as low as practical. At speeds approaching 400 knots injury was likely, though not necessarily fatal.

Going to the other extreme, after being involved in a mid-air collision, a pilot flying Meteor WA777 on 20th June 1952 actually baled out - preferring not use his ejector seat at all!

CHAPTER 10

I Return to 257 Squadron

I rejoined the squadron to find that a number of my friends had been posted away and new pilots had replaced them. We also had a new CO, Squadron Leader John Steele, affectionately known as 'Farmer' because he looked as if he would be more at home with a tractor strapped to his backside than a jet fighter. He had previously been a 'trapper' at CFS which caused a bit of a flutter when he arrived, but such fears were without foundation, and he quickly became a very popular boss. 'JB' Carruthers had been posted in to replace 'Chalky' White as the 'B' Flight Commander, and Johnny Barwell had taken over 'A' Flight. Also we had acquired a 'fishhead' in the shape of Lt 'Freddie' Mills RN, a fellow ejectee who had banged out of a Sea Hawk.

I was given a room in the main building of the mess, quite an elevation in status as previously I had to make do with a room in a Secco hut next door to the garages.

Prior to my bale-out, contractors had built some blast pens on the far side of the airfield, but they were never used - not even during exercises. Now another firm of civil engineers were on the base putting concrete roofs over them. The rumour being that someone in Fighter Command wanted to make a name for himself, so the pens got roofed in - but when finished they were still unused.

Whilst I was in hospital, Colleen came to see me every Sunday. This happened to be her only day off from the show at the Adelphi Theatre, and I looked forward to her visits very much. Now that I was back on the squadron we met in London at every opportunity, but somehow things were not the same. She was restrained and unhappy, but she would not tell me what was wrong. Then eventually she confessed that she had been seeing someone else and they were thinking of getting married. I was devastated. She handed me her engagement ring and we parted for the last time.

By now all the pilots had converted to the Hunter, and the squadron had regained its operational status. No.43 Sqn had flown down from their base in Scotland in February to join Nos.257 and 263 Sqn's for an open Press Day - to introduce to the media the new swept-wing fighter which was now in operational service with Fighter Command.

Then a few weeks later, four Hunters from the squadron escorted the *Queen Mary* down the Solent in a final farewell to Howard Tanner and his family, as they sailed back to the USA.

Wondering into the crew room on my first day back I was shocked to be told by the adjutant that I was no longer on the squadron strength. I had been posted to a holding unit at RAF Innsworth, near Gloucester, standard procedure for anyone who was injured or sick for any length of time. The boss said he would get it sorted out, and in the meantime I could get my hand back by doing a few dual trips in the Vampire T.11, which the squadron was now using for instrument rating checks.

My first flight was with Fred Hartley, a gentle introduction back into flying, followed by another trip the next day. I then kicked my heels doing nothing for three weeks while still awaiting the posting notice, but nothing happened so I was given two more dual trips in the T.11. Still nothing happened, so I then did a stint with the Wattisham Station Flight, swanning about as second pilot on the Avro Anson for a while. I also helped out in wing ops, mainly on the switchboard. Whilst doing this during a Fighter Command exercise a pair of 257 Hunters were scrambled by the sector controller. But the leader's aircraft failed to start so his No 2, Flying Officer 'Slash' Slaney, was scrambled with another Hunter from No.263 Squadron. The problem with this hurried change of plan was that 263 Squadron had Hunter F.5's with a fuel capacity of 388 gallons whereas the F.2's of No.257 only had 314 gallons. Anyway, they got airborne in pretty grotty conditions and successfully carried out their interception. On the way back they were told that the Wattisham weather was below limits and they were being diverted to Biggin Hill. Then 'Slash' had complete radio failure!

Approaching Biggin 'Slash's' leader discovered that their weather was equally grotty, so they carried out a pairs QGH and fed into a GCA for landing. At 200 ft the leader had no contact with the runway, and the pair overshot for another approach.

By now 'Slash's' fuel gauges were reading practically zero and he had two choices. He could eject but he was over a heavily populated area, and in any case it might not be successful at such a low altitude, or he could continue the approach in the hope that they would make it before he ran out of fuel. He chose the latter.

Desperately hanging onto his leader's wingtip as they flew down the glide path for a second time, he suddenly caught a glimpse of runway lights out the corner of his eye. Chopping the power and stuffing the nose down he landed a bit on the fast side, quickly hurtling off the end of the runway, going through two hedges and then crossing a main road before coming to rest unhurt. It was not Biggin but Kenley - which had only 800 yards! Back at Wattisham we all thought 'Well done Slash', and wandered back to the mess in anticipation of an invitation we had to a party that evening at the nurses' hostel in Ipswich. We all had the surprise of our lives when at 11 o'clock, with the party going full swing, in walked 'Slash', full of apologies for being late. He hadn't anticipated having to travel to the party from south London!

But I was getting frustrated with inactivity. I just wanted to fly solo again as a squadron pilot, hopefully in a Hunter. There was still a Meteor with the station flight, but all my requests to be let loose in it fell on deaf ears, simply because I was not yet back on the posted strength. Until I was, I could not fly solo in any of the Wattisham aircraft.

I made up for it with a pretty active social life. With my accumulated pay I bought an immaculate 1938 Morris 10 from an old chum Ted Gibbons in Maidenhead for £180. I bought it on hire purchase with a deposit of £100 and 12 monthly payments of £7.13s.4d. I only had a provisional driving licence, but felt that as jet pilot I should be capable of driving a motor car on my own, which I did. Needless to say I nearly copped it when I was stopped by the police driving the wrong way round Parliament Square in London. Fortunately I was in uniform, and was let off with a caution by a very understanding police officer.

After a few months swanning about the country lanes of Suffolk I applied to take the test. On the appointed day I borrowed some 'L' plates, and bribed one of the lads, Harry Martin, with free beer to come with me and set off for the test centre in Ipswich.

The examiner looked at my uniform and said "This should be a piece of cake for you, shouldn't it?"

"I hope so" I replied.

All went well on the test and, after telling me that I had passed, he mentioned that he thought I had a slight limp as we walked to the car before the test.

"Yes I have, and it's because I lopped half my foot off banging out of a Meteor last year."

"Bloody hell, and they still let you fly those things!"

It was not until I got back to the mess and looked at the chit he had given me that I noticed he had changed the normal wording to read 'Licensed to drive a motor car only'.

A few months later, and before I had finished paying the instalments, I wrote it off. I had taken a nurse from the Borough General Hospital to a dance in Felixstowe. After dropping her back at the hospital I set off back to Wattisham in the early hours of Sunday morning. Hurtling down a hill out of Ipswich on the main road to Needham Market I hit a patch of black ice. The car skidded out of control for 50 yards before hitting the kerb on the opposite side of the road. It then rolled down a steep embankment, coming to rest on its side in a field with a concrete post having smashed its way through the rear door. I escaped through the passenger side and, with blood pouring from my head, I staggered back up the bank. Standing at the side of the road wondering what to do next, I saw the headlights of a vehicle approaching. After waving it down I was delighted to discover that it was an empty ambulance, and within 30 minutes I was back in the Borough General getting my head stitched up. As dawn was breaking the Station Medical Officer came and took me back to base.

At the beginning of March I received the long awaited posting notice, but to my dismay instead of being posted back to the squadron I was instructed to report to RAF Innsworth in Gloucester. I was devastated. Having spent 8 months in hospital with high hopes of flying again, and now this. It was an enormous disappointment.

RAF Innsworth was an admin records centre, which among other things looked after officer postings. I booked into the mess in the early evening, and after dinner found the bar, which was empty. An hour later it was still empty with just the barman to talk to. He said it was always like that during the week;

"They're all in their married quarters".

My God, I thought, I'm too young for this I've got to get away. The next morning, after going through an arrival process, I was interviewed by the wing commander in charge of postings.

"We're going to keep you at RAF Innsworth, Carter, as there are no other jobs available. This is because you will have completed your four year engagement in a few months' time, so you will remain with us at Innsworth until you leave the RAF."

"In that case can I put a proposition to the RAF?"

"You can try", he replied with a wry grin.

"I'll sign on for a further 8 years if I am posted back to No.257 Sqn!"

He thought for a while as to the implications of such a request.

"Is 257 up to strength?" He asked an airman at another desk.

"Yes sir, at the moment they are, but they do have two pilots due to be posted out next month".

He looked at me for a while and then said

"OK then, go home on leave for two weeks and then report back to No.257 Sqn"

"Oh, and by the way, sign here on the way out!"

On my first day back I did three dual trips in the T.11. Then the boss said that before doing my first flight in a Hunter it would be a good idea for me to get my hand in first by flying the two Meteors which had been left with the squadron for target towing. So I did a dual trip in the T.7 and then went off solo in the F.8 on 4th April 1956. This was my first flight on my own since ejecting 15 months previously. By the end of the month I had flown 12 trips in the Meteor and found it quite exhilarating, even the tail chases!

The Squadron had a difficult time introducing the Hunter F.2 into service. A serious lack of spares, numerous modifications, and a chronic shortage of qualified ground crew meant that the serviceability record was poor. For long periods we were reduced to having only four aircraft available on the line. With my posting now confirmed, I was anxious to be let loose on the Hunter. Then, out of the blue, came an instruction from HQ 11 Group telling me to report to RAF Oakington for a flying refresher course on Vampires. Was there no end to this buggering about? Someone had obviously discovered that I had been off flying for 15 months. A phone call from the boss to say that I had already done over 10 hrs refresher flying Meteors and Vampires on the squadron fell on deaf ears, so off to Oakington I went. I wasted my time doing a further 7 hrs dual in T.11s. The only thing I can remember about the four week stay was being allowed to do two trips on my own in a single-seat Vampire Mk 5. A delight to fly and great fun, but after the 'Meatbox' a bit of a 'dinky toy'!

Whilst I was at Oakington the squadron took part in a massed fly-past for the Soviet leaders Bulganin and Khrushchev at RAF Marham. No doubt they had wry smiles on their faces as Fighter Command proudly demonstrated its new-swept wing jet fighter. The Soviet Air Force had been equipped with an equally good fighter, the MiG-15, for more than six years already. After the flypast Mr A.N. Tupolev, who was accompanying the Soviet party, turned to the Chief of Air Staff and said, "You train your pilots magnificently!"

I also missed taking part in a fly-past for Princess Margaret when she visited RAF Horsham St Faith. Rumour has it that, within hours of her departure, the loo seat had disappeared from the ladies' room in the Mess and reappeared in the 74 Sqn crew room, with a suitable inscription to commemorate her visit!

I returned once again to the squadron and the boss said

"Enough mucking about, swat up on the pilot's notes tonight, 'cos tomorrow you're down to go off in the Hunter"

As we still had no two-seat version of the aircraft it was a case of, have a chat with the 'chiefy' about what to do on the pre-flight, read up the pilot's notes, scribble a few speeds on your knee pad, and off you go. This seemed a bit strange, as new pilots on the Hunter were being sent to RAF Chivenor, the Hunter OCU, to do the conversion. But I was not about to argue after all this time - let's get on with it.

When I jumped into the cockpit the next day I had not even taxied one before, neither had I any experience of flying in a 'G' suit. The powered controls were also new so, before leaving dispersal, I selected them on and checked the doll's-eye indication. The brakes whilst taxying were a hundred times more effective than the Meteor, and after a slow meander round the peri track I was cleared to line up.

"Rainbow 21 you're clear for take-off, surface wind 250/10 knots".

I opened up the throttle to 7,500 rpm and let off the brakes. With an enormous surge of power, I was pressed into the back of the seat, and before I had time to collect my thoughts I was doing 140 knots with the aircraft hurtling skywards.

When flying a powered-control aircraft for the first time it is easy to over-correct, especially after having lived with the heavy controls of the Meteor. I levelled off at 25,000 ft, not by choice but because that was the height the Hunter had reached by the time I had sorted myself out, and then I did some general handling, which in practice meant swanning about and thinking what a great day it was.

Now while this was happening I was also experiencing for the first time the sensual effect of the 'G' suit. This was a new piece of clothing not unlike a zip-up corset with bladders stitched inside covering the abdomen, thighs and calves. Compressed air was supplied to the bladders through a valve which cut in at about 2G, increasing the pressure as the 'G' increased. The average pilot could withstand up to +5G before blacking out; the 'G' suit increased this to +7G as the bladders expanded and restricted the blood flow to the abdomen and legs.

For greater elevator control the Hunter had an electrically operated variable-incidence tailplane in place of the conventional elevator trim tabs. This took some getting used to, as there was a tendency to over or under trim, having lost the feel of the conventional trimmer.

The take-off was easy, but after twenty minutes swanning about, I had the more difficult problem of getting the thing back on the ground. It landed faster than the Meteor, and had a longer landing run, but the runway at Wattisham was still the same length so it called for a bit of concentration. Back into the circuit for a couple of overshoots to get the feel, then a final landing; a long downwind at 180 knots whilst doing the landing checks. Maintaining 160 knots turning finals and, after dropping full flap, crossing the hedge at 135 knots. Approaching touch-down the rate of decent is checked, and the aircraft being flown onto the runway at 120 knots. Holding off was not recommended for fear of a wing drop. The undercarriage was firm and you knew when you were down, there then followed a fair amount of braking as you saw the end of the runway coming up a bit faster than previously experienced.

I did a second trip that afternoon, then three trips per day for the next three days. On the fourth day I did five sorties, and my conversion was complete! Probably the most exciting part of the conversion was on the fifth trip, when I went supersonic on 14 May 1956. A slight forward movement on the stick and the Hunter settled into a shallow dive, when the Machmeter indicated 0.98M you were through the barrier - heady stuff. The only indication you had in the cockpit was a slight twitch on the control column. It was Heaven, like sliding downhill in a vacuum. Now, with a

Hunter, you could roll it on its back and pull through and be in complete control, a perfect fighter.

In fact it was impossible to fault this excellent aircraft, so easy to fly and a good looker to boot. But the F.2 and F.5 did have a few teething problems, the most serious from the pilot's point of view, being the tendency of the Sapphire engine to either flame-out or catch fire. These marks of Hunter carried no fuel in the wings, it was all in fuel bags wrapped around the engine so any suggestion of an engine, fire called for some rapid action. Practising dead-stick landings became a regular feature in our training programme. 'Dusty' Rhodes had an engine failure at 40,000 ft some 100 miles out over the cold North Sea, but managed to glide back to Wattisham for a safe landing. 'Curly' Smith was another member of the 'dead stick' club, he put his Hunter safely down at the USAF base at Wethersfield after descending through 30,000 ft of cloud. And Tony Weedon had an engine failure whilst actually practising a flame-out landing!

Sadly, we had a fatality when Eddie Mussett had his fire warning light come on during a night take-off. This was the second time in three weeks that this had happened to him. On the first occasion the light went out when he throttled back (it was a cracked jet-pipe) and he got the aircraft back, but the second time he was not so lucky. The engine was on fire and, although he ejected, he suffered fatal injuries. It was Eddie's second trip of the night, and as he strapped himself into his ejector seat he failed to notice that the release wheel on the parachute box had been left in the unlocked position. After inserting his parachute straps into the box he then fastened the seat harness over the top. Tragically, either before or during ejection, pressure from the seat harness unlocked his parachute harness so when the seat separated he fell out of the seat and his parachute. There had been at least one other known instance of this happening: a pilot on No.79 Squadron ejecting from a Meteor a year previously was killed in exactly the same way.

A well-publicised fault in the early days was discarded ammunition links being sucked into the engine air intakes when the guns were fired. This problem was overcome by fitting two blisters under the forward fuselage to collect the discharged links. Because of this and other problems the squadron had to wait 15 months before being cleared to fire the 30-mm Aden guns. Another problem, and a disappointment to those of us who found manual ranging difficult, was that the much promised radar ranging failed to work. Throughout my time flying Hunters it never did.

The Handling Squadron at Boscombe Down had not yet produced any Pilot's Notes, so we made do with typewritten handling notes given to us by the Hawker test pilots. Also the old-type oxygen mask was not suitable for use with the pressure-breathing system on the Hunter, so we were issued with new American masks. But there was a snag, these were too big to be worn with the new RAF 'bone-dome' so we had to cut them down to size with a pair of scissors!

But despite everything I was back - on a front-line squadron flying the latest jet fighter. A privilege indeed.

Photo courtesy of MoD.

No.257 Sqn Hunters on the pan at RAF Wattisham.

CHAPTER 11

Deployed to RAF Wymeswold

No sooner had the contractors finished roofing-in the blast pens than another lot moved onto the base to resurface and extend the runway by 500 yards. The reasoning behind this was not clear, unless of course the Air Ministry were thinking ahead to the next generation of supersonic fighters. Operationally we were quite happy with 2,000 yards for the Hunters. Some wag suggested it was probably the work of the same chap who had made a name for himself with the blast pens. Anyway, the upshot was that we were temporarily deployed to RAF Wymeswold in Leicestershire.

On our arrival the local paper carried pictures of the squadron with the caption

'One of the crack front-line squadrons flying their supersonic swept-wing Hawker Hunter jets'.

This failed to impress the weekend flyers from No.504 Sqn, Royal Auxiliary Air Force, who until then had the place to themselves. We had taken over the whole airfield for six months, to be operated as a major fighter base - not a weekend flying club.

Wymeswold was a wartime hutted camp, with most of the habitable accommodation being occupied by a large number of Polish families. It was therefore decided that the pilots would be billeted in the Officers Mess at RAF Newton, some 20 miles up the Foss Way not far from Nottingham. This had its advantages in that, although the mess itself was pretty dull, we were able to take full advantage of the night life in the Nottingham area.

Our technical support became somewhat fragmented. With only sufficient facilities at Wymeswold for first-line servicing, the Technical Wing personnel remained at Wattisham, but doing all the major servicing on our aircraft at RAF Martlesham Heath. As the aircraft came up for second-line maintenance, we flew them down to Martlesham, and then picked them up again after the checks had been completed. These positioning flights to and from Martlesham became quite popular, as they enabled you to do a spot of pleasure flying en route. With all the airfields the RAF had at its disposal, Wymeswold did seem to be strange choice for a six-month detachment. The sheer delight of flying an aircraft with powered controls was tempered every now and again by the need to practise manual flying; and in manual the controls were very heavy. Ten times heavier than the Meteor, so much so that it took two hands to fly it, which made the landing a bit tricky because your left hand was working like a one-armed paperhanger, switching between the throttle and the stick.

There was a tendency when in manual to cross the hedge just that bit faster. Within a week of arriving at Wymeswold, whilst landing off a QGH/GCA in manual, my aircraft burst a tyre. This was probably due to a hasty touch of brakes before the wheel was firmly on the runway. Perhaps the extra 500 yards they were adding to the Wattisham runway was sensible after all.

But I had an even bigger problem, which I kept to myself - I could not fire the guns!

When I was being patched up in hospital, the RAF specialists said that if I was to fly again I needed to have at least half wrist movement, and a strong enough grip in my right hand to hold the control column. What they overlooked, not being fighter pilots, was that I needed a strong first finger to pull the trigger, and an equally strong thumb to press the cine' camera button located on top of the control column. Although collectively my grip was reasonably good, the first finger was rather weak, and my thumb was there for show only!

The only way to overcome this was to take my left hand off the throttle to press the cine' button or to fire the guns. Having done that, I was then not able to range on the target, because the range setting control was on the throttle. The standard procedure was to range and track using the range setting control on the throttle from 600 yards down to 200 yards and to fire in short bursts when both were on target. This I was unable to do, so instead, and without mentioning it to anyone, I set the range to 400 yards and left it at that. Then I would move my left hand to the trigger and, when approaching 400 yards I would fire the guns or press the camera button. It was good fortune that, during debriefing, nobody noticed that all my attacks started and finished at 400 yards!

During June and August we spent a great deal of time practising target interceptions with our new fighter controllers at RAF Neatishead. One day it was for real, when I was scrambled leading a pair to intercept an unidentified aircraft over the Dutch coast heading fast towards the UK at Angels 35. We were vectored onto the bogey over the North Sea, which turned out to be a USAF B-47. It was a simple case of a misplaced flight plan, but the interception was a change from Hunter intercepting Hunter, and I took full advantage by getting in close to have a good look at this large bomber.

Things then went a bit quiet for a while, until one late afternoon when Dick Millward was leading a pairs take-off and his Number 2 called "Blue One, I think you've lost a wheel!"

At the same time the tower came up and told him that his starboard wheel was disappearing at a fast rate of knots far into the distance! A slow flypast over the tower confirmed that the wheel was indeed missing. As was customary on such occasions, the Wingco Flying, supported by the Wingco Tech and his experts congregated in the tower to consider the options and to offer advice. After much discussion on the R/T it was agreed that Dick should land it on two wheels and a stump. It was a spectacular sight, in the fading light, to see the stricken Hunter settle on the runway and then generate a sheet of sparks two hundred yards long behind it. After scraping along the runway for some distance the leg eventually broke away, and Dick went hurtling through the boundary fence. The aircraft eventually came to rest astride the main Melton Mowbray to Loughborough road.

The squadron still kept a Meteor F.8 on strength, for towing the banner during air-to-air gunnery exercises. It was also used as a squadron hack, and I took it in late August to Llandow in South Wales 'on a navigational exercise' to spend the weekend with my aunt who lived in Cardiff. On my return on the Monday I found the lads getting briefed for a very large 'Balbo' which was due to take place in ten days' time. The C-in-C of the Russian Air Force was to be entertained at RAF Honington, and there was to be a massed flypast of Hunters and Javelins. Nothing too spectacular, but get as many aircraft in the air as possible, we were told. After a few practices we were ready, and on 5th September we flew into Honington. There were Hunters everywhere and the mess was bulging with pilots, which did no end of good for the bar takings that night.

*Massed start up by Hunters at RAF Honington
for the C-in-C Soviet Air Force.*

Photo courtesy of MoD.

The next morning at the appointed hour we were already strapped in our cockpits and, as the Russians appeared, we did a mass engine start and within 20 seconds the first pair were rolling. There followed a continuous stream of take-offs, and within minutes we were all airborne. Very quickly we formed up into a loose formation before turning back inbound over Thetford. As we approached the airfield we descended to 500 ft and were in close formation at 400 knots. If the Russians were not impressed, we were. We then finished off with a high-speed run in on the deck for a break and landing.

Later, whilst at lunch in the mess we saw our Russian adversaries for the first time. Eye-to-eye contact perhaps, but nothing else - they seemed a miserable bunch. Once they had gone, we jumped into our aircraft and flew back to Wymeswold another day's work completed.

The squadron strength at the time was 18 pilots, but we had a new member join us, a Major Gerhard Barkhorn from the Luftwaffe! The West German Air Force had just been reformed. In the spring of 1945 he had been a member of an elite unit (JV 44) commanded by Adolf Galland, where he flew the Me 262 jet fighter in a last stand against the Allies in Europe, but he obviously had no recent air combat experience. He was reputed to have shot down 301 Allied aircraft during the war. We were told he was joining us for a short time to get updated on modern techniques. His arrival coincided with our Battle of Britain Open Day, when the RAF and the public would be remembering Fighter Command's great victory over the Luftwaffe. The irony of the situation was not lost on us at the time.

He flew as my No.2 on a number of occasions, mainly practicing cine' quarter attacks. Most of the time he had little to say, but one day, whilst we were both sitting in the 'chiefy's' hut waiting for a Form 700 to be signed up, I asked how he managed to shoot down so many aircraft during the war.

"By getting fifty yards line astern and coming up from below" was his reply.

Then as a quick afterthought,

"But they were all on the Russian Front!"

Station parades were not held all that often, but when they were they were a right pain, I felt that I had joined the Air Force to fly. If I wanted to stomp around on parade grounds I would have joined the Army, so I went to the Station Medical Officer and convinced him that square bashing was having an adverse effect on my damaged right foot, and it might even affect my ability to perform my flying duties. He agreed, and I was duly given a chit which said I was excused parades, and with that vital piece of paper I never did another parade during my time in the RAF. I used the same argument when petrol was about to be rationed during the Suez crisis, and was given another chit which said:

'As a result of injuries sustained on 21.12.54 whilst on an operational sortie, this officer should not walk more than short distances and cannot carry loads with his right arm. This makes travel by public transport difficult and undesirable, especially when luggage is involved. I consider he has very adequate grounds to claim supplementary petrol issue on account of these disabilities.' S.M.O RAF Wymeswold

Whilst with the Doc I took the opportunity to mention that I was getting this uncomfortable stinging sensation in my backside.

"You've got the fighter pilot's complaint – piles," he said without even bothering to look.

"If you must go hurtling around the sky pulling 6g two or three times a day, what do you expect? Stuff these up your bum twice a day and that should fix it." It did.

It was customary to hold a major air defence exercise every year, usually in August or September. One requirement of the forthcoming exercise, code named 'Stronghold' was to see how quickly various squadrons could deploy to other airfields. Which squadrons were to be deployed, and to where, would not be known until the exercise started for real. Well that was what they thought at Fighter Command, but with a fair amount of subterfuge we found out that they were planning to send us to a little-known airfield near Mablethorpe called RAF Strubby.

Within an hour of the exercise starting we received the expected signal from Group Headquarters deploying us, surprise surprise, to Strubby. Half a hour later the ground crew with all their equipment were on the road and we were waiting to leap in our aircraft as soon as the advance party arrived.

Four hours later the boss signalled Group to say we were fully operational at our new base! Of course we achieved the fastest deployment in Fighter Command by a long way, but we heard later that there were some questions as to how we managed it so quickly.

Strubby was used as a satellite by the RAF Flying College at Manby. Although we were billeted in some comfort in the mess, our squadron accommodation was in tents, a bit reminiscent of

No.257 Sqn Hunter pilots on standby at RAF Strubby during 'Exercise Stronghold'. The author is in the foreground reading a paperback.

World War One. It was good fun though, and we managed to fly quite a few sorties on the first day. I became involved in a huge dogfight over The Wash, with aircraft milling about all over the place. We were being attacked by a large number of aircraft from 2nd TAF in Germany. My Number two called 'bingo', which meant his fuel state demanded we head for home, but then our controller said he was going to recover us to West Raynham in Norfolk. In less than thirty minutes we had landed, been turned round, and were on standby ready to go again. And so it went on, seven days of intensive and very exciting flying.

After the exercise we learned that we were to go to Horsham St Faith to do some live firing on the flag. A treat indeed, because the squadron had been flying the Hunter without ever being able to fire the guns. But now all the problems had been overcome, and we were keen to have a go.

About this time a limit of 15 hours' flying per pilot per month was applied throughout Fighter Command, reportedly due to a shortage of Avtag fuel. Probably more a case of building up stocks in the light of possible troubles in the Middle East. In fact this hardly affected us as what with the short duration of the F.2 and aircraft unserviceability we rarely achieved 15 hours anyway.

In preparation for the gunnery I was told to get myself checked out on how to tow the banner with the Meteor. There was no great difficulty with that, you lined up on the centreline about 300 yards down the runway. The ground party would then lay out the flag behind you, and hook the tow line to the back of the ventral tank under the belly. Off you went, full poke, straight into a steep climb to avoid trawling the banner across Norwich. I had not towed the flag before but, as on this occasion we would be firing real 30mm shells, it was felt that everyone should take a turn. It was not unknown for the occasional 'ace' to miss the flag and pump one or two bullets into the towing aircraft!

On our arrival back at Wymeswold we were told that the runway work at Wattisham had been finished, and that we were just awaiting clearance from the Clerk of Works to move back after we returned from Christmas leave.

I had already been told to go direct to Martlesham Heath after Christmas to do some air tests. On the third day I had a phone call from the squadron telling me that, if the air test on WN920 was satisfactory, I was to land it back at Wattisham. I immediately saw this as a golden opportunity to put my name up in lights, as being the first pilot to land on the new runway, but just as I was carrying out the pre-flight checks on the aircraft I was called into the engineers' office.

"257 Ops on the line"" said the Chiefy.

"Nick - if you had any ideas of being the first to land at Wattisham - forget it. The Station Commander is just walking out to his Hunter, and it would be in your best interests to see that he gets there first!"

An hour later, as I crossed the threshold, I saw a set of tyre marks on the virgin concrete and quietly accepted second place!

CHAPTER 12

Fighters are Obsolete!

In May 1957 the Minister of Defence, Mr Duncan Sandys, presented a White Paper to Parliament which said, more or less, that the days of fighter aircraft in the RAF were over. In future the defence of the country would be dependent upon ground-to-air missiles and the nuclear deterrent. Needless to say, the morale in Fighter Command plummeted overnight.

It was no coincidence that at the same time we were told that both the national airlines, BOAC and BEA, were short of pilots. Should any of us wish to move into civil aviation, interviews would be arranged, and if offered employment we would be released from the RAF. I desperately wanted to stay in the Service because I liked the life. I also doubted whether the civil airlines would accept the injuries to my arm and foot. But I was also aware that I could find myself in a desk job, and civil flying would be better than that, so I presented myself before a BOAC selection board at Heathrow to see what it was all about.

I was eventually ushered into a room and was invited to take a seat opposite four very serious looking gentlemen, each one a Captain O.P. Jones look-alike! A few general questions, then one of them passed me a map asking what its projection was. It was of course a Lambert, which was nothing like the topographical maps used by single-seat fighter pilots. I remembered vaguely being shown one whilst doing navigation at flying school, but for the life of me I could not remember what it was called. I could see they were not impressed. What I did not know at the time was that BOAC were not recruiting pilots to fly aircraft, but pilots to be navigators with a promise of reverting to piloting some time in the future. This of course fitted in nicely with the Corporations' future policy where pilots would hold navigation licences, removing the need for specialist navigators on the flight deck. Even worse, some RAF chaps taken on by BEA were employed as stewards until they had piloting vacancies. The letter of rejection received from BOAC was not a great shock, neither was it a disappointment.

The squadron was short of an Instrument Rating Examiner (IRE), so the boss asked if anyone would like to go on the next IRE Examiners' Course. Strangely, I enjoyed flying on instruments, and I thought this might be an easy way to get another string to my bow so I indicated my interest. Three days later he said my application had been accepted, and I was due to join No.78 course at the Fighter Command Instrument Training School at the Central Fighter Establishment at RAF West Raynham in Norfolk. In the three weeks spent on the course I completed 28 hours' flying, of which 18 were either actual or under the hood. We also spent some time in the classroom because the instrument rating renewal was in two parts, a flying test and an oral examination. The latter included such subjects as the principles of flight, pressure instruments, gyro instruments, pilot navigation, range and endurance, air traffic control (Rules of the Air), approach aids, meteorology, safety equipment and technical questions on the aircraft which the candidate was authorised to fly. To help us, as future examiners, to conduct an oral test we were given a question and answer book, which was to prove invaluable for those of us who were probably not quite so bright as some of the chaps we were going check.

The RAF still had no two-seat training version of the Hunter, so most of my flying on the course was carried out on the single-engine Vampire T11. Consequently, as an IRE I would be qualified to carry out instrument rating renewals on pilots flying single-engine jets like the Hunter; although the course syllabus did call for us to do a few trips in the Meteor T7 – for experience! Anyone thinking a Meteor was a handful on one engine should try it on one engine under the hood on primary instruments! On the test the hood was down from brakes off, to simulate zero runway visibility. It was therefore vital that you lined up exactly on the centreline with the nose wheel straight. Also, to ensure that the heading index on the G4B compass was set to the runway QDM to help you keep the aircraft on the centreline during the take-off run. Many a renewal got off to a shaky start by the IRE having to take control before you were even airborne!

After take-off the candidate established the aircraft in the climb at the correct speed, with a couple of turns thrown in to remain in the local area, levelling off at 8,000 ft on a cardinal heading. Then followed the most difficult part of the test, a climbing turn at Rate One from 8,000 ft to 14,000 ft, through 360 degrees, in exactly 60 seconds. This was then repeated from 14,000 ft to 20,000 ft in the opposite direction!

Once at 20,000 ft you would be told to open the throttle and allow the speed to increase to the limiting Mach number, encounter compressibility, then maximum deceleration down to the stall and recover, whilst still remaining within limits.

As if that was not enough, the examiner would then take control and topple the artificial horizon with a series of aerobatic manoeuvres, leaving the aircraft in an unusual attitude, usually in a climb, upside down with the speed falling fast, then being told to recover!

Then whilst still on primary instruments, a QGH let-down was followed by a GCA approach and overshoot.

To reach the required standard to become an IRE needed skill and aptitude, and an ability to fly the aircraft within half the limits normally allowed for Instrument Rating Renewals. It was a very demanding course. Some years later I was being interviewed for a job as an Operations Officer with the Civil Aviation Authority. They noted on my application form that I had served with the Royal Air Force, and that I had also been an IRE. They were a bit miffed, and even intimated that I had tried to mislead them, when they discovered that I had been an RAF IRE and not a CAA IRE. In their eyes the Service qualification was somewhat inferior to its civil counterpart!

I passed the flying test, and then on the last day took the written exam. It was customary for the results to be announced by one of the instructors during the end of course drinks party in the mess. There was only one failure and it was me, having achieved only 30% for Principles of Flight. Perhaps I had not been paying enough attention when shock waves on a double wedge aerofoil were discussed! Anyway I was given another paper and told to go away to a spare room and take it again - not very easy with a skinful inside you, but I managed to scribble some coherent answers and returned to the bar.

"Drinks all round, and you've passed!" they all shouted.

Returning to the squadron, I discovered that 'Farmer' Steele had rather surprisingly been posted to RAF Acklington as the station administration officer, this was only four weeks after he had returned after having completed the Day Fighter Leaders' School at CFE West Raynham. 'JB' Carruthers, the 'B' Flight Commander, had taken temporary command of the squadron pending the arrival of a new boss.

The weather was kind to us in February 1957, and we even managed to do some night flying which for many of us was the first time with the Hunter. We also had two visits from Squadron Leader Walker who called in to introduce himself as our CO designate.

But then on the morning of 1st March it all changed. 'JB' said he wanted all the squadron pilots to assemble in the crewroom after met briefing. This we did, and to our surprise the Station Commander was there. He came to the point quickly,

"It's with great sadness that I have to tell you that 257 (Burma) Squadron will disband at the end of this month."

There was a deathly silence, then as if to soften the blow, he said that we were only one of a number of squadrons suffering the same fate as a result of severe cut-backs in Fighter Command. He said that people from Air Ministry would visit the squadron in a few days' time to discuss what postings might be available to us, but we were not to hold out much hope of getting further flying jobs because the RAF would now have a large surplus of pilots. We were victims of the Duncan Sandys Axe.

When we realised that we might not be fighter pilots much longer we tried to get in as many flights as we could. On 12th March I did five trips, leading a battle four at 45,000 ft twice in the morning, an air test after lunch which turned into an emergency with a fire warning, which fortunately turned out to be false, local flying and dusk circuits during the early evening, then after supper a night cross country to Lincoln, Luton and back.

Nearing the disbandment day, the postings people from Air Ministry arrived as planned – and the outlook was bleak. Twenty glum pilots sat in the crew room listening to what they had to say over numerous cups of coffee. Even my recently acquired IRE status was of little significance. There were promises of flying appointments in the future if we first accepted a two-year ground job, but that did not appeal to me so I listened and waited. Then one of the team who had been searching through his files said,

"I suppose nobody's interested flying Meteors, target towing at RAF Chivenor?" (A dead-end sort of job, with always the possibility of getting a bullet up your backside from a trigger-happy novice.)

"I'll have it" I blurted, before anyone else had time to think about it.

"OK old boy, it's yours" he said.

"Deputy Flight Commander of the Target Towing Flight, but as you don't have to be there for a couple of months you can stay here and help wind up the squadron."

I was elated because, with Chivenor being the Hunter OCU, I might get the odd trip to keep my hand in and there were already a number of ex-257 chaps on the staff there.

Then we had a pleasant surprise. Although we were within two weeks of our disbandment date, we were suddenly told that the squadron was to take part in an exchange visit to the Belgian Air Force at Chievres, near Brussels. For three days we would be operating jointly with the Belgian and French Air Forces, and their ground controllers. Eight aircraft were to go on the detachment, and I was lucky enough to be flying one of them. We were to go out in two battle-four formations under positive radar control the whole way.

We had heard some whispers in the bar that 263 Sqn intended to bounce us as we climbed out across the Thames Estuary. We would be sitting ducks, because we would not have enough fuel to get involved in a dogfight on the way. Our estimated flight time to Chievres was 35 minutes and the endurance of the Hunter F2 was about 40 minutes! As it happened, there was no sign of them. On our return we were told they had been bounced by other aircraft so had to call off the interception - a likely story, they probably never saw us!

Operating from a Belgian airfield, being controlled by French fighter controllers, practising interceptions and dogfighting with Mysteres was exhilarating. On the second day we got involved in a hell of a battle with some French Mysteres and we soon

No.257 Sqn on detachment with the Belgian Air Force at Chievres. Author second from left.

discovered that with a bit of flap we could out-turn them. I claimed two 'shot down' and had the cine' film to prove it. The following day we did PI's with both French and Dutch GCI stations who vectored us onto a variety of targets, and also two sorties of formation aerobatics.

We were entertained lavishly by our hosts, and on the second evening they took us to *Le Boeuf Sur Le Toit*, a top night club in Brussels, for some entertainment! It was all over much too quickly, and we left our hosts with sad hearts, knowing that in just over a week's time we would all be going different ways and our famous fighter squadron would be no more.

As was the norm on such occasions, a disbandment parade had been arranged to take place on 29 March 1957, with a final flypast of squadron aircraft. The parade was taken by the AOC No.11 Group, Air Vice-Marshal Bowling CBE, who was accompanied by the Burmese Air Attache'. Two formations of four was all we could muster, as both pilots and ground staff were already being posted out. As we were overhead the parade, doing 400 knots, I had a power control failure. I told the others, who moved slightly away to give me room so that I could gently ease the aircraft out of the formation. Whilst they went around and landed, I did a twenty-mile circuit in manual before returning back for a manual landing. I was not aware of any reaction from the AOC, but having a sudden manual reversion at 400 knots in close formation at 500 ft made me sit up. On the previous day I had carried out five taxi flights in both the Meteor T.7 and the Vampire T.11, taking some of the lads to new postings at Leconfield, Horsham St Faith and Little Rissington. Within a day or so of the disbandment only 'JB' Carruthers and myself were left. It was pretty lonely, a complete family of men gone. I did a few air tests on aircraft which had been in the hands of the engineers, and which were now ready to be taken to their final resting place at RAF Kemble. Every other day a Varsity would land and drop off a couple of ferry pilots to fly the aircraft away. I felt it was not right that complete strangers were flying our beloved Hunters to their final resting place in the Cotswolds, so I asked one of the visiting pilots if I could ferry a couple. He suggested I ring his boss, which I did.

"Sure I'll put you down for one tomorrow, and you can also have the privilege of taking the last one."

Excellent! The next day the Varsity arrived and dropped off one pilot who also had the paperwork for WN915 which I was to ferry. We took both sets of documents into stores to get the aircraft struck off squadron charge, and with the storekeepers' signature we were ready to go. It had never occurred to me that you actually had to hand aircraft back into stores! We agreed that we would fly down individually, and not in formation. I had drawn a line on my map, and studied the route carefully. Pride was at stake, it was WN915's last flight, and it would be flown as a fighter with honour. Balls out, low level and tell Kemble when I was five miles for a break and landing. In true fighter tradition, I was determined not to have to call Kemble for bearings, but equally it would be an enormous embarrassment to miss the airfield or, worse still, to break and land over the wrong place. It had been done before - but not by me! But I had never been to Kemble or flown over that part of the country before, so it needed extra careful planning.

Oxford came up on my port side right on time, a minute later Witney was on my starboard side, only four minutes to overhead Kemble, but with five more airfields on track, in that short distance there was always the possibility of a cock-up. Once abeam Cirencester I knew I had cleared the others, and the only airfield ahead had to be Kemble, although in the haze I could not see it.

"Kemble Tower, Ferry one zero, five miles for break and landing."

"Ferry one zero Roger, runway 25, surface wind 270/10, call downwind"

"Roger one zero."

I saw a railway line flash past underneath and knew I had a mile to run, just then the runway approach lights came into view at twelve o'clock. A 4G left-hand break, and seconds later I rolled out of the turn and greased it on to the runway.

"We don't see many ferry flights arrive like that" said the chiefy as I clambered out of the cockpit.

"Fitting for a special aircraft, and a special squadron" I replied.

The Varsity pilot gave me a bit of dual on the way back to Wattisham. A few days later the boss of the ferry pool rang again to say he was sending the documents down for the very last flight,

"But Carter, I would be a lot happier if you arrived in the circuit at Kemble a bit slower and somewhat higher than 50 ft!"

"Yes sir".

Before going to the aircraft I again went to stores with the paperwork for WN920, our last Hunter, to be struck off charge - and then ran into a problem.

"This aircraft isn't on charge to 257 Sqn, so you can't hand it back."

"In that case, can I have it."

The stores basher failed to see the joke, and called over his governor who promptly told me to stay put until it was sorted out. Must be the only time that stores grounded an aircraft. After a few phone calls they were happy and WN920 arrived at Kemble in a more genteel manner. It was a very sad moment as I walked away from a hanger completely full of Hunters. All with the Chinthe and No.257 Sqn yellow and green colours emblazoned on the nose. None ever to fly again.

What was worse, 257 Sqn was reformed on 1st July 1960 at RAF Warboys - as a Bloodhound Guided Missile Squadron - Duncan Sandys had got his way!

CHAPTER 13

No. 229 Hunter OCU

The moment I drove my Vauxhall Velox through the gates at RAF Chivenor I knew I was going to enjoy the posting. Chivenor was a wooden-hutted ex-wartime airfield situated between Barnstable and Ilfracombe on the estuary of the River Taw. The approach to the runway from both directions was over water. In charge of the Target Towing Flight was Flight Lieutenant Sid Cooper, an ex-Battle of Britain Spitfire pilot. The flight had five Meteor F.8s and one T.7. Another chap, Flying Officer Tom Price, arrived at the same time. This brought the complement of pilots on the flight to five, making it somewhat over-staffed, with air-to-air firing being carried out only on four days of each month, but we were not complaining.

Target towing, enabling students to fire live at the flag, was always going to be hazardous. It was not unknown for a budding fighter pilot to come back with a picture of a Meteor and not the flag on his cine' recorder! But accidents were not always in the air. Shortly after arriving, an airman towing a fully armed Hunter to the pan had a very rude awakening. The armourer sitting in the cockpit doing his pre-flight inspection pulled the trigger to check the operation of the cine' camera. Unknown to him, the safety switch in the wheel bay had been set to live, and three 30mm shells smashed their way through the Land-Rover, only missing the driver because he was turning at the time.

Chivenor was one of two Operational Conversion Units flying Hunters. The task was to convert pilots, fresh from the FTS's, into day fighter pilots prior to joining front-line squadrons. There were on average some 50 aircraft on strength, mostly Mk 1s which were slowly being replaced by F.4s although the difference between the two was insignificant for OCU purposes. All the aircraft carried the No.229 OCU war code of ES on the fin. It was one of the last RAF flying units to do so.

My plan was simple, to ease my way into flying the Hunters by first offering to do the odd air test. The Wingco Flying, Wing Commander Peter Ellis, also lived in the mess, so I took the opportunity to suggest this to him when were talking in the bar one evening. He thought it a good idea, and suggested I offered my services to the two squadron commanders as and when I had no target-towing commitments. I was also able to get the ex-257 pilots to put in a good word.

"Don't worry 'Nickers', we'll see you get some trips", they said.

Previously I had only flown the Mk 2 with the Sapphire engine, so it was suggested that I first get acquainted with the Rolls Royce Avon which powered the F.1 and F.4. A quick look though the pilot's notes, and I was then sent off on a familiarization flight - I was in! After that, the Hunter trips started coming thick and fast. When not doing air tests I flew either as a No.3 in a finger-four or as leader of a pair. The flying was exactly the same as I had been used to on the squadron, but the wingmen were students and we were instructing them to become fighter pilots. In most cases they came to the OCU straight from flying school, but quite a number of the more experienced pilots came on the course following a ground tour, or having been posted in from another Command.

My mates on the Target Towing Flight insisted that I still did my share of banner towing, but I did not mind. I would fly anything at any time, given the chance. In fact life on the TT Flight was quite good fun. We ran it a bit like a flying club, doing aero's, low flying, QGH/GCAs, even battle formation if and when four out of the five of us turned up for work at the same time!

Chivenor also provided a summer camp for the Air Training Corps, and a Chipmunk was given to the flight to give the cadets pleasure flights. I got checked out on the 'Chippy' by Sid Cooper one morning, and then took the Station Medical Officer up on a weather check before settling in to a routine of 10-minute hops.

By keeping the 'passenger' talking during the flight you got a fair idea of how he was taking it. Lots of chatter and enthusiasm and you would extent the flight and perhaps let him have a go, possibly with a few gentle aerobatics. No noise from the back, and you scuttled back into the circuit as quickly as possible, so as to avoid the lad having to do a cleaning-up job. It all brought back memories to me. Exactly ten years earlier, as a 17 year old cadet, I had attended a summer camp at Chivenor and was given two flights in an Anson.

The TT flight also became the unofficial communications flight for the OCU, using the two-seat Meteor T.7. As an IRE I was authorised to fly the two-seat Vampire T.11, which was also used to run the odd bod to far-away places from time to time. These trips were most enjoyable, especially for fighter pilots who very rarely 'landed away'. I was now flying four different types of aircraft in a variety of roles; that, combined with a superb social life, made the posting just out of this world.

It goes without saying that we were never short of female company, both local ladies, and those on holiday. We were in our mid to late twenties, and nearly all single. We had a 'hoolly' in the mess every Saturday night, a darkened room adjacent to the bar being set out for dancing. Frank Sinatra, Eartha Kitt and the like into the early hours. Nothing too strenuous! It was always high tea on a Saturday, which gave us enough time to do a tour of the local hostelries before arriving back in the Mess long before the bar closed, nearly always accompanied by a young lady. But one had to be careful, there were those ladies you brought to the mess and those you did not! At one stage we had a fad for collecting trophies - a suspender belt, a bra and even the odd pair of knickers being donated by accommodating young ladies in North Devon.

For a more serious relationship I should have paid more attention to Pauline, but she lived in Maidenhead and I saw her only infrequently, when home on leave. She was the only girl-friend I knew who had her own sitting room, next to her bedroom.

When her father answered the door he would welcome me by saying 'Pauline is waiting for you upstairs!' A lovely girl, but I was too wrapped up flying to embark on a steady relationship. Later she married an American, and went to live in the States.

We had the usual monthly dining-in nights when all sorts of games would be played, not with the same determination as between front-line squadrons but competitive none the less. On one occasion, a student did his future no good by breaking the arm of the Station Commander, Group Captain 'Flash' Pleasance, during a bout of high 'cockaloram'. Naturally this act of sheer madness caused a few giggles, but the unfortunate student still survived the course. Plans were well advanced for Chivenor to be open to the public with an air display on Battle of Britain Day. The programme called for a display by a Meteor F.8. I put in a bid do it, and as nobody else on the TT flight was interested, I got the job. I had not given much thought previously to aerobatic displays, and had no idea what should be included in the display programme, but after chatting with the other four chaps on the flight we worked out a suitable sequence. I had been told to practise over Winkleigh, a disused airfield south east of Barnstaple. I went off down there whenever the opportunity arose, starting at 5,000 ft and then slowly reducing the height to 500 ft above ground level. Quite a few pilots had been killed doing low-level aerobatics in the Meteor, and I had no wish to join them, so my sequence contained no high-speed beat-ups, that being left to 'Bodger' Walker who was the Hunter display pilot. I also performed no manoeuvres involving bunts, because not only were they uncomfortable but I had no desire to have my eyes permanently bloodshot.

Peter Ellis called me into his office a fortnight before the display, and asked how my preparation was going.

"Fine" I said,

"In that case, perhaps you would like to show us what you can do - make it about 5pm so that your peers can enjoy the fun whilst taking tea!"

The Mess was in an ideal location, overlooking the runway with uninterrupted views across the estuary of the river towards Bideford. As I walked in the bar for a well-deserved beer afterwards, the Wingco said

"Nice display Nick, try not to kill yourself on the day"

Another string to my bow, but no big deal.

I was still getting plenty of flying on the Hunters. Most of the Mk 1s had now been replaced by the Mk 4s, and in addition to flying as a tactical instructor I was still managing a few air tests, which from time to time made me sit up and take notice. A flap failure required them to be blown down using the emergency air bottle, on another trip the undercarriage failed to retract, and on another some wing and aileron panels came adrift. Nothing serious, but enough to keep you alert.

As the festive season was approaching, I felt the time was ripe to make my move. I asked the Wingco if I could be formally posted from target towing to tactical instructor duties with one of the Hunter squadrons. "I'll see what I can do", he said.

Within the week I was on the staff of 'C' Flight, No.1 Sqn, with Sqn Ldr Kendall as my new boss.

On only my second trip with 'C' Flt I was leading a formation back to base when, after joining the circuit, I found my port wheel would not unlock. I was getting green lights for the nose and starboard wheel, but nothing for the port wheel. I overshot to let the others land whilst I tried re-selecting a couple of times, but to no avail.

"Chivenor - Blue one, I've got a problem"

"We can see that" they replied

"The Wingco Tech is on his way to the tower, in the mean time perhaps you can try bouncing the good wheel on the runway - the jolt might release the other one."

Seemed hairy to me, but I had a go - without success.

"Any other idea, Chivenor?"

"Give us a low fly-past over the tower so we can see what it looks like", Said the Wingco Tech. Now that is always an open invitation to do a legal beat-up. I took my opportunity to show the belly of the aircraft to the assembled observers - about ten feet over their heads. They confirmed what I already knew, it was fully locked in the up position.

"Shall I blow it down using the emergency air?"

"Not a good idea, the Hunter you are flying hasn't yet been modified so you will lose your powered controls."

"I see. Well I won't do that. How about if I retract the other two wheels and land it on the grass, on its belly?"

"Not to be recommended"" they said.

"Tests have shown that if the Hunter is belly landed there is a risk of the fuselage breaking just behind the cockpit".

Seemed a bit odd to me, but bowing to their technical expertise I prepared myself for the inevitable two-wheel landing. There was always the choice of flying out to sea and ejecting, but once was enough in a lifetime, plus I would finish up in the 'oggin' and that would be no fun - I couldn't swim! It was obvious that when the wing dug in the aircraft was going to swing some distance off the runway to the left. If I went far enough I might, at worst, slither across the dispersal into a hanger or at best finish up crashing into the Officers Mess, which would not be much of a problem because it was only made of wood. I released my parachute harness so that I could evacuate the aircraft as fast as possible and then I told the tower that I was on my final approach. Crossing Saunton Sands at 150 knots I jettisoned the hood and then crossed the runway threshold at 135 knots. I gently eased the starboard wheel onto the runway and did a trick-cyclist act balancing on one wheel for a few seconds whilst getting the nosewheel down. It seemed relatively easy until with maximum right aileron and at a speed of about 90 knots the left wing dropped and survival was in the lap of the Gods. I chopped the HP cock, pressed the engine fire-extinguisher button and switched off the battery master. Whilst doing this I had no idea where I was heading, the aircraft being enveloped in a cloud of dust and smoke. Eventually, it came to halt without having hit anything. I released my ejector-seat harness and jumped out quick.

The medics whisked me off to sick quarters in the 'blood wagon' where they pronounced me fully fit and I was back in the Mess in time for lunch. That evening Peter Ellis, the Wingco Flying, presented me with a mounted mangled runway light as a momento of my morning's work. In due course it was established that a corroded door spigot was the reason for the wheel failing to unlock. Faulty maintenance.

Early in the new year we had a change of boss. Sqn Ldr Kendall was posted to Aden, and we were to miss seeing him in his white tailor-made flying suit walking out to the flight line! His last act before departing was to assess each pilot's ability. I got an Above Average assessment as a Fighter Tactical Instructor and, with my IRE qualification, Above Average for instrument flying. His replacement, Squadron Leader Neville Howlett, was to become very popular with all the staff pilots on the OCU.

The Suez Crisis gained momentum during 1956/57 and rumours persisted that some Hunter squadrons were to be sent to Cyprus to take part in a Franco/British attack on Egypt. It was unlikely that they would send aircraft or pilots from the OCU, as they would not wish to disrupt the OCU training programme, especially as the only other Hunter OCU, at RAF Pembrey, in South Wales, was in the process of closing down.

It was quite a surprise then, when Mike Stabler and I were told that we had to go to the Royal Navy Dockyard at Plymouth to get a yellow fever jab, to be on standby to join the Suez Task Force which was being assembled in Cyprus.

"What are we going to fly out there?"

"Nothing" they said. "You'll be down a deep hole as members of a fighter control team"

"Bloody hell, there's enough chaps across the water at Hartland point controlling us every day - why not one of them?" but protests fell on deaf ears.

In the end only Mike went, and I was left to continue a life of wine, women and flying, with another summer to look forward to in North Devon.

The AOC carried out his usual annual inspection, and we laid on a flypast for his benefit. On the day preceding his visit I did eight trips. In the morning a sortie of aerobatics and a practise flame-out landing in manual, in the afternoon a flypast rehearsal for the AOC, then at night a long cross country in the Vampire T.11 from Chivenor to Valley, Valley to Leuchars, Leuchars to Lyneham, Lyneham to Marham, Marham to St Mawgan, St Mawgan back to base. I don't recall there being any flight-time limitations for fighter pilots in those days! I shared the night flying with another pilot on the base, who was shortly leaving the RAF and who wanted the extra hours, and away landings, to qualify for his civil licence and rating.

Pilots on a ground tour were still required do a number of hours each year in order to retain their flying pay. It was sometimes made difficult if a pilot was on a base equipped with aircraft on which he was not qualified, or perhaps not on a flying station at all which meant a visit to another airfield or to go on a refresher course. Our Wingco Admin fell foul of the system when he was court-martialled for making false entries in his log book.

I had my IRE qualification renewed, and continued to carry out instrument rating renewals in the Vampire T.11 and, because of this, I became pretty proficient with the aircraft. Air Marshal McEvoy was staying with the Station Commander whilst doing a Hunter conversion, and I was told to take him to Filton and pick him up three days later. Not the sort of job given to anyone who might not know where the all the knobs and tits were. That weekend he came into the Mess, bought me a couple of beers, and introduced me to his daughter. On my best behaviour that night - no trophies!

My confidence was now at its peak, and after brushing briefly with formation aerobatics, the Hunter individual aerobatic slot became available - and an Avro Anson arrived on the station. The Wingco asked if, in view of my previous display in the Meteor, I would like to become the display pilot in the Hunter. I jumped at the opportunity, and then was cheeky enough to suggest that perhaps he was also looking for someone to fly the Anson as well!

Within three days I had gone solo on the Anson, and done the obligatory tea-time display overhead Chivenor in the Hunter.

I was destined to give my first Hunter display at Plymouth on Saturday 14 June. Not as easy as it sounded, Plymouth (Roborough) was a small grass airfield on the north side of the city. I was told it was difficult to find, the makings of a glorious cock-up I thought, so with the Wingco's blessing I flew down there, joined the circuit and had a look around. I could see a problem. The Hunter was to be the main attraction, and as such the viewing public would want to see it flying fast, and making a noise. I normally opened my display by approaching the airfield low, and fast. At the end of the display I again put on full power and stood it on its tail from overhead the airfield. Made the windows rattle, which was what the punters wanted. With that sort of opening, I could easily miss the airfield and be halfway across the English Channel before I realised it.

It was customary to call the tower and say you were running in fast from whatever direction, and would be overhead in one minute. The commentator would than say 'If you look to your right you will see the Hawker Hunter flown by Flying Officer Nick Carter from RAF Chivenor running in to commence his display.' Now if at that stage you missed the airfield completely......... Added to that was the fact that the show was to be opened by Air Marshal Sir Phillip Wigglesworth KBE, CB, DSC, and the AOC of No.19 Group, Air Vice-Marshal Saye CB, OBE, AFC, was the chairman of the organising committee. A cock-up here would certainly nip a blossoming career as an individual aerobatic display pilot in the bud. I saw that answer was to pick up the A386 leaving Yelverton, keep the road on my starboard side and it would be impossible to miss the field. This I did, and to my relief all went well.

In between everything else I managed to get in some Anson trips to St Athan, Leconfield, Lyneham (with Group Captain Morant, the new Station Commander as passenger!) and Exeter. Then I was told to take a stretcher patient to the RAF Hospital at Wroughton near Swindon. No problem, off I went with Tom Price as my second pilot and navigator, and with an airman who had come along for the ride. All went well until we landed at Wroughton. It was mid-day, and Air Traffic Control said the duty crew had gone for lunch. Then, contrary to all rules and regulations, I was told to hold at the intersection of the two runways, to keep the engines running, and the ambulance would come out to me and collect the patient. I was a bit apprehensive about this, as there would be no chocks under the wheels and no fire extinguishers but I really had no alternative but to comply if the patient was to get to hospital. The ambulance arrived and backed up to the door and, after a while, the airman came up and said the transfer had taken place. I let off the brakes and, as the aircraft moved slowly forward, I felt the rear end move a bit sideways. Thinking it was the tailwheel straightening up I carried on taxiing to the holding point of the runway. I was about to line up for take-off after doing my checks when the airman came up front,

"I think we've got a problem, sir"

"What sort of a problem?" I asked.

"The tailplane looks as if it's bent" he blurted.

Tom went back and confirmed that the leading edge of the tailplane was indeed damaged. I told the tower, and they suggested I taxied it over to the MU for a technical inspection.

I was anxious to get it fixed and to be on my way, it was Friday afternoon and Chivenor was closing down at 4.30pm for a long weekend.

"If you can do a quick patch job on it, I'll be on my way".

"You're not going anywhere in that aircraft young man" said the Wing Commander in charge of the MU, "The aircraft is a write-off!".

After he had shown me the wrinkled fuselage I was inclined to agree with him.

I had to phone the Wingco Flying at Chivenor, Peter Ellis, who took it quite well in the circumstances. Two Vampire T.11s and Meteor T.7 duly arrived in the circuit to take the three of back to base. The following day I was told to attend the inevitable Court of Enquiry, which was due to be held at RAF Wroughton to determine how Anson VV362 and an ambulance happened to collide on 4th July 1958. Tom Price was also required to attend as a material witness to events. We drove up to Swindon in my car, the use of an aircraft to fly up had not been offered by the Wingco and I thought it prudent not to ask!

Tom and I arrived in the mess in time for dinner, and then drove out to a local hostelry for a couple of beers. We got chatting to a couple of chaps in the bar who were obviously RAF types who said they were also visiting Wroughton.

"Some silly bugger pranged an Anson, and we've go to do the court of enquiry!"

After a pregnant pause we came clean. I think they were as embarrassed as we were, in fact we had a bit of laugh about it and then had a few drinks together. As we left the pub they said

"see you in court"

The inquisition lasted about three hours, but in the end it was impossible to determine whether the aircraft hit the ambulance or vice versa. The Court decided that both drivers (ambulance and aircraft) were to blame, but Air Traffic Control were also guilty for allowing the transfer to take place in the middle of an airfield, without any ground crew being present. The verdict of the Court was that the ambulance driver, the air traffic controller and I should all be 'interviewed' by our respective bosses.

A month later the Wingco called me into his office:

"We've been given a replacement Anson, go up to Horsham St Faith and bring it back, and for God's sake don't prang it, or we're all in trouble."

I was now flying the Hunter F.1, F.4, the Meteor F.8 and T.7, Vampire T.11, the Anson and the Chipmunk.

My next aerobatic display was to be at RNAS Culdrose. In between my OCU instructional flying I was squeezing in a practice over Winkleigh at least every other day. The Operation Order called for me to position to Culdrose the previous day, and because of this it was decided that Fred Hartley should come down with me in a spare aircraft just in case mine went unserviceable.

During the briefing the following morning for participating pilots it was announced that the Russian Air Attache' would be a guest at the display - at his request. It was no coincidence that the Scimitar had just entered service with the Fleet Air Arm, and one was scheduled to take part in the flying display at Culdrose. Clearly the Russians wanted to have a closer look at this new aircraft.

After lunch Fred and I were sipping our coffee in the Wardroom when in walked three high ranking Russian Air Force officers, escorted by some equally senior Naval people. Fred and I watched the gathering with interest, especially when one of the Russians put a packet of cigarettes down on the table adjacent to my elbow as they sipped their pre-luncheon drinks. They were strange cigarettes, in that they seemed to be half a fag on the end of a tube.

"Do you think we should have that packet Fred, it would make a smashing trophy to show the lads back at Chivenor?"

As we got up to leave I absent mindedly picked up the packet as if it were mine, and walked out. The display went OK and that evening back at Chivenor we produced our trophy to a crowded Saturday-night party in the Mess.

In preparation for the 1958 Battle of Britain display season I spent a weekend at RAF Valley doing a display there, and at Shawbury. On my return to Chivenor I learned that my Battle of Britain Day programme on 20th September would include displays at Valley, Ternhill, Cosford and Gaydon.

I was handed Gaydon Operations Order 5/58 which, among other things, stated:

'Hunter Mk 4 will arrive overhead at 1429 hrs for immediate landing at 1430 hrs then go to the MoS dispersal. At 1518 hrs enter active runway to backtrack whilst Whirlwind performing. Take-off at 1521 hrs after Javelin has completed low run in opposite direction. After take-off do a wide turn to the south, and orbit Edgehill airfield at 3,000ft. To commence the display overhead at 1531 hrs and to be back on the runway at 1539 hrs.

Then depart Gaydon for Chivenor at the close of the display at 1730 hrs'.

A footnote to the operation order stated that a glider on tow would be over Edgehill at the same time at 2,000 ft, and three Douglas B-66s would be crossing the area below 2,000 ft! It occurred to me that the whole day was going to need a bit more planning than I normally did, so I was quite pleased when Gaydon said that a rehearsal would take place three days beforehand. It was a good opportunity to contact the other airfields and rehearse my complete programme. Two things concerned me on the planning, fuel, and arriving at Gaydon on time. It was obvious that I would need to land at Valley first in order to refuel, so I decided to do it the easy way and go up the afternoon before and night-stop in their excellent Mess.

The Hunter gobbled fuel at low level, especially whilst doing aerobatics, so I was quite relieved to learn that my 'show' at Valley and Ternhill would be only a couple of low fast runs. Cosford would be a full display, as would be that at Gaydon.

I calculated that my flight time from Valley to Gaydon, including the displays en route would be 29 minutes. If therefore I took off from Valley at 1355 hrs I would be five minutes early arriving in the Birmingham area, giving me a flight time of 35 minutes with a five-minute fuel reserve.

I also had to consider a safety-altitude problem, due to the close proximity of Mount Snowdon on the first leg out of Valley. A cloud base lower than 5,000 ft would either involve a detour around the north coast of Wales, which would have an adverse affect on timing and fuel reserves, or climb above it and do a QGH let-down at Ternhill to get back below cloud. In the end I flight planned for three alternatives. Good weather, bad weather round coast, and bad weather Ternhill QGH.

On the day of the rehearsal the good-weather plan went like a dream until the last leg into Gaydon when I became 'uncertain of my position' (fighter pilots are never lost!). I had not flown over this area before, and the smog and the vast urban area around

Birmingham made pilot navigation difficult. To make matters worse I was flying into sun. For a 'country lad' up from Devon it was unpleasant. I had to ask Gaydon radar for help, something they would not have much time for on the day.

In those days single-seat fighter aircraft had no radio navigational aids to call on. CRDF bearings to or from an airfield could be requested, but you could only work one at a time, to get a fix it was necessary to change frequency to obtain a cross-bearing from another station. It was tedious and time-consuming. In any case, at low level the bearings obtained were prone to some inaccuracy.

It was clear that on the day it would be better to do a detour around Birmingham to the west. With a westerly wind (hopefully) the smog would be blown to the east, thereby making map reading easier. It did mean that the extra distance would eat into my fuel reserves, but at least I would know were I was. I decided that my track would be Cosford, over open country to Kidderminster, then to Droitwich following the railway with the BBC transmitters on my left, then direct to Stratford upon Avon. I could then leave Stratford on an easterly heading, over Wellesborne Mountford, where I would see Gaydon in the one o'clock position for a run-in, break and landing - hopefully.

The weather on the day was excellent, everything went according to plan, and I touched down at Gaydon precisely on time at 1430 hrs.

My mother had not seen any of my displays, and a friend offered to drive her to RAF Gaydon to see this one. I had told her where the Hunter would be parked, and met up with her at the crowd barrier, having taken a mac with me to wear over my flying suit. Mixing with the public in your 'working clothes' was not approved of in those days.

At the end of the show, with 50,000 spectators streaming away from Gaydon, I flew back to Chivenor in time to shower and pick up the current girl-friend in Barnstaple for the Battle of Britain Mess Ball being held that night.

Chivenor was one of the few front-line bases, if not the only one, which had a private flying club located on the airfield. It was

called the Puffin Flying Club, aptly named after the birds inhab-
iting Lundy Island, and it became a second officers' mess for the
staff pilots at the OCU. A good place to meet the locals and of
course there was always a common interest in aviation. Their
flying activities were severely curtailed during the day, because of
the intensity of our flying, but at weekends and during the
summer evenings they were quite active, doing trips to Lundy
Island in an old Miles Aerovan!

This popular watering hole had a bit of a set-back when the
police caught a large number of drinkers on the premises after
hours. The raid took place during the August Bank Holiday, when
fortunately most of us were away on leave.

With so many second- and third-tour fighter pilots on one
station it made sense that, in the event of hostilities, training
would be transferred elsewhere and the OCU staff would become
two operational day fighter squadrons. This happened during the
annual defence exercise, code-named 'Sunbeam' when we
became No.127 (R) Sqn. We were then detached to RAF Stradishall, and the following day the exercise started with a fair number
of 'bandits' penetrating UK airspace. I was scrambled four times,
once from RAF Odiham after being diverted there by the sector
controller at Wartling. I had two more scrambles on the third day,
before returning to Chivenor in the late afternoon. I had managed
to get some F-86s and Canberras on my cine' film, but whether
they could be claimed destroyed was another matter. Some of the
lads actually saw F-100s and we all 'shot down' other Hunters -
hopefully not our own.

In September 1958, we had a fatality. Paddy Harper, an A2 QFI,
took off in a two-seat Hunter T.7 for a detail of instrument flying
and circuits with Lt Fatouk of the Royal Jordanian Air Force.
Nothing further was heard from the aircraft, and repeated calls
from Air Traffic Control brought no response. I little later the local
police telephoned to say that an aircraft had been seen diving into
the sea in Barnstaple Bay. Anticipating that the pilots may have
used their ejector seats, a sea search was immediately set in
motion, but despite covering a large area of the Bristol Channel

for over two days nothing was seen of Paddy or his student. A week later both bodies, together with some small pieces of wreckage, were washed ashore further down the coast. It was a sad loss, Paddy was an extremely popular member of the Chivenor staff.

The T.7, the new training version of the Hunter, had been delivered to 229 OCU in the middle of 1958. Within a very short space of time we had no fewer than 14 of them. Many of us had hundreds of flying hours on the Hunter, which had been accumulated over three or more years. We did not relish the thought of being checked out by some clever Dick, now we had a two-seater. Our worries were unfounded. They were used mainly by the QFIs on the staff to convert students on type before they came to us for tactical training. But of course, we all had to be able to fly them, so a simple programme was devised - we would check out each other. This meant that I was checked out by one of the lads in the morning, and in the afternoon I checked out someone else, who would in turn check out another, and so it went on until we all knew where the important knobs and tits were. This enabled me to do instrument-rating renewals on the Hunter T.7 as well as the Vampire T.11.

It was whilst debriefing a fellow instructor, after having completed his Instrument Rating renewal in the Hunter T.7, that I received a phone call that was going to change the course of my career.

"Nick, it's a call from Air Ministry"" shouted the chap in operations.

"What - for me?"

"Yes, you - its the second time they've rung."

Our masters in the 'Air Box' rarely made phone calls direct to the 'workers', certainly not mere Flying Officers. Such contact was always through Squadron Commanders, Wing Commanders, or even Station Commanders, depending on how serious the matter was.

""This is Wing Commander Fullerton. We would like you to attend a meeting at Air Ministry at 1100 hrs tomorrow. There will be a pass waiting for you at reception, and you will be shown to my office. Will keep you only for about an hour, old chap. Is that OK?"

"Yes sir."

Next day I flew a Hunter up to North Weald, changed and caught the tube into London, arriving at the Air Ministry in plenty of time for a cup of coffee before being escorted along the corridors of power to the Wing Commander's office. He introduced himself, and the two Squadron Leaders who were with him, then without stopping to draw breath said,

"We would like you to volunteer to go to Jordan!"

I needed less than five seconds to decided this was not for me. There was turmoil in that part of the Middle East, the Syrians had just tried to shoot down King Hussein's aircraft, the Parachute Brigade had been deployed to Amman in a desperate attempt to stop Nasser taking over the country, Glubb Pasha had recently been sacked by Hussein, and the Russians seemed to be everywhere.

"Its very kind of you to think of me, but no thank you, I'm quite happy in North Devon". I felt like adding that I didn't join to get hurt but thought better of it!

They ignored my refusal.

"The Americans have bought 12 Hunter F.6s for the Royal Jordanian Air Force, and they need three RAF pilots on secondment to train them up to an operational standard. There will be a further three pilots doing the same on the Vampires they already have. There will also be an RAF ground party, comprising of an engineering officer and 12 groundcrew, plus a small number of technicians who will set up a training school. You would be based on the civil/military airfield at Amman. You would be a member of the British Training Mission under the direct command of Wing Commander Dalgleish, the Air Attache'. The tour will be for 12 months only."

I was still unconvinced, but then came the punch line,

"We've also noted, Carter, that you have in fact sat the promotion examination for Flight Lieutenant twice, and failed on both occasions; if you volunteer for this posting we will immediately promote you to Flight Lieutenant, and you can have the posting of your choice when you return"

"Would the promotion be acting, or substantive."

"Substantive."

"You've got a deal"" I said with indecent haste!

"Excellent, now don't tell a soul. Details of your posting is restricted information at the moment. If asked where you're going, just say you're being posted overseas. Now let's have a chat with the chaps down the corridor and get you fixed up with a suitable passport"

I left the building wondering what on earth I had let myself in for.

On the way back to Chivenor I did a small detour and did a couple of slow rolls over my home in Maidenhead for old times' sake.

Officers Mess Ball at RAF Chivenor. Left to right 'Kiwi' Frances, Terry Thornton, 'Bodger' Walker, 'Nick' Carter, Fred Hartley, USAF exchange pilot, 'Paddy' Harper.

CHAPTER 14

Posted to Jordan

I had already met three of the Jordanian pilots whilst they were going through the OCU course at Chivenor. They were likeable chaps and keen to learn, much like the Lebanese who went through at the same time. We also had some Iraqis, who were a different kettle of fish altogether, stand-offish and arrogant. You were unable to teach them much, and they lacked the warmth and friendliness of their fellow Arabs.

Perhaps it was thought appropriate that a staff pilot from the OCU should go to Jordan, especially someone already known to the Jordanians. On the other hand perhaps someone in the 'Air-box' thought it might be better if I flew someone else's Hunters! Whatever the reason, my masters had overlooked the fact that I was purely a day fighter pilot. Pilots in the RJAF needed to be trained in the ground-attack role, as well as day fighting. I knew nothing about firing rockets at tanks, in fact I thought it was positively dangerous, hearing stories about chaps getting the 'chop' with target fixation and all that.

Somebody must have latched on to this oversight because, shortly after arriving back at Chivenor, I was hastily despatched up to CFE at West Raynham to do a quick five-day course in ground attack. On arrival I was introduced to Squadron Leader (just made up from Flight Lieutenant) Erik Bennett, who was on the staff of CFE but who was now earmarked to be my immediate boss flying the Jordanian Hunters. A short, dapper man, always on the go, hopping about from one foot to the other, but he seemed to have a sense of humour which was OK with me.

We did three trips in a Vampire T.11 firing rockets at ground targets on the Holbeach Range in The Wash. He seemed to be satisfied with that, but he then said,

"Are you qualified to fly the two-seat Hunter T7?"

What's this then? I thought, another check-out

"Yes".

"Good - Just that CFE has been allocated one and you might as well collect it from the MU at RAF Kemble, and I'll come with you.

Back at Chivenor the chaps gave me a farewell party, and as was customary the boss, Neville Howlett, presented me with a suitably engraved pewter tankard. The following day I renewed his instrument rating, and that was my last flight at Chivenor. It was the happiest station on which I had served in the Air Force - great flying, great mates, great social life, and all in a lovely part of North Devon.

I went home on leave for a week, and my mother greeted me by saying,

"I know where you're going, the Americans have bought twelve Hunters for the Jordanian Air Force and you are going to fly them - it says so in yesterday's *Daily Telegraph*"

Not wishing to leave my Vauxhall Velox unused at home, I put an advert in the local paper which came out on the Friday. Fortunately I had a buyer on the Saturday afternoon, prior to catching a train the following morning to Swindon. Late that night I flew from RAF Lyneham in a Comet to Nicosia.

On arrival in Cyprus, just as the Sun was coming up, I was met by an RAF Movements Officer who escorted me away from the barbed-wire military enclosure into the civil area of Nicosia Airport. He gave me a ticket to Beirut with Middle East Airlines, and another ticket from Beirut to Amman with Air Jordan. I presented myself at the departure desk and handed over my luggage, one suitcase full of personal clothing and another full of flying gear. I presented my passport for examination, which said my profession was a 'government official'. I then joined a motley group of people waiting to board a very clapped-out Dakota.

Officials at Beirut Airport seemed to take more than a passing interest in my passport, but as I was in transit they eventually waved me though and I boarded the Air Jordan Convair. After take-off the aircraft had to climb in a racetrack pattern overhead Beirut to gain sufficient altitude to cross the Jebel esh Sheikh mountains, which run along the Lebanese/Syrian border. The route would take us over Damascus before turning South for Amman. It was a bit uncanny overflying Syria and seeing a large number MiG fighters sitting on the ground and knowing that they were a potential enemy.

The desert became bleaker the further we went, until between the hills in the middle of nowhere I saw the ancient city of Amman, where we landed. In the arrival hall, amid a mass of milling people, I saw Erik Bennett who had arrived a day or so earlier. With him was a Jordanian Air Force officer, who guided us through a side door, completely by-passing the formalities of immigration and customs. Once outside, we were quickly whisked away in an RJAF staff car.

It was a short ride; the airfield was joint civil and military, being the Headquarters of the Royal Jordanian Air Force and the home of a squadron of Vampires, as well as a communications flight with a Dove, Heron and a Republic Seabee. We were accommodated in the old Officer's Mess, built by the British in the 1930s. It was a single storey building, built around a square with the resemblance of a garden in the middle. On one side were the public rooms, dining room, ante-room, etc, and on the other three sides were officers' quarters. In each of the bedrooms was an old iron bed, with a horsehair mattress, and a wardrobe. Heating was by way of oil dripping from a pipe on to a bed of sand; once the sand was moist, it was ignited. Having the drip too slow meant the fire would go out, but if set too fast the whole room become full of soot. Eventually this problem was overcome by scrounging some electric fires.

I met 'Splinter' Browne, who was the third Hunter pilot and Squadron Leader John Greenhill, Flight Lieutenant's 'Puddy' Catt and Brian Entwisle, who were going on to the Vampires. 'Nobby'

Clarke joined us as the Hunter Technical Officer, with a complement of RAF NCOs who were all Hunter qualified technicians, and Flight Lieutenant St John was the Admin Officer. In addition a number of RAF NCOs had arrived six weeks earlier to set up a ground school to train RJAF personnel. The only problem was that few had any previous instructional experience, and none were technically qualified on Hunters. A terrible cock-up resulting in most of them being sent back to Cyprus for training.

The situation in the area had become quite tense. There had been considerable unrest in Jordan, as the result of propaganda broadcasts from Cairo and Damascus aimed at the Palestinian refugees and left-wing extremists in the country.

The Baghdad Pact had been signed between Turkey and Iraq in 1955, which became the basis of a Muslim defence agreement, with Britain joining later together with Iran and Pakistan. President Nasser of Egypt, seeing his influence in the region being eroded, was hostile to the pact, as was Syria. Britain tried to influence King Hussein to join the pact, with promises of increased civil and military aid. It was at this time that the twelve Vampire jets arrived in Amman. It was not to be and there was rioting in the streets, followed by the resignation of the Prime Minister. There was a barrage of anti-Hussein propaganda from Cairo, calling for the Jordanians to get rid of the British Officers and to get rid of the King. The King asked the British Government for help in restoring order, but it was suggested to them that they might like to seek assistance from Iraq - we had more important matters to attend to - namely sorting out the Egyptians over the Suez Canal!

Free elections in Jordan returned a Government with leanings towards Moscow and Communism. The Jordanian Army (previously the Arab Legion) also became increasingly disillusioned with Major-General Glubb (Glubb Pasha) for a variety of reasons. The British Government paid for the Arab Legion, but not direct to the Jordanian Government but to a special account controlled by Glubb. The Arabs had come to mistrust Glubb which led to his sudden dismissal by the King in 1956; together with a large number of British Army officers who were in the country at the time.

An attempted coup to overthrow the King, let by the Commander of the Army, General Ali abu Nowar, was averted by Bedouins of the 1st Amoured Brigade, who were strongly loyal to Hussein. However, the loyalty of many other officers in the Jordanian Army was now in question, and would be for a number of years. Many were imprisoned, and martial law was imposed. In desperation, the King appealed for help from Britain and America. The Americans were already committed to sending troops to the Lebanon, and historically it was more appropriate for British troops to go to aid the Hashemite Kingdom. Two days later units of the British 6th Parachute Brigade arrived in Amman, as did six Hunters from No.208 Sqn who had been cleared to overfly Israeli airspace. Wing Commander Dalgleish was also posted back to Amman, arriving on one of the first Beverley aircraft. The co-operation of the Israelis was short-lived when they suddenly withdrew diplomatic clearance for the RAF to overfly their country. Supply flights were of course essential, so an urgent request was sent to the Americans, they eventually got approval to fly in supplies for the British troops using huge C-124 aircraft, providing the flights were made at night.

Some degree of stability then returned to the country, although there was still some doubt as to the loyalty of some elements of the Jordanian military. The presence of British troops on Amman airfield was clearly a deterrent, but commanders back in Cyprus and London were uneasy about this deployment, and were looking to withdraw the force as soon as possible. As a result, and following further talks with the King, it was agreed that the British would stay in Jordan only until the end of October. As a gesture of thanks King, Hussein sent the Queen two thoroughbred horses.

On 7th November the *Daily Telegraph* reported:

'This morning it was announced by the British and American Embassies in Amman, Jordan, that under an agreement con-

*cluded on 8th June the United States undertook to provide 12
Hawker Hunter aircraft for the Royal Jordanian Air Force. A
group of Jordanian pilots has recently undergone flight training
in Britain, and the aircraft purchased under the off-shore
procurement programme will shortly be delivered. Additional
operational training will be provided by a special RAF training
mission which is expected in Amman shortly.'*

The British Training Mission, of which I was now a member, was
under the overall command of Brigadier M Strickland, the senior
military adviser to the King. The RAF element was commanded
by Wing Commander 'Jock' Dalgleish, who was now the British Air
Attache'.

The Vampire Squadron was already in existence, but operationally non-effective due to poor serviceability and lack of
tactical training. The twelve brand new Hunter F.6s would
constitute an additional fighter squadron at Amman.

Jock Dalgleish was a legend. He was in Jerusalem standing
beside the young Hussein when his grandfather, King Abdullah,
was assassinated. They subsequently became firm friends, and in
due course the Wing Commander would teach the King to fly.
Although eventually fully qualified, the King never flew on his
own for obvious reasons.

Three weeks before our arrival the King and Dalgleish were
overflying Damascus on their way to Europe in the RJAF Dove
when they were intercepted by two Syrian MiG fighters. Dalgleish
thought this was strange, as they were flying along a recognised
airway and their flight plan had been accepted by Syrian Air Traffic
Control. But they were told by Damascus that their clearance had
been withdrawn and they were instructed to make an immediate
landing at Damascus. Sensing they were in trouble, Dalgleish took
command and stuffed the nose down until they were just above
the ground, and started heading back to Amman. The MiGs then
attempted to force the RJAF aircraft into the hills, but were
defeated by the skilful flying of Jock Dalgleish, who most certainly
saved the King's life.

The Hashemite Kingdom of Jordan had hostile neighbours to the north, west and south. Egypt and Syria, who had signed an agreement in February 1958 to become the United Arab Republic, were both engaged in subversive attempts to topple the Monarch. The Israelis to the west were the natural enemy but, although they had no desire to de-stabilise Jordan, there was always the possibility of conflict on the Jordanian/Israeli border being created by extremists on either side.

In the summer of 1958 Jordan then found itself completely encircled by enemies when Hussein's cousin, King Feisal II of Iraq, was assassinated in Baghdad following a military coup by the Iraqi Army. The King and members of his household were gunned down in the palace garden. Senior members of the Jordanian government who were in the Iraqi capital at the time were also brutally murdered, and the following day their bodies were dragged through the streets by a jeering mob. The British embassy was looted and set on fire.

Fuel supplies to Jordan were cut off by the new rulers in Iraq, then Saudi Arabia stopped flights by the Americans carrying fuel from the Gulf to Amman over Saudi airspace. In the end under pressure from the USA Israel allowed aircraft to overfly their country with fuel from the Lebanon until supplies could be shipped in through Aqaba.

This was the situation when we arrived. We were aware of the politics of the region from newspaper reports, but we had not been briefed on the local situation or what our task would be in the event of civil unrest, or direct military action by another power. This lack of information was not just confined to us. HQ MEAF, in Cyprus, send three signals to London asking for a statement of policy with regard to the RAF Training Mission in Jordan. There was no response to these requests. In contrast, the Americans would send their officers on a military advisers' course prior to any deployment of this nature.

What did concern us right from the start was who among the officers in the military would be loyal to the King, and who would not, if it came to a punch-up. We already knew that some army officers were to be treated with suspicion, but our immediate concern was the Jordanian pilots. One bad apple in a fully loaded Hunter could create havoc. We considered their attitude, family background, any Palestinian connections, did they mix or were they loners? All these factors influenced our thinking, but in the end is was all supposition and guess-work. Radio Cairo was continuously beaming propaganda to the population, especially to the Palestinians in the refugee camps, inciting them to riot and telling them that the presence of British pilots would not save Hussein. The Jordanian pilots told us of these broadcasts, and made great fun of them, which was a welcome sign.

Captain Fakhri Abuhmaidan was the most senior, a portly gentlemen and a bit older than the others, but quite capable. Lt Salah Kurdi was an excellent pilot and an asset to the squadron, he eventually became the Commander-in-Chief of the Royal Jordanian Air Force. Lt Nasri Jumiean, another keen fighter pilot was to switch to civil flying, taking a senior position with Alia Royal Jordanian Airlines. The squadron joker was Lt Marwan Zakaria, an extrovert and the life and soul of the party. Lt Firas Ajlouni was a likeable chap, and an excellent pilot. Later, after we had all left, he showed great courage and bravery when fighting the Israelis during the Six Day War in 1967. Sadly he was killed by Israeli fighters strafing King Hussein Airbase (Mafraq) as he was preparing to take-off on his second mission of the day. A sad loss.

The sixth Jordanian pilot was Lt Jamal, a nice chap who came from the West Bank. He eventually left the RJAF and went to fly MiG's for the Libyan Air Force after Gadaffi had sacked all his Pakistani pilots. Jamal later died from a heart attack.

CHAPTER 15

The Desert Kingdom

On the pan at the military side of Amman Airport stood 12 new Hunter F.6s - well 12 ex-RAF aircraft, which had been refurbished by Hawker Aircraft prior to delivery. Whilst en route at Nicosia, the Air Ministry instructed HQ Middle East Air Force (MEAF) to fit rocket rails to the aircraft. MEAF signalled back that they had no facilities to undertake this task, so they were never fitted.

The F.6 was slightly heavier than earlier Hunters, at 17,750 lb, and it had 'saw tooth' leading edges to overcome a tendency of the earlier versions to 'dig-in' in tight turns.

The main difference from an operational aspect was the addition of two 300-gallon under-wing long-range drop tanks. The radar ranging still did not work!

Before we arrived, Wing Commander Dalgleish had put out feelers to Air Ministry via MEAF as to the possibility of the Jordanians purchasing a two seat-Hunter, most probably for him to fly with the King. He was told that he could put forward a case for the purchase of this aircraft through normal channels, but that the chance of one being available was remote.

The ground crew under 'Nobby' Clarke were anxious to start acceptance checks, but were handicapped by not having the necessary servicing equipment. They spent the time going through the manuals with the Jordanians, and Erik Bennett, Splinter Browne and myself started work forming a new squadron. Bennett would be the Squadron Commander, and Splinter and I would be the two Flight Commanders. Although Splinter obviously had more seniority as a flight lieutenant, and was an ex-Cranwellian to boot, Bennett appointed me the senior flight commander and therefore his deputy. Probably my previous experience staff pilot at the Hunter OCU was the deciding factor.

Within days we came to realise just how isolated we were; completely on our own in what could become a very hostile environment. There were gun emplacements around the airfield, as well as a large number of armed guards looking after us and our aircraft day and night.

Apart from the odd Air Jordan flight, there were very few civil aircraft movements into Amman. The national carrier had, by virtue of the political situation, a somewhat restricted network with routes only to Beirut, Jeddah and, occasionally, Cairo. There were no tourists, and the only non-Arabs in the Kingdom seemed to be staff working in the various embassies - and us! On the third day, much to our surprise and delight, we saw a USAF C-124 Globemaster appear in the circuit and land. As it taxied to our dispersal we had a phone call from the tower to say it was carrying our spares and ground equipment. Within an hour the cargo had been unloaded and, with a 'best of luck to you guys', the crew got back in and were gone.

We soon learned that there were two things about Amman airfield which, from a pilot's point of view, needed watching. These were the hills half a mile to the south, the tops of which seemed to be pretty damn close when doing low level circuits, and the sheer drop at the far end of the westerly runway into downtown Amman. There was no overshoot area; if you ran off the end, not only were you a 'goner' but you were going to take a few Arab families with you.

Much happened in the first month. We air-tested all 12 aircraft, which also enabled us to do sector recces, plus it gave me the opportunity to familiarise myself with the Mk 6. But what concerned us most was that the whole of the Royal Jordanian Air Force was concentrated on Amman airfield. One strike would wipe us out completely.

There were three other airfields in Jordan: Aqaba, Jerusalem and Mafraq. Aqaba was out of the question, the runway was dirt and much too short. Jerusalem had a long enough runway, but it was only a mile or so from the Israeli border, the 'front line' to the Arabs! Mafraq had been built by the RAF in the early 1950s as a potential V-Force dispersal airfield. It was dead flat with a 3,000 yd runway, but on the downside, it was only a few miles from the border with Syria. We looked at Jerusalem and Mafraq from the air, and decided to visit them both to see how they might fit in with our future planning. Apart from the tactical necessity of being able to deploy in the event of hostilities, there was also a need to have a diversionary airfield available for both the Hunter and Vampire squadrons, should the runway at Amman, be obstructed.

We were flown first to Jerusalem in the Dove, and as soon as we touched down it was clear that this airfield should be used only in an emergency. The circuit took aircraft very close the border, with little or no margin for error, plus there was a bump in the middle of the runway, which meant that the end was not visible until you came over the brow of the hill. Best left alone, we thought.

Old Mafraq was a dirt landing strip that had been an RAF staging post since the 1920s. It was conveniently situated alongside the pipeline that carried oil from Iraq out to a Mediter-ranean terminal at Haifa. Needless to say, the pipeline had been empty for some time. It was painted black and sat on top of the desert, running in an easterly direction as far as the Iraqi border. The only railway line in Jordan also ran through Mafraq in a southerly direction, past Amman and on to Ras en Naqb just short of Aqaba. This seemed ideal, just follow either the pipeline or the railway track and you arrived back at Mafraq - my type of navigation!

In the early 1950s it had became apparent that old Mafraq would not be suitable for jet aircraft, so a completely new airfield was built on a new site a couple of miles east of Mafraq town, and it was at this airfield that we landed on the 15th December.

New Mafraq was intriguing, a massive base with hangars, barrack blocks, married quarters, and an enormous runway - but completely deserted. In one of the married quarters we discovered that No.249 Squadron had been in residence at some time, but with the squadron crest still over the bar it was evident they had made a hasty departure some time previously. Since the British military had hastily departed in 1956, the airfield had remained empty, the Royal Jordanian Air Force having little or no desire to utilise this abandoned asset. The Vampires had no difficulty operating from Amman, and the RJAF personnel much preferred being in the capital with their families.

Entering one of the huge hangars, we had the surprise of our life. In one corner were three Arab Legion Austers looking quite forlorn and covered in dust and sand. One was a dual-control Autocrat, and the other two were AOP.6 spotters. Clearly, we were going to have some fun flying those in due course. Splinter and I both agreed with Erik Bennett that we should move the Hunter squadron to Mafraq as soon as possible. Bennett then floated the idea back at Amman, with both Jock Dalgliesh and Col Othman, the Commander in Chief of the RJAF.

In the run up to Christmas we settled into a routine quite different from what we had been used to in the UK. We could low fly anywhere without prior approval. In fact, we were encouraged to 'show the flag' to let any potential rioters see that trouble of any kind would be countered from the air. We did joint exercises with the army, where they called us up on a common frequency to carry out dummy attacks on targets. Within days it was perfectly clear to most army commanders that the Hunters and Vampires could mount an attack on any objective within minutes. In contrast to UK regulations, we were allowed go supersonic anywhere over the country, and were even encouraged to drop sonic bangs over populated areas.

On Christmas Eve we visited the Holy Places in Bethlehem, and then went on to a carol service in the Field of the Shepherds. It was uncanny, we were the only foreigners there, and we stood out like sore thumbs. The Jordanians thought so as well, because on all subsequent excursions outside Amman we had a discreet armed guard. As a further safety measure, we were each issued with a Berretta pistol, which we wore under a jacket or in our flying suit. Luckily we never had to use them, which was fortunate as we regularly missed hitting oil drums at 10 yards! Christmas day was spent in our mess. A local Arab company, Flouty Bros, had a contract to run the mess and provide for our needs. It worked quite well, and Mr Flouty did us proud. We also had a fair number of invitations out to the homes of people working in the Embassy. The officers' mess was built on the side of a hill, which at the time would have had superb views across one of the many valleys in Amman. Now it overlooked a mosque, ringing out the good news at all hours of the day - and Amman Jail!

Early in the new year, Nobby Clarke and a couple of his chaps came with Bennett and myself to Mafraq to check on the state of the Austers. Luckily, there had been some attempt to inhibit the engines, and as far as they could see the airframes seemed to be OK. Having said that, Nobby pointed out that none of his chaps could sign the Form 700, but they would look at them from time to time if we wanted to take a chance and fly them! We had no pilot's notes, but by trial and error we considered that a comfortable speed for take-off was about 40kts, climb 60kts, stall 30kts and approach 50kts, nice round figures! In fact the Autocrat's ASI was calibrated in mph, but we considered it simpler to use the same speeds for both types of aircraft! Once happy with the handling we headed off across the desert back to Amman, Bennett in the Autocrat and me in a AOP.6. We soon discovered that the Auster Mk 6 was quite a nippy little aircraft, but the Autocrat was sloppy on the controls and terribly underpowered, although the seating was more comfortable.

We had another problem - what should our squadron number be? Bennett wanted the Hunters to be No.1 Squadron RJAF, but the Vampire and the transport squadrons were already numbered No.1 and No.2 respectively. This meant that logically we should have been No.3 Squadron. Bennett was not keen on being third in the pecking order, and he eventually got the RJAF Commander to agree that we should become No.1 Squadron, much to the annoyance of our British and Arab colleagues in Amman. Next, we needed a squadron crest. One of the RAF chaps was a bit arty, and he came up with a black wolf's head superimposed over an Arabic figure one in red. An order was placed with a firm in Pakistan to produce squadron badges in wire, to be worn on our flying suits, and for a number of wall plaques from a firm in the UK for presentation to the King and high-ranking military commanders, as well as one each for ourselves.

We adopted red and white as the squadron colours, and the aircraft were painted accordingly. The logo was similar to that of No.34 Squadron RAF, which had been deployed to Amman the previous year. Bennett wanted to go further, and have the rudders and wingtips painted with red and white squares. Nobby was against this, because in the Royal Air Force the painting of control surfaces was forbidden. But Bennett told Nobby 'They're not RAF aircraft, so get 'em painted'. This he did, and we finished up flying aircraft looking a bit like a Christmas Card! Strangely, we did very little productive flying in January. There might have been some training on the ground, but little in the air. I did only three sorties with a Jordanian on my wing, all the rest were individual flights where I seemed to do aerobatics and low flying sorties. Included in the low flying would be practice ground attacks on the odd train or truck travelling down the desert road to Aqaba. Occasionally we intercepted the odd civil aircraft that had failed to file a flight plan or missed a reporting point. There was no radar control, either military or civil, and what airways existed were only advisory. We understood that a military radar unit had been set up in the hills on the West Bank some time previously, but for a variety of reasons it was no longer operational. I checked Splinter out on the Autocrat, and did a few trips back and forth to Mafraq in the Auster in preparation for our move to Mafraq, which had by now been approved in principle. Nevertheless, there were a number of problems to overcome, not least the additional cost of supporting an extra airfield, as well as laying on all the necessary technical and administrative services.

Military expenditure accounted for over 50 per cent of the Jordanian budget. It was an enormous drain on the country's economy. It was only possible to maintain this by an annual grant from the British Government. In the late 1950s this amounted to JD 10,000,000 (1 Jordanian Dinar equalled £1 Sterling) which went some way to covering their expenditure on defence. There was no restriction on the number of hours flown, but shortage of cash showed up in other ways.

A very good deal had obviously been negotiated with an oxygen supplier in downtown Amman, who in turn was getting his supplies from an unknown source in Beirut. We had been using this oxygen for over four months before we discovered that it was low-grade industrial oxygen only to be used for welding! With the blessing of the Jordanians, HQ Middle East Air Force sent over an expert who carried out a complete inspection of the oxygen supply and aircraft systems, and at the same time an RJAF NCO was sent to Nicosia to do a course on oxygen production.

What did concern us was the lack of any information about ammunition stocks and fuel reserves, two vital elements in the assessment of our fighting capability. The Jordanians were very coy about discussing this with us, and we never knew if we had enough 30mm ammo for 10 or 100 sorties - or perhaps none at all.

There were historical reasons for this sensitivity. They had felt they were badly let down during the Arab-Israeli conflict in 1948 when the supply of ammunition was suddenly stopped by the British Government. With all their military equipment being of British origin, they had no option but to cease fighting. The Jordanians also felt that Glubb had a policy of keeping the ammunition stocks low for reasons best know to himself. Right or wrong, the effect of this mistrust was still apparent in 1959. During my 12-month tour, I only fired the guns twice, and the Jordanian pilots never!

Early in February, the Commander-in-Chief Middle East Air Force, Air Marshal W.L.M. MacDonald, paid a courtesy visit to the King, and we laid on a flypast in his honour. He was pleased with what we had achieved, and in the crew room after the show he asked if I had ever thought of applying for a permanent commission. I said I hadn't.

"If you are interested, now is the time" he said.

I thanked him, and said I would give it some thought. I was on a Short-Service engagement, which meant that I would go no higher in rank than Flight Lieutenant, and I would leave the Service after my contracted 12 years, with a lump-sum gratuity of £4,000. Should I wish to stay on in the hope of a career to retirement, with the prospects of further promotion, I would need to apply for a Permanent Commission (PC). All I wanted to do was fly, I had no desire to do anything else in the RAF. I remember at ITS being told we were officers first and pilots second. At any time we could be posted into jobs which might be nothing to do with flying - the reason why all pilots were in the General Duties Branch of the RAF.

In general, the majority of officer aircrew were serving Short-Service engagements and, because of the cost of training and relatively short time they spent in the Service, they did nothing else but fly. Once you changed to a Permanent Commission, it was a certainty that you would have to mix flying with general duties. I still remembered the effect of the Duncan Sandys Axe whilst I was on 257 Squadron, some of the chaps with PCS were sent into all sorts of dead-end jobs, could that happen again? In addition, there were exams and courses to complete to achieve higher rank. For someone who had to have his flight lieutenant's rank given to him I could see problems there! Clearly, with a recommendation from the C-in-C there was little doubt that I was onto a good thing if I applied, but I was uncertain. The thought of becoming an administrator didn't really appeal at the time, and in the end I let the opportunity slip. In retrospect, I made two mistakes in my life and that was one of them!

CHAPTER 16

Lifesaving

February went out with a bang: we woke to find three inches of snow had fallen overnight, and more was forecast. Not just in Amman either, reports were coming in of drifts of up to five feet deep in many parts of the country caused by the high winds. The worst areas were from Amman down the eastern side of the Dead Sea as far as Ma'an and Petra. The main desert road from Amman to Aqaba was blocked in a number of places, as was the railway. There were reports of drivers stranded in their lorries, and even a train on the single-track railway was snowbound.

Amman airfield was closed; snow clearance was not something the military or the civil authorities had envisaged. The Army was making attempts to rescue beleaguered drivers on the desert road, when news started to come in of the plight of the Bedouins in the valleys around Petra. They were stranded, with drifts completely covering their tents. There was no way the Army was going to reach them, so they approached the Air Force for help.

Could we drop supplies to them from the air? The cloud base was down to 500 ft at Amman, and in the Petra area, low cloud was covering the hills. It was impossible to use the Dove or Heron in these conditions, and it seemed that there was nothing we could do - until someone said, how about the Austers?

The idea did not appeal to the Jordanian pilots. They were reluctant to fly the Austers in good weather, let alone with a 500 ft cloud base, 30 kt surface wind, and with only limited panel instrumentation, and who could blame them. Then, in a moment of shear madness, we said 'We'll do it' - we being Erik Bennett and myself on the Hunter side and Brian Entwistle and 'Puddy' Catt from the Vampires. Brian and 'Puddy' must have been out of their minds as, to the best of my knowledge they had done little or no flying on the Austers until then!

The plan was simple; we would fly down to Ma'an, a small old Arab Legion garrison town and staging post along one of the early trading routes leading into the ancient Nabataean city of Petra. Adjacent to the Fort was a small dirt landing strip, which we were told would be cleared of snow in time for our arrival. We would be met by the local army commander who would provide the food and clothing to be dropped and brief us as to where the Bedouins were located. Previously we had only flown the Austers in good weather, and only in the immediate vicinity of Amman or Mafraq, mainly because we were uncertain about the reliability of the engines. We were now about to fly them for 130 miles over snow-covered inhospitable desert! Somebody told us what we needed to know about carb-air heating, and we then drew lots to see who was going to fly the under-powered Autocrat. I got the short straw, but it did have one advantage over the other two, it had an artificial horizon - sheer luxury! The Boss and I decided to fly down in loose formation so, should one of us have engine failure, the other would have a rough idea of the location and summon help. We would follow the Hejaz Railway where we could, but it was only single track and it was most likely covered by snow for long stretches. Just before the halfway mark was the small settlement of Qatrana, which would be an ideal fix.

With full tanks we guessed we had an endurance of about 2.30 hrs, and with an estimated flight time of 1.45 hrs it was obviously a one-way mission! There was no way we could get back to Amman if we ran into bad weather and were unable to land at Ma'an. As the landing strip was on a rock plateaux about 2,500 ft above sea level this was a real possibility! We had no radio, so were unable to talk to each other, or to anyone else for that matter. We decided that if either of us had a problem before the point of no return we would come into close formation and signal thumbs-down to the other, and we would return to Amman together.

The following morning, 28 February 1959, I lined up on the westerly runway and opened up to full power. The acceleration was virtually non-existent, due to two factors, there was two inches of snow on the runway and someone had decided I should take a passenger! Passing the halfway point on take-off I noticed that the speed was reluctant to increase beyond 55 kts so I eased back on the pole and we staggered into the air, then followed a slow and unsteady climb straight ahead until we reached our cruising altitude of 250 ft. A left turn on to track, and I saw Erik Bennett coming up on my inside to take up a loose formation position. As I was in the slower aircraft, I would lead the way. We soon saw the extent of the havoc. Lorries and cars stuck on the dirt road going south, with Jordanian Army vehicles desperately trying to reach them. The railway line was completely covered in snow, but we could see the tops of telegraph poles running alongside.

The cloud base seemed to be about 1,500 ft for two-thirds of the way, and although we ran into snow showers, they were short-lived. After being airborne for only 55 minutes, we saw a few buildings come into view which seemed to be Qatrana. If that was the case, we were running ten minutes ahead of our flight plan time. Clearly we had a stronger tailwind component than we thought.

The settlement seemed to be completely cut off by drifts; in the station was a train which looked stranded. We did a quick orbit and continued on our way. I anticipated that we would be overhead Ma'an about 15 minutes early if the wind stayed the same for the remainder of the flight. If it was that strong in the Ma'an area I hoped that the landing direction didn't present us with an difficult crosswind. It would be a bit of a disaster if we wrote off both aircraft attempting to land.

About 40 miles from our destination we came to the real test. We could see the ground rising ahead of us as we approached the plateaux on which Ma'an and the landing strip were situated. We just hoped that there was sufficient clearance between the high ground and the cloud for us to find the strip and land. We were in a lot of trouble if the cloud was on the deck - it would mean flying back along the railway until we saw signs of life, preferably an army unit - and crash land in the snow.

We started climbing, the ground got higher and the cloud lower, until we levelled out 100 ft above the plateaux and about 200 ft below the cloud base. We saw the town ahead, but where was the Arab Legion base? Then suddenly off to one side we saw a ring of military vehicles with their headlights on, on what seemed to be a marked landing strip. After a couple of orbits we were pleased to see the strip was roughly into wind, which was a stroke of luck as the tatty old wind-sock was nearly horizontal, telling us the surface wind was a bit on the strong side. After landing we were warmly greeted by the base commander, who quickly briefed us on the situation and what he was expecting from us.

The main problem was in the Wadi Musa (close to the ancient city of Petra) where the Bedouins had been cut off by deep drifts for days. All attempts by the Jordanian Army to reach them had been unsuccessful. The plan was that we would each take a soldier with bundles of food and clothing loaded on the back seat. We would then fly up the Wadi until we found a Bedouin encampment, then the soldier would open the door and throw out the parcels.

Within half an hour I was on my way up the valley. I was maintaining a steady track with 15 degrees of drift in severe turbulence, with shear rock faces on either side closing in on the aircraft the further we went. After a while we saw a group of brown tents which were only just visible above the snow drifts. The Bedouins waved to us, and we could see blood in the snow where they had slaughtered their goats to eat. We did an orbit overhead and eventually succeeded in dropping our supplies from 50 ft.

After a couple of close encounters with solid granite I realised how important it was always to turn into wind, and to keep the speed up. Any error would result in a terrible death, being smashed against the mountains.

It also became obvious that carrying a passenger to throw out the supplies was a waste of payload, and I took this up on my return.

"But how are you going to get the parcels out of the aircraft?"

"Simple - I'll fly with the passenger seat and the door removed – we can nearly double the payload that way"

Any possible changes in the flying characteristics of the Auster as a result of such action did not enter my head but it seemed worth a try. It turned out to be far from easy. Approaching the overhead position I would lean back, grab a parcel and place it on the passenger door step. When overhead I would loosen my straps, ease myself out of my seat and while flying the aircraft with an extended right arm I kicked the bundle out through the gaping hole with my left foot. It got easier with practice. It was freezing cold, and the only clothing we had was our standard RAF issue flying overall. My biggest dread was an engine failure, which would have been 'curtains'. We were being refuelled with petrol purchased from the local garage in Ma'an, with no checks as to its quality or for possible water contamination. It was best not to think about it.

During the remainder of that first day I managed six trips up the Wadi, going further each time and still finding people in desperate need. As darkness fell we were taken to the Jordanian Officers Mess, which was in an old Arab Legion fort, steeped in history from the time when the Emir Abdullah set up camp there in 1920 as did Lawrence of Arabia some years later.. After a welcome meal of rice and boiled mutton, we flaked out on horsehair mattresses ready to start again at first light.

Operations on the second day were restricted, as by mid afternoon the cloud base was right on the deck. Even so, I managed another six trips, each flight being nearly an hour in duration.

We were grounded throughout the third day by continuous low cloud and further snow showers, the following day was better, with a good viz below 8\8ths cloud at 1,000ft. The surface wind was still very strong possibly gusting 35 to 40kts, but luckily still more or less in the direction of take-off. The army updated us on new areas to search, which were even further into the Esh Shara Mountains. It was gratifying work, knowing that you were helping these proud nomadic people to survive. They waved their arms in thanks after each and every drop. But I was concerned that we seemed to be dropping much more clothing than food. I sensed that in some cases the recipients were also expecting more food, a point I mentioned to the army chaps back at base.

As darkness was falling, King Hussein arrived at Ma'an in the RJAF Dove, and he joined us in the army mess for supper. We sat around in a group describing to him what it was like and what we had seen. He was most concerned for his people and the suffering they were having to endure. As he left he turned to us RAF chaps and said

"The Jordanian people will always remember you for what you have done - I thank you from my heart".

I had completed ten sorties that day, and it was a fitting climax.

We continued to fly mercy missions for a further two days, by which time the weather was beginning to ease, and the army had reached all the cut-off areas. We had completed a difficult task at great personal risk, way above what was required of us. Many months later, whilst home on Christmas leave, after having returned to the UK, I received a parcel in the post - it was a medal. The covering letter said I had been decorated by King Hussein with The Hashemite order of Independence.

I also received a Royal Warrant from The Queen.

ELIZABETH THE SECOND, by the grace of God of the United Kingdom of Great Britain and Northern Ireland and of our other Realms and Territories QUEEN, Head of the Commonwealth, Defender of the Faith, To Our Trusty and Well-beloved John Graham Carter, Esquire, Flight Lieutenant in Our Royal Air Force. Greetings! WHEREAS his Majesty the King of The Hashemite Kingdom of Jordan has been pleased to confer upon you the decoration of the Order of Independence (Class IV), in recognition of valuable services rendered by you during the distribution of supplies by air to the Bedouin of southern Jordan

after the disastrous snowstorms of February and March 1959,
resulting in the saving of lives: AND We being Graciously Pleased
to approve thereof: Know Ye that We of Our Special Favour have
given and Granted, and do by these Presents give and grant, unto
you the said John Graham Carter Our Royal Licence and
Authority that you may avail yourself of the said mark of favour
and wear the decoration of the Order of Independence (Class IV)
and that you may enjoy all the Rights and Privileges thereunto
belonging.

The medal was a great honour and totally unexpected, but it was
a big disappointment having it presented by the postman! Being
invited back to Jordan to receive it from the King might have been
asking a lot, but perhaps an invitation to a presentation at the
Jordanian Embassy would have been nice.

Elizabeth R

ELIZABETH THE SECOND, by the Grace of God of the United Kingdom of Great Britain and Northern Ireland and of Our other Realms and Territories QUEEN, Head of the Commonwealth, Defender of the Faith, To Our Trusty and Well-beloved John Graham Carter, Esquire, Flight Lieutenant in Our Royal Air Force,

Greeting!

WHEREAS His Majesty the King of the Hashemite Kingdom of Jordan has been pleased to confer upon you the decoration of the Order of Independence (Class IV), in recognition of valuable services rendered by you during the distribution of supplies by air to the Bedouin of southern Jordan after the disastrous snowstorms of February and March, 1959, resulting in the saving of lives:

AND We being Graciously Pleased to approve thereof: Know Ye that We of Our Special Favour have given and granted, and do by these Presents give and grant, unto you the said John Graham Carter Our Royal Licence and Authority that you may avail yourself of the said mark of Favour and wear the decoration of the Order of Independence (Class IV), and that you may enjoy all the Rights and Privileges thereunto belonging:

The Author's Royal Warrant

CHAPTER 17

Attempted Coup

Within days of returning to Amman, we escorted the King to the Syrian border at the start of his world tour. Since our arrival in the country, whenever the King or senior members of the Government were airborne we always provided an escort of four Hunters. Everyone was concerned that the Syrians might be tempted to repeat their previous attack on his aircraft. The leader of the escorting formation would be either Erik Bennett, Splinter Browne or myself, and we would remain at the border at 40,000 ft until his aircraft was clear of Syrian airspace. The object was to let the Syrians see us on their radar and to hear us on the R/T.

Everyone seemed to use the same frequency in that region, so we all knew what was going on. We used this openness to our advantage, to convey to the Syrians that we would be over the border to sort them out at the slightest sign of any provocation. What they did not know was that our aircraft were unarmed!

We had been told that there might be some unrest in certain elements of the Army during the King's absence, so it was suggested that we do some joint exercises to keep them occupied. These exercises also provided us with excellent air-to-ground practice, as we were due to take part in the King's Review of the Army and the Air Force on his return.

Whilst all this was going on, we decided to spend one of our off-duty weekends visiting Petra. The plan was to drive down in Land-Rovers, but Nobby and I decided to fly down in the Autocrat and leave the aircraft with our Army friends at Ma'an before meeting up with the others. The entrance into Petra is through the most spectacular gorge, which in places is only a few feet wide. You either walk, or ride a horse or donkey. News that we were the chaps who only a few weeks previously were dropping supplies to them had preceded us, and we were treated like heroes. There was much shaking of hands and heartfelt thanks, and of course there was no question of having to pay for the transport.

The sight of the Treasury as you enter this ancient city, carved out of solid rock, is awe-inspiring. What also gave it an eerie atmosphere was that the whole of Petra was empty - not another soul in the place.

We were the guests of the Jordanian Army, who had arrived before us and pitched tents for us to sleep and to provide us with food, complete with the customary armed guard. There was a small guest-house, but this was in disrepair and had not been used since before the Second World War. The only item of interest in the building was a visitors' book dating back to the early 1930s, which was still in the foyer. We spent two whole days exploring this historic site, along with a very young Bedouin boy who appeared from nowhere. He carried an old Lee-Enfield rifle slung across his back. The army chaps said his family had received some of the parcels from the sky, so they sent him to guard us!

At the end of our two-day visit Nobby and I returned to the Autocrat for our return flight, a quick pre-flight check, and off we went - well, nearly. It was plain that, following my previous exploits at Ma'an, a degree of over-confidence was creeping into my Auster flying. I had failed to take into account the fact that Nobby was a big bloke, that we had numerous iron tie-down stakes and much baggage in the back, and the temperature was a good 25 degrees C higher than when I last took off from this strip. Well, during the take-off run we trundled on, and on, and on, but the aircraft seemed to have little or no inclination to get airborne. On reaching the end of the strip I gingerly eased back on the stick, and hoped for the best. Much to my relief, the wheels left the ground, but I could tell by the sloppiness of the controls that we were just on the stall, and hanging on the prop. Any further attempt to climb or turn would be disastrous. Nobby was conspicuous by his silence, and I could sense that he was increasingly aware of our predicament. I was beginning to sweat – what a way to finish the tour! Fortunately the terrain was flat, we continued straight ahead for a good five miles, no more than ten feet off the ground. After five miles, we gained height, not because we were climbing but because the ground was falling away as we left the plateau behind. When we had gained what I thought was a couple of hundred feet clearance I dropped the nose, the speed increased to 65 knots, and I started to turn north for Amman. I imagined Nobby was not all that impressed but, being a gentleman, he said nothing!

Once back at base we got intelligence updates from Wing Commander Dalgleish as to the current state of unrest in the army. The information was sketchy but it was thought that some very high-ranking officers in the Jordanian Army were involved. More importantly for us was how the Jordanian pilots would react to any revolt by the Army. The crunch came one evening, when the Wingco called us together for an urgent briefing. He said reports had been received that there was likely to be an attempted coup in the early hours of the following morning. Needless to say, this made the three of sit up and take notice. Suspicion was centred on the Armoured Brigade based at Zerka, a large garrison 13 miles north-east of Amman. It was exactly two years since a previous mutiny at Zerka, which had to be put down by Bedouin troops loyal to the King. It was considered to be a hot-bed of unrest, constantly targeted with propaganda from Radio Cairo.

Intelligence reports were coming in from officers close to the rebels, but who were in fact loyal to the King. They said the tanks were going to roll down the main highway, and take Amman at daybreak.

Under great secrecy, ammunition for the Hunters and Vampires was released from the armoury, and the RAF ground-crew armed the aircraft overnight. The few Britons resident in Amman at the time had already been warned of possible unrest, and to stay indoors, by a simple but effective system of a coded telephone message which originated from the Embassy and was passed on from household to household.

The following morning as dawn broke we were sitting in three fully armed aircraft, ready to be airborne within seconds. We had been briefed to attack the tanks as they rolled into Amman. There was an early-morning mist which kept a nip in the air as we read our paperbacks. From time to time one's thoughts drifted to other things, how effective would our 30mm Adens be against their tank armour, how much ammunition was available for another sortie, what if the runway was blocked on our return, what if we got shot down? I had taken the precaution of making a note of the heading and fuel required to make it to the RAF base at Akrotiri in Cyprus - perhaps even to Tel Aviv should the need arise!

As it was, there was no need to worry. An hour after sunrise we were told to stand down - the leaders of the coup had been arrested, and the tanks were still safely inside the garrison compound.

The King was due to arrive back in Jordan on 2nd May. As was our custom, we were loitering at 40,000 ft as he crossed Syrian airspace. As he entered Jordan we formatted on his aircraft for the short leg into Amman, and then we welcomed him home with a close formation flypast after he landed.

What we did not know was that the Chief of Staff of the Jordanian Armed Forces, General Sadiq Shara, was suspected of being the ringleader of the military coup. King Hussein had been told of this and had decided at very short notice to take the General with him to the USA, thereby thwarting any ideas he may have had while he was out of the country. The General was arrested as he left the aircraft back at Amman, was court marshalled and sentenced to death (this sentence was later commuted to life imprisonment by His Majesty).

In spite of being somewhat preoccupied with the abortive coup, we had been busy practising for the Royal Review of the Armed Forces, which was to be held at the end of the month. It was a three-day event, with RJAF participation throughout; each day the King would be present, together with military and diplomatic representatives from many Western nations. The first day was totally RJAF and would be in the form of an air display at Amman. I was involved in three of the display items; a dog fight with a Vampire flown by 'Puddy' Catt, leading the second section of four Hunters in a close formation flypast low over the saluting base, and finally an individual aerobatic display.

Perhaps I was getting complacent, even over-confident, because on the day of the display, in front of the King and his many guests, I broke a cardinal rule of all display pilots and very nearly wrote myself off. It happened towards the end of my aerobatic routine. I had already performed a bit lower than was the norm and then, with a sudden rush of blood to the head, I decided to changed my programme! That alone was bad enough, but to try a 'Derry Turn' at 200 ft, a manoeuvre I had never practised before, was sheer lunacy. It all happened in a fraction of a second; even with the high rate of roll of the Hunter I lost height, and my port wing missed the high ground on the far side of the airfield by inches. The Arab spectators were most impressed, but my RAF colleagues knew it had been a close call.

The dog fight with 'Puddy' Catt proved what we already knew, that the Vampire was capable of a much tighter turning circle, which meant the Hunter was on a hiding for nothing. Inevitably, 'Puddy' was on my tail in no time at all, as he had been on every occasion during rehearsals - but on the day I had other plans. As he closed in for the 'kill' I opened up to full throttle, heaved back on the pole, and left him stranded as I climbed away. The next day was the start of the Army Review. This was held at Zerka, and we did an eight-ship flypast in close formation whilst the King was inspecting the Army parade.

The third and final day was more interesting. We were to demonstrate a ground attack on tanks and armoured vehicles in the desert. This caused some concern for two reasons: there was the safety of the Monarch to consider, with live 30mm shells flying about, and in front of so many dignitaries the attack had to be a success!

The question as to whether the Jordanian pilots should take part in this live demonstration did not arise, because they had not carried out any air-to-ground training with live ammunition. The official programme simply stated that all the Hunter displays during the three-day event were by aircraft from No.1 Squadron RJAF.

Bennett was of course the ground-attack expert, having served on the staff at CFE in the UK. Even so, we thought it sensible to check out the site of the proposed targets, especially as we were planning to fly to the target low level, and then pull up into a wing-over before commencing the attack from 1,500 ft. We took the Autocrat, flew along the route and did a sector recce around the range before landing next to the vehicles that we were hopefully going to hit the next day. We flew back to Amman and then did a dummy run in the Hunters, which seemed to go well, and as the time approached, I felt confident. In any case, the Boss was leading, so all I had to do was stick on his wing until we came to the firing bit. As we were operating as a pair, the only problem for me was making sure Bennett was clear of the target area before I opened fire. The next day all went well, and as I turned in to commence the attack, I could see at the left of the targets a large bevy of observers. There was no room for error. I got my gun sight on the target at about 1,200 ft just as I saw my leader breaking away. At 800 ft I opened fire and, although I could see my bullets hitting the ground in the area of the tank, I was somewhat surprised to see the whole thing explode as I was pulling out. Whether we had both got direct hits on a tank full of explosives, or whether it had been blown up by others we never knew, but the demonstration was a huge success.

A few days later, the boss said I was to meet someone from the Embassy at dawn the next day, and fly him in the Auster down the Aqaba road, so he could see the construction work that was going on. I was not to enter the flight in the authorisation book, nor to put it in my log book, and I was to be back on the ground before the rest of the squadron turned up for work. It all seemed a bit melodramatic to me but, on checking with the mysterious passenger, it was simply that the British Government was financing the construction of the road, and people in the Embassy wanted to see how the work was progressing!

Early-morning cloud covered the route, and the further we went the lower the base became. The 'passenger' was keen to see as much of the road as he could, but I was conscious that we had been forced down to 100 ft in order to remain visual. Then we were in it, which made me sit up because I was flying the Auster Mk 6 with no artificial horizon! A very nervous rate one turn through 180 degrees on limited panel was hastily made to get back out of the murk; very much IRE conditions. Whether it was worth all the trouble, when he could easily have driven down the road on his own, was arguable.

CHAPTER 18

Move To Mafraq

We now had formal approval to open up Mafraq as an operational base, and it was planned that we would move the Hunters up there on 1st June. Erik Bennett would become the Station Commander, and I would command the Squadron, heady stuff for a couple of chaps who had only been promoted a few months earlier. We also thought it would be nice if the airfield had a different name, and we were quite pleased when His Majesty agreed to our suggestion that it should be called King Hussein Air Base (KHAB).

On the day of the move, it was arranged that we would fly the Hunters into KHAB as soon as the advance party had arrived. I was the first to go, so I got airborne in 'C-Charlie' for the short ferry flight, but on arrival I had an undercarriage malfunction - the port leg would not come down. Two or three attempts at recycling had no effect, it would not unlock, so I returned to Amman and after a low run over the tower they confirmed the wheel was firmly retracted. How many Hunter pilots had a port wheel refusing to come down twice in a lifetime? I thought it must be a record of sorts.

I did a couple of circuits while I assessed the situation, and air traffic control alerted the crash crew. I really had two choices; I could return to KHAB and crash land it there, where there was plenty of open space, but limited crash facilities and no medical back-up or I could do the same at Amman, which had excellent crash and medical services. However, there was a down side to Amman. Close to the left-hand side of the westerly runway was a high fence supported by 6 ft concrete posts every 50 ft. If the swing was anything like what I experienced at Chivenor, then I stood a pretty good chance of crashing into a few of them.

By now Sqn Ldr Bennett was in the tower along with Lt Col. Othmann and other airport officials. Bennett naturally told me to do what I thought best but the Arabs suggested I head off into the desert and eject. Clearly, the last thing they wanted was a smoulder heap in the middle of their airport! My response was quick and to the point

"Amman Tower - I'll land on the perimeter track - can you keep it clear of other aircraft?".

The peri track was no wider than the average road on a housing estate but, as it was on the opposite side of runway to the concrete posts, I thought it might allow more room for the aircraft to swing before hitting them.

I then saw another aircraft scurrying back like a scalded cat to the safety of the Terminal, as the fire engines and blood wagon took up their positions. I did a dummy approach and overshoot to check the drift, and then commenced a nice long low approach at 150kts, slowly coming back to 135kts at the point of touchdown. I felt the starboard wheel touch, and progressively applied right aileron to hold up the left wing for as long as possible. It then dropped on to the drop tank at 90 knots and, much to my surprise (and many others), the tank took the full weight of the wing and with a little right brake, I found myself still on the peri track when the aircraft came to halt. I was quite chuffed with this achievement and wanted to hang about to savour the moment. But no, as soon as my feet hit the deck I was whipped away, back to the confines of the military area by the Colonel.

Eight weeks later, I received the following Green Endorsement from Air Marshal W.L.M. MacDonald, Commander-in-Chief, Middle East Air Force:

INSTANCE OF AVOIDANCE BY EXCEPTIONAL FLYING SKILL AND JUDGEMENT OF DAMAGE TO AN AIRCRAFT. On the 1st June 1959, Flight Lieutenant J G Carter RAF attached to No.1(F)

Squadron, Royal Jordanian Air Force, was authorised to fly RJAF Hunter No. 702 from Amman to King Hussein Air Base. As a result of faulty servicing, malfunction of the undercarriage occurred, and CARTER was obliged to return to Amman and make a landing with the port main undercarriage leg retracted. To give more room for the anticipated swing this officer elected to land on the taxi-way instead of the runway and this decision, together with the cool calm manner in which he tackled this emergency was a fine example of superb airmanship. By exceptional flying skill and judgement Carter certainly avoided a major accident. The resulting damage to the aircraft was confined to one drop tank and a slightly damaged port flap. After four hours the aircraft was again serviceable for flight.

The first ten days at our new base were spent getting organised. The airfield was huge, and with a combined strength of less than 50 personnel, we were rattling about like peas in a pod. There

Jordanian Hunter F.6 after author landed it with port wheel stuck up. Note distance wing tip off is off the ground.

were also considerable logistical problems to overcome; especially concerning water, which had to be brought in daily by tanker, as of course was the aviation fuel. We took over one of the married quarters as a Mess, and the NCOs did likewise. Erik Bennett set up office in Station Headquarters, and it was decided that the squadron crew room would be in an isolated building on the far side of the airfield. We felt that in the event of an attack it would be better for the pilots to be as far away from the maintenance area and aircraft as possible. In retrospect, a very strange decision! It meant that we needed two Land-Rovers for pilot transportation, and each journey took nearly ten minutes.

The British do some strange things when they are overseas, and we were no exception. The boss, who had previously done a tour in the Canal Zone in Egypt were they did strange things, said we should have a lawn outside the crew room. This had the Jordanians rolling about in hysterics, but he was adamant so grass seed was scattered. Sure enough, after countless gallons of water had been applied to a barren patch of desert, we saw some grass growing, but it took a bowser-load every week to stop it dying. Although a negative exercise in many ways, it brought home to me how easy it would be to reclaim the desert if minds and resources were put to it.

We realised that we should look at the condition of the perimeter fence, after seeing a young boy one day herding goats into one of the hangars. Inspection revealed that the fence was down in a number of places, and they were quickly repaired. To avoid a repetition, we periodically had great fun flying the Austers around the perimeter fence at 10 ft, looking for any new holes which might have appeared.

We had not been at KHAB very long before we had what could have been a serious incident. Whilst briefing for the first training sortie of the day, we heard the sound of jets overhead. As the early-morning mist had not yet burned off we could not see who they were.

"It's those buggers from Amman in their Vampires," someone said. "Get on the blower to our chaps down there and find out" I shouted. Back came the reply - there were no Vampires airborne! This caused a bit of a flutter as this meant they were most likely Syrian MiGs. Our Land-Rover had gone to the maintenance area, so we had no transport. Even if we had it, it is doubtful if we could have been airborne in time from where we were. So we just sat there and, after a short while, they went on their way. The incident raised some doubts about the defence of the airfield, and shortly afterwards units of the Jordanian Army equipped with anti-aircraft guns started digging in around the perimeter.

There was a salt flat to the east called Dawson's Field, and further on an airstrip at the H4 oil pipe pumping station. The boss and I thought we might have a look at them, to see if they could be utilised as dispersal airfields. As the track would be over some inhospitable territory we again took an Auster each, so if either of us had a problem we could land in the desert and come back in the serviceable aircraft. Although we had accumulated quite a number of hours on the Austers, we were still unsure about the reliability of the engines, especially on the Autocrat, which I seemed to fly most. We landed at Dawson's Field, and found it ideally suitable for the Hunters, it was rock hard, dead flat and about five miles long. An excellent dispersal, but the logistics needed to be sorted out. On we went to H4, where we were met by the maintenance staff who had not seen an aircraft - or any oil for that matter - in years. The pipeline was no longer in use, because its outlet to the Mediterranean was now in Israel. We enjoyed our brief visit, but it was obvious that H4 would not be suitable for the Hunters, but it might be of interest to the chaps on the Vampires.

Dawson's Field had been used many years previously by the RAF, but not by swept-wing jet fighters, which were more at home on concrete runways. We laid on an exercise to assess its feasibility. Nobby Clarke led a ground party with two trucks and a fuel bowser out across the desert. On their arrival, Erik Bennett and I got airborne, arriving overhead ten minutes later. After checking all was OK with Nobby on the R/T, Bennett landed whilst I circled overhead.

Author about to take-off from Dawsons Field in an Auster, under the watchful eye of a Bedouin guard.

"It's a piece of cake Nick - come on in" he said, before shutting down.

I followed and, although the shimmer of the sand made it just a bit difficult to judge your height in the final stages, the landing presented no problems. What was unusual was being able to let the aircraft run on until it stopped without using the brakes, and still having two miles of runway left. I got out and admired the scene, whilst the ground crew went about turning the aircraft round.

Wherever we went in the desert, it was not long before a Bedouin, armed to the teeth, appeared from nowhere. This day was no different; there he was already sitting in the shade under the wing! The vehicles had been positioned under camouflage netting, which was just as well as all RJAF vehicles were painted bright blue, standing out like 'dog's balls' against the desert sand. The Hunter camouflage, although not perfect, was better. We returned to KHAB convinced we had a good, if not perfect, dispersal strip. Although we drew up a plan for the deployment to Dawson's we never did it again. This was unfortunate, because during the six-day war the Israeli Air Force destroyed most of the Hunters whilst they were lined up on the dispersal at KHAB. Dawson's Field later came to prominence when a BOAC VC10 was hijacked, and forced to land there by the PLO and then blown up.

I was extremely happy in Jordan, as one could imagine, but I felt that there was a personality clash developing between Erik Bennett and the rest of us; this affected me more than the others because he was my immediate boss, flying the Hunters and running KHAB. He was not the easiest of people to get on with, even socially we were never on first-name terms with him, which was a bit unusual for three officers stuck out in the desert. I got to the stage of looking forward to weekends, when we would fly down to Amman and join the Vampire chaps in the mess. There was no questioning his ability as a fighter pilot, and he did have a genuine desire to help the Jordanians, but he did rub people up the wrong way whilst doing it. Once he suggested, half jokingly, that we drive through Syria to the Lebanon one weekend, stopping at Damascus Airport to have a look at their MiGs which were based there, and if possible, to take some photos. I dismissed the idea as being foolhardy, not wishing to finish up in a Syrian Jail. In any case, every time we went to Cyprus in the Dove for spares we flew right over Damascus, and could see and photograph all we needed. However, the Arabs were fascinated by him, which is probably why he remained in the Middle East on and off until the present day.

In a news item in the *Sunday Times* on 17 September 1995 it was reported that Sultan Qaboos Bin Said of Oman had been injured in a car crash in the Oman desert. Also in the vehicle was the Deputy Prime Minister, who was killed, and a wealthy businessman. The report went on to say that no official mention was made of the fourth person, who was sitting in the front seat next to the Sultan, 'dapper ginger-haired Air Vice-Marshal Sir Erik Bennett, who was also recovering in hospital.' The report went on to say that Bennett, who was unmarried, like the Sultan, stayed on after retiring from commanding the Omani Air Force as the Sultan's special adviser, and they became close friends.

Our relationship hit a low when one day he booked himself out for local flying. Instead, without saying anything about his intentions, he flew to Jerusalem and landed, despite having previously rejected this airfield as being unsuitable for Hunters. Unfortunately for him he landed a bit on the fast side and, caught out by the bump in the middle of the runway, ran off the end into the rough overshoot area.

The first indication I had of the incident was when a Dove arrived at KHAB to take three ground engineers to recover the aircraft and to inspect the airframe. On their arrival, they found

Party time in the Philadelphia Hotel. Left to right, 'Puddy' Catt, Maurice Raynor, Manager of the Royal Garages, Egyptian belly dancer, author, and 'Nobby' Clarke.

some damage to the nose wheel, and the pitot tube was bent. They then enlisted the help of a large number of watchers who finally managed to push the aircraft back on to the runway.

After carefully examining the damage, and now doubt being under some pressure, they agreed that Bennett could fly the Hunter back to KHAB with the undercarriage down. Their main concern however, was a cut in the nose wheel tyre, and because of that, it was suggested that he lowered the nose very gently on landing!

In view of all this it was all the more important that I, or air traffic control, should have been in the picture as to what was happening - but we were not. For reasons best known to himself the boss decided not to tell me about the incident, what the damage was, or that he intended flying the aircraft back that afternoon. All I knew was what the Jordanian pilot in the Dove told me – that the Hunter was unserviceable in Jerusalem. So at our normal finishing time at 1630 I closed down the base, and Splinter and I went back to the mess for tea.

Needless to say, he was less than pleased to find the shop shut when he eventually landed back some time later. I pointed out that I took the decision to close up, based on the information available to me at the time, which was zilch; I had made my point.

CHAPTER 19

Social Life!

Before leaving the UK, Bennett told me to take a dinner jacket with me, as we were 'sure to be invited to a number of social functions during our tour in Jordan'. I thought this a bit strange as, since being commissioned six years previously I had never come across a serving officer wearing a DJ at any function, dress on social occasions being always uniform or lounge suit. However, I took the hint, and off I went in great haste and bought one. I need not have bothered; I took it home again, covered in sand, not having worn it once! As expected, it was either uniform or lounge suit depending upon the event and the location.

Three weeks after our arrival it was Christmas, and the RJAF laid on transport for us to visit Jerusalem and then go on to Bethlehem. We visited The Church of the Holy Sepulchre, The Church of the Nativity, and then went to the Shepherds' Fields and sang carols in the moonlight. We then saw the New Year in at the Philadelphia Hotel in Amman. Philadelphia being the old Roman name of Amman and across the road from the Hotel was the ruins of the Roman theatre. It became our main 'watering hole' when in town, with many a happy night being spent being entertained by the resident belly dancer in the basement nightclub.

We soon became very friendly with Maurice Raynor, who was the manager of the Royal Garages. He lived in a bungalow in the grounds of Basman Palace, which was the Kings' residence in Amman. He had met Hussein whilst he was as pupil at Harrow School, and Maurice was the proprietor of a local garage. When Hussein returned to Amman to take the throne, which had been vacated by his father, King Talal, through illness, he asked Maurice to go with him. Maurice and his wife were to become extremely close to the King, and he would often visit them informally in their home. Hussein was living alone in the palace at the time, having divorced Queen Dina some two years previously. In due course Maurice showed us around the royal garages, and when we jokingly asked 'Are there any for sale?' he said he would enquire! A few days later we were invited to take our pick!

I bought a two-year-old Austin Healey for 125 Dinars (£125) that the King had used as a racing car - belting it round the perimeter track on Amman airfield. In lieu of a log book, I received a letter from the Royal Palace saying that the car was now mine. The sale was further confirmed in a letter from the Jordanian Ministry of Foreign Affairs to the British Embassy in Amman. Erik Bennett bought a Mercedes, and collectively we all chipped in and purchased a pre-war bullet-proof Buick which had previously been used by King Hussein's grandfather King Abdullah. It was a lovely car, steeped in history.

At the same time, we were issued with Jordanian driving licences. Our instructions, from the Army, were that in the event of an accident we were not to stop, but to drive as quickly as possible to the safety of the nearest police post or army check-point. Seemed like a good idea to me, after witnessing how quickly a hostile-looking crowd could suddenly appear at any accident.

Often the Buick was recognised by older Arabs as we drove around the country, so we took great care of it. We had little unserviceability with it, except that early on, the windscreen wipers packed in. Spares were unheard of, so when it rained the front-seat passenger had to lean across in front of the driver and work the wipers by hand. No mean feat, negotiating the seven hills of Amman or the steep inclines into and out of the Jordan Valley.

I made enquires about driving the Healey home to the UK at the end of my tour, but after looking at the likely route and taking into account the mechanical condition of the car, I decided against it. When I left I sold it to Dave Dorwood, one of our ground-crew chaps, for the same price I paid for it.

With the purchase of the cars we became much less dependent upon RJAF transport, and were able to get around the country quite a bit more. Jerusalem was quite popular, and at times we would stop overnight in the Shepherd's Hotel, which was situated on Mount Scopus overlooking the Old City. It was in Shepherd's that we would have the odd glass of beer with the United Nations Peace-keeping Force, who of course could move freely across the 'front line' into Israel.

"Why don't you come over with us one evening, and see a bit of night life?" they said half-jokingly.

"Nice of you to offer, but no thanks, not this time!'"

We also picnicked in the old Roman ruins of Jerash, visited Jericho, swam in the Dead Sea, and were guests of Jamil's family at a wedding in the town of Jenin on the West Bank. We were made very welcome, but it was a bit unusual having sweets passed around instead of large gin and tonics!

Twice we flew to Nicosia in the RJAF Dove. These trips were primarily to collect spares, but they were also arranged at weekends so we could have some time off in Cyprus. It was a bit 'out of the frying pan into the fire', because the Eoka emergency was at its height, and we were restricted as to where we could go. On one trip we had to land in Beirut on the way back, for some reason or other. Whilst on the ground we managed to convince the Jordanian pilot that he had a snag on the aircraft, which meant we would have to night stop - whoopee. We got fixed up with some rooms in the St George's Club, and at the same time the Boss thought it prudent to check our presence in Beirut with the Air Attache' at the British Embassy. This was rather a good move, as it got us an invitation to a reception which was being held in the Embassy that evening. The guests were rather sombre-looking Arabs and Eastern Europeans, I remember. Perhaps Philby was there as well! We left about 8pm fully primed for a memorable night out on the town.

I went back to Beirut a few weeks later, as the guest of the Lebanese Air force. Two of their pilots had been students of mine at Chivenor, and they had rather foolishly said 'If you ever come to Lebanon, give us a call', probably never thinking the RAF would send me further than the English Channel. I wrote to Lt Sammy Abdullah and told him I was just down the road in Jordan. He arranged for me to stay a weekend in their luxurious Officers' Club, which was right on the beach in Beirut, and in the evenings I would be taken up into the mountains and he would introduce 'Captain Nick' to his friends.

We dined with King Hussein in the British Ambassador's residence, and were also guests at dinner with him at the American Embassy. The King also invited us to dine with him in the palace, and afterwards we joined him watching movies in his private cinema. It seated about two hundred, but on this occasion there was just the four of us in the front row! Dinner was very informal, with just the one servant waiting on us.

On more than one occasion, Hussein invited us to join him at Shuneh, his holiday retreat in the Jordan Valley, which had been built by his grandfather, King Abdullah. He was very much into Scottish dancing, so invariably the young ladies from the Embassy, who all seemed to be experts, no doubt having been taught at Roedean or Cheltenham Colleges, would be invited. The King would not directly ask a particular lady to partner him. The request, at the appropriate time, would come via Jock Dalgleish, who would then ask a particular lady if she would care to partner the King. In fact, it was a pleasure for the ladies to dance with him, because he was good at it - no doubt having been taught at Harrow and later at the Royal Military Academy, Sandhurst, whereas us RAF chaps were quite hopeless, and kept cocking it up!

Another party at Shuneh in the Summer was much more fun, because there was a treasure hunt followed by a sumptuous barbecue. The guests were split into four teams, and the first to find and produce all the items on a list would be the winners and get a prize. It was clear that the King had thought up the list, because some of the items were personal to him, for example a royal sock which entailed - after some hesitation - rummaging around in the royal bedroom!

We attended Jordanian Air Force dining-in nights, when the King was nearly always present. During one such dinner, a group photograph taken of us with the King was subsequently published in *Flight International*. I appeared to have my eyes closed, having blinked as the shutter went down. A friend of my mother who was working at the Air Ministry at the time sent her a copy with the comment "Seems he's had too much to drink" – We should be so lucky, tell her!

Erik Bennett was very good in manipulating Mr Flouty, who was responsible for our catering. By clever bargaining, Flouty was able to produce some excellent meals, after some flannel and arm-twisting. Our Sunday curry parties on the patio, which overlooked Amman Prison, were the talk of the staff at the Embassy who became regular visitors – especially the ladies

Many a time, Maurice Raynor and his wife would invite us to their home for a meal, which was most enjoyable. On one occasion, we had just finished a superb dinner when the phone rang. It was Prince Muhammad, King Hussein's younger brother, an unpredictable and impulsive young man who at the time seemed to go around with an armed bodyguard much larger than anyone else. He had heard of a cabaret show which was currently appearing at the Dead Sea Hotel in the Jordan Valley, and would like to go and see it. Would Raynor come round with the car and collect him? Maurice, as diplomatically as possible, said he was entertaining his RAF guests, in the hope that he might postpone it to another night. No luck - "Bring 'em with you" said the Prince.

So at ten o' clock we all set off for the Dead Sea, driving along a tortuous road which twisted and turned as it went down into the valley. The convoy consisted of two very large Mercedes, one for the Prince and the other for us, plus a Jeep front and back carrying the Prince's heavily armed bodyguard. On arrival over an hour later we all trooped into the hotel lobby, only to be told that the cabaret was finished for the night. However, the manager hastily appeared and said he would summon the entertainers to do another show for his Royal Guest. We took our seats in a near-empty lounge, with our minders close by, resting their Sten guns on their laps. Eventually the show started with a belly dancer, who was well into her act when I noticed Muhammad lean across and speak to the commander of his bodyguard. A few words in Arabic were then exchanged with Maurice, who said,

"Sorry lads, we're off, stick close to the soldiers until we get to the cars".

Whereupon, we all jumped back into the Mercs, and off we went, back to Amman at high speed. We were later told by Maurice that the Prince had been suspicious of a group of men who had suddenly appeared in the room. We discovered later that the Prince often suspected that he was in danger, hence the large number of heavily armed soldiers who accompanied him everywhere. But who could blame him, when there had been so many attempts on the life of his brother?

Dining-in night at RJAF Officers Mess. Back row L/R. Flt Lt 'Nick' Carter, Flt Lt 'Nobby'Clarke, Sqn Ldr Erik Bennett, H.M. King Hussein, Air Marshal W.L.M. MacDonald, Flt Lt 'Splinter'Browne, Lt Firas, Capt Fakhri. Front row L/R. Lt Nasri, Lt Saleh, Lt Jamal.

CHAPTER 20

No. 1 (F) Sqn RJAF

We had by now completely settled in, after moving up from Amman, and were savouring the unique experience of having this large airfield to ourselves. Just nine pilots with 12 Hunters to play with, it was unbelievable. There were no flying restrictions, so we could low-fly and drop sonic booms to our heart's delight. In fact, we were actively encouraged to do both, to let everyone on the ground know we were about. Having said that, it was important to have a good idea of where you were, there was no radar to call on, and no CRDF for steers back to base, it was all down to pilot navigation. One piece of desert is like any other when you're lost, though east of the River Jordan we relied on the pipeline, the Hejaz Railway and the Dead Sea for position fixes.

The further east or southeast you went, the wilder the terrain became. Years ago some of the more savage tribesmen in the desert did some very painful things to airmen unfortunate enough to finish up in their hands. This was primarily due to the policy of using the RAF in the 1920s and 1930s to 'control' dissident tribes by pre-warned bombing raids. As a result, any pilots falling into their hands were ruffed up a bit – generally by having a knife taken to their testicles.

Eventually RAF aircrew carried a 'goolie chit', which was a letter in Arabic to 'whom it may concern' which said in effect that, if their captive was returned intact the King of England would be very pleased and money would change hands!

Navigating over the West Bank of the Jordan was more difficult. The Armistice cease-fire line with Israel was difficult to pinpoint accurately. When leading four aircraft in battle formation at 30,000 ft you are only sure of your actual position to within say 10 miles at any one time because of your height. Consequently, most of our flying over the West Bank had to be at medium or low level. Only once did I have a problem, and that was when leading a pair low-flying in the Nablus area. My No.2 was Lt Jamil, and whilst briefing for the flight I agreed that we would do a couple of beat-ups over his mum's house, which happened to be a mile or so from the 'front line'. As pre arranged I allowed him to take the lead when we got into the area, so he could locate the family home. We had done a couple of runs, with me sticking close to his wing, when I heard another voice on the R/T. The transmission was not in English, so I was not aware of what was being said, but Jamil instantly turned on to an easterly heading and returned the lead back to me. I could sense he had heard something, but said nothing until after we landed when he told me it was Israeli radar getting a bit twitchy.

With the first anniversary of the assassination of King Feisal of Iraq approaching, there were fears that some of Hussein's enemies would take the opportunity to bring the mobs on to the street, and there was some obvious concern for his safety. As a result, he opted to spend the day with us at KHAB. He arrived quite early in the morning with Wing Commander Dalgleish in the Vampire T.11, and he joined us in our crew room. Later, he was joined by his young brother, Prince Hassan. It was to be a busy day. The King and Jock Dalgleish led a Balbo of nine Hunters and nine Vampires on a low-level close formation sortie over all the major towns on the West Bank. Most of the time we were down among the chimney pots as we passed over the towns, in order to make our presence felt. We did the same thing in the afternoon, but this time in low-level battle formation, which enabled us to fly at a faster speed, and being more spread out we were seen and heard over a much greater area. We also did beat ups over a few places on the East Bank, including, for good measure, a few sonic bangs over the army barracks at Zerka. The day passed peacefully with no disturbances, and the King went back to Amman in the late afternoon.

In between our operational commitments we slowly began introducing cine' ranging and tracking. Everything took a long time to be actioned by the Jordanian military, and it was only constant pressure from Erik Bennett which produced the necessary cameras, film, projectors and developing facilities. We continued to teach the Jordanians the basic elements of high-level fighter tactics, but in my own mind I considered that in any future conflict the role of the Royal Jordanian Air Force would be low-level interceptions and ground attack in support of the Army. I started to initiated more pairs flying, as opposed to fours, with low-level attacks on selected targets sometimes more than one hundred miles away. One such exercise was to fly at 250 feet to Ma'an for a simulated rocket attack on the railway station. The pumping stations along the IPC pipeline, the Allenby Bridge over the Jordan, and some targets on the West Bank were all 'visited' at regular intervals. Apart from this being more appropriate to the threat, it was a lot more interesting than waffling about at 40,000 ft playing silly buggers.

I was constantly on the lookout for new targets that would test the Jordanians low-level navigational skills. I also had a sneaking desire to try and find the spot where Lawrence blew up the Hejaz Railway. I knew that it was somewhere between Ma'an and the Saudi, border so off I went on my own for a look. I followed the railway to its present terminus at a place called Ras en Naqb, halfway between Ma'an and Aqaba. Hopefully I would find some clues as to its routing from there on. The railway had been constructed by the Ottoman Turks, and it originally ran all the way to Medina in Saudi Arabia. I found some old sections of railway track and the odd wheel set, left in the sand, but little else. If I was in the area of Lawrence's exploits, there was little left to see.

My return route turned out to be a lot more interesting. Flying at 2,000 ft I saw a dirt road heading off into the desert due east from Ma'an. 'I wonder where that goes?' I thought - 'let's have a look'. I followed it for a good 40 miles, with the terrain becoming more bleak and uninviting. I was on the point of turning left and heading back north when I saw something ahead. It was a very large compound, with half a dozen buildings and a fair number of people wandering about in it. It was completely enclosed with what I could only imagine was barbed-wire fencing. It also had the mandatory watch towers, which confirmed to me that I had discovered a detention camp of sorts. I did a couple of orbits, the inhabitants waved, I waggled my wings and set off back to base. After landing I mention this 'find' to the Jordanian lads, who said 'Oh yes, that's a camp for the bad boys', but they were reluctant to enlighten me further, so I thought perhaps it might be wise to leave it off my ground-attack list!

A couple of years later the mirage scene for the film *Lawrence of Arabia* was filmed in that area.

The shift in emphasis to ground support was fortunate, because in September we took part in 'Exercise Subbr', a joint RJAF/Army exercise where we achieved some excellent results, establishing a much stronger operational link with the Army which had been missing before. Even so, we had little personal contact with the Jordanian Army except for the soldiers manning the anti-aircraft guns around the KHAB, and they disappeared back to their families at sunset. We never met the officers.

Brigadier Strickland visited us from time to time, and we were often in his company at social functions in Amman. In the summer, his children came out from the UK, and I had the pleasure of giving all four of them trips in the Auster 6. They all loved it. A charming man and a lovely family.

Sadly, that summer, a Major Ali Shoqum was killed in an accident, and we were asked to do a 'missing slot' fly-past at his burial. Such fly-pasts were a regular feature in other air forces, but rarely in the RAF.

Disaster struck a few days later. Whilst I was doing an air test, Lt Barakat, our one and only air traffic controller called me on the R/T. He said that there were reports of an aircraft having crashed in the Zerka area, and would I go and check it out. Within minutes I had located a smouldering crater some distance out of the town.

Attempts to raise Lt Marwan Zakaria on the R/T were unsuccessful. He had been briefed to fly his Hunter on an individual sortie, to practise flame-out landings, some aerobatics and to finish with a manual landing. At the time of the accident it would appear that he was doing unauthorised low-level aerobatics, and misjudged the height required for a loop and went straight in.

The next day we were doing the missing slot formation again. The Jordanian pilots were all at the funeral, so it was left to Erik Bennett, Splinter and myself to do the flypast. The boss was to lead us in echelon starboard, with the number two slot vacant. I was to fly at number three and splinter at number four. Not easy, trying to judge a full aircraft distance out from the leader was more difficult than the customary couple of feet that we were used to. Timing was critical, as it would not look good if we arrived overhead too early, so we arranged for someone near the graveside to have a mobile transmitter who could then call us in when ready. That, coupled with a powerful light that had been placed on the Jebel, meant we made it over the top at exactly the right time.

It was a sad day for me. I had first met Marwan when he was a student at the Hunter OCU at Chivenor. He was a most pleasant and likeable young man, with a strong sense of humour. It was a pity that his life had been lost through an act of stupidity, but there but by the grace of God went all of us at some time or other.

No sooner had we landed than we were told to do a patrol along the border with Iraq. There had been reports of heavy troop movements within sight of the Jordanian frontier post, and it was felt that we should make our presence known. We had never flown that far east before, simply because there was never any need to, plus it was over some pretty inhospitable desert should we have an emergency. However, with one of the Jordanians as my wing man, we set off by following the main road to Baghdad, which ran alongside the IPC pipeline. After passing overhead the H4 pumping station we commenced a maximum-rate decent from 40,000 ft, levelling off at 2,000 ft with about 20 miles left to run. If all went to plan the frontier post would come into view after 3.5 minutes. As the ETA came up, all I could see was uninviting desert. Either the headwind component was stronger or, heaven forbid, we had missed it and were merrily heading into Iraq! At low level we were gobbling up fuel at an alarming rate. I was beginning to get concerned when there it was - about a mile ahead, a big pole with the Jordanian flag flying above a small group of huts. A hundred yards or so beyond was another flag on a pole, which we were rapidly approaching at 350 knots.

"Red, brake port - go" I shouted, and threw the Hunter into a 6G turn to the left to avoid a diplomatic incident, and hoping my number two was still with me!

We then did a couple of beat ups-over the Jordanian post and got some welcoming waves from the soldiers based there. Unfortunately, we had no common frequency enabling us to talk to them, so we then climbed back to altitude and patrolled along our side of the border, but nothing was seen of the Iraqi Army, so we eventually headed back to base. I did a repeat sortie four days later, but again nothing was seen. It is extremely difficult to see well-camouflaged vehicles in that type of rocky desert, so they could well has been there. If they were, our presence gave them food for thought; all cat and mouse, really.

CHAPTER 21

State Visit of the Shah of Persia

When we discovered the three Austers in the hanger at Mafraq I never thought they would play such an important part in our activities. We had been sent to Jordan as a training mission, flying their Hunters, but at the end of my tour I had completed 144 hrs on Hunters and no less than 105 hrs on the Austers. I loved them, and they were great fun to fly, despite my having doubts about their serviceability. Nobby and his lads did their best, but without service manuals or technical records, they were up against it. The engines were an unknown quantity, the hours previously flown were unknown, and from time to time, they had been flown on unfiltered MT fuel.

I went so far as to write to the Auster Aircraft Company asking if there was any way we could improve the performance of the Autocrat. They wrote back saying they were surprised to hear it was still flying; they had sold it to the Jordanians at least 10 years previously and had never received any requests for spares! The letter went on to say the performance of the aircraft could only be improved if we installed an upgraded Gipsy Major engine at a cost of £900. They had no record of the two Auster 6s having been sold to the Jordanians, so we assumed they were ex-Army Air Corps aircraft that had been left behind during the hurried British departure in 1956. It is a tribute to the design of the airframe and engine that throughout my 105 hrs Auster flying I never had a single unserviceability - well, not one that I was aware of! We used them extensively as communications aircraft between KHAB and Amman. Although we checked out the Jordanian pilots to fly them, they were less than enthusiastic about them.

I toyed with the idea of buying one, as clearly, the Jordanian Air Force had little interest in them, but like the car, the route home would be either across the Med or over some pretty unfriendly Eastern European or Arab states. Neither option seemed very attractive so, with some reluctance, I dropped the idea.

Throughout the summer and autumn we continued to provide escort and top cover for the royal family and senior members of the government whenever they visited towns and villages outside Amman. As the escorted party were landing or arriving at their destination, we would do a beat-up to let everyone know that we were about. After a while we started to drop the odd sonic boom over places being visited, followed by a maximum-rate descent with a fast flypast at 500 kts, similar to the early displays by Neville Duke at the Farnborough air displays. It might have rattled a few old places such as Kerak, Petra and Jerash, but at the time our main concern was to deter any demonstrations or hostile action by local hotheads.

But our main test was yet to come, when it was announced that the Shah of Persia would make a state visit to Jordan during the first week in November 1959. At the same time, the Jordanians put in a request to the British Government for the British Joint Training Mission to extend its stay by a further six months. Jock Dalgleish said that it was up to each individual whether he wanted to stay or not. I gave it careful thought but decided against it, not because I was unhappy in Jordan or with the job, but because I found it had become a strain working with Erik Bennett, perhaps he felt the same about me! Anyway Splinter Browne decided to stay, as did Puddy Catt and Brian Entwistle on the Vampires, but they were fortunate in that they had a happier relationship with John Greenhill, their immediate boss. The Shah arrived after overflying Saudi Arabia, and we intercepted his aircraft as it entered Jordanian airspace. We put one pair on each wingtip until his aircraft was overhead Amman, when we carried out the usual fly-past as the King and the welcoming party were greeting the Shah on the tarmac. This seemed simple enough after all the times we had done it, but this one was special. It was a State Visit, and they wanted no cock-ups. As the Shah's aircraft was on final approach we started an orbit six miles from the airfield at 2,000 ft. As the Shah appeared at the top of the steps the tower cleared us to a run in. The objective was to be overhead just as the Shah was being greeted by the King. On this occasion, as with many others, we were pretty much spot-on.

We had no commitment on the second day of the visit. Early on the third, we took the opportunity to carry out a rehearsal for an air to ground attack on a tank, which was scheduled to take place on the following day. It was to be similar to the demonstration we did earlier for the review of the army, and again with live ammunition. As before, it would be Erik Bennett and myself doing the flying. Although I had become more competent at ground attack, it was always a comfort to get in a rehearsal before doing a demonstration in front of an audience, especially on this occasion when performing on behalf of a foreign air force in front of a visiting head of state.

In the afternoon the Shah was to visit Jerusalem, and we had to provide top cover in the usual way. It needed some careful planning, with Jerusalem airport being so close to the Jewish controlled area, and any navigational error could cause a diplomatic incident. Although we were obviously on the Arab side in the on-going Arab/Jewish conflict, we were in fact less concerned about Israel than some of Jordan's unpredictable Arab neighbours. The Israelis knew that the Jordanian Air Force was being led by RAF pilots. They could hear us on the R/T every day, and they knew we were unlikely to do anything silly.

On the following day we did the ground-attack demonstration for the Shah, each of us letting fly with a long burst of 30mm cannon fire at a number of tanks just outside Zerka. In the afternoon, we escorted the Shah and the King on a visit to Petra. They flew in a Twin Bonanza, which had been specially flown in from Tehran for this particular trip. They stayed overnight in Petra, and we then picked them up the following morning and escorted them back to Amman.

We had just enough time to get back to base and refuel before getting airborne again to escort the Shah out of Jordan at the end of his visit. This escort was different: it was led by the King and Jock Dalgleish in the Vampire T.11. On reaching the border the two monarchs bade farewell to each other over the R/T, and then finally the Shah said in English,

"Good day, gentlemen, and thank you." We took this to be a personal thank you for having escorted him within Jordan during his visit.

On the 10th November the King flew to Europe, and I led the escort for the last time to the Syrian border. Knowing that I would be gone before he returned, I asked Maurice Raynor if he could ask the King, if he would sign a photograph for me. Two days later Maurice gave me a photograph of the King on which he had personally written *To Flt Lt N Carter with our best wishes, Hussein.*

My last flight in a Hunter was on 23 November, when I hurriedly returned to KHAB with what I thought was anoxia, but could have been the after-effects of a pretty wild leaving party which had been arranged for me by the ground crew in their mess the previous night. They made a huge squadron tie, and presented me with a tankard. It is not often that NCOs give farewell parties for officers, and I was quite moved by this gesture.

My tour with the Royal Jordanian Air Force was coming to the end. I boarded an Air Jordan Convair at Amman airport on 7 December 1959 for Beirut. There I had tickets for a Lufthansa Super Constellation flight to Frankfurt, with an onward connection to London on a BEA Viscount. As the Convair was climbing away from Amman I could see the passengers, who were mostly Arabs, getting very agitated and peering out of the windows. The public-address system came alive.

"This is the Captain speaking, would Flight Lieutenant Nick Carter care to come to the flight deck and speak to his friends!"

A photograph presented to the author by King Hussein.

I trotted up front and there, much to my surprise, were three Hunters in formation on either side of the Convair, led by Erik Bennett.

"Just wanted to say thanks for all you've done, Nick, and have a safe journey home".

A lump came in my throat - perhaps he wasn't so bad after all!

After two weeks' leave I reported back to my 'handler' in Air Ministry. After the customary debrief, the question of my next posting came up. Remembering that I had been told I could pick my own job on my return, and having spent the past six years steaming up to 40,000ft two or three times a day, I thought I would like a change.

"I'll take Comets," I said.

"Sorry old boy, you can't have Comets."

"Why not? You promised."

"There's no vacancy," was the smart reply.

"We can offer you Britannias," they said.

"But they've got propellers!"

"Sorry, but that's all we've got… anyway, you'll soon pick it up!"

Being rather keen to see more of the world at Her Majesty's expense, I accepted.

CHAPTER 22

Back to the RAF

I was posted to No.511 Sqn, which had been reformed a month earlier at RAF Lyneham, Wiltshire. They were flying the Bristol Britannia long-range turboprop, newly built by Shorts of Belfast. I also knew that their Proteus engines had a tendency to ice up and flame out!

In true RAF fashion, I sat around doing nothing for the next three months, whilst I awaited the next conversion course to start. Much time was spent in the local pubs, especially *The Duke* at Hilmarton, and *The Currier Arms* at Wootton Bassett, where you could always squeeze in a few after hours. We even followed the hounds until it was time to join No.14 Course at the Bristol Aircraft Technical School at Filton, travelling each day from Lyneham. Much of the technical stuff was well over my head, but with a flight engineer in the crew, I thought it best not to worry myself too much on that score. Similarly, the aircraft's scheduled performance was a bit of a handful for a jet jockey who had no need to consider such things previously.

The Brit, to all intents and purposes, was to be operated closely to civil requirements, but there were some exceptions. For example, take-off weight was not restricted to enable the En Route Terrain Clearance Regulations to be adhered to. It was sufficient, should you lose an engine, to have a stabilising altitude that was simply above the safety height. One area where we did have to comply fully with civil regulations was in respect of fuel planning. Ministry of Aviation Inspectors had authority to check our fuel planning down the route, although I never heard of it happening.

In order to comply with the new regulations, both civil and military, Transport Command produced Scheduled Performance Notes for the Brit, they were written by the Command Navigation Branch, and it took a navigator to understand them! Each pilot was given a copy, but my philosophy was again that we had a navigator in the crew, so put the notes in your bottom draw and leave it to him! If he said the weight was right for take-off, it was OK by me. Fortunately, there were no exams at the end of the three-month course!

Conversion training started in early September, and I soon realised that operating as a crew member was totally different from what I had been used to. It was like flying an aircraft by committee, with long hours where you did nothing. Nevertheless, hopefully I would see a lot of the world in the four years that I would spend with the squadron. It was an easy life, good fun in excellent company, but I was to find the flying boring.

There was a flight-deck crew of five: Captain, Co-pilot, Navigator, Flight Engineer and Signaller. The navigator was probably the most important member, for two reasons. First, the only radio navigation aid on the aircraft was a solitary RMI (Radio Magnetic Indicator), and secondly most pilots find it difficult to navigate when there are no railway lines to follow! The presence of the flight engineer was also quite comforting. "Sort it out Eng!" was the cry as soon as we had the slightest problem – plus he understood propellers!

What I did find extraordinary on my first flight was that neither pilot was allowed to use the R/T, not even in the circuit. The signaller had to do that.

'Sig. Tell the tower we're downwind'.

'OK'.

'They say we're clear to finals with one ahead – do we have contact?'

'Hang on I'll have a look,'

'Tell 'em negative.'

'They now say the one ahead is on short finals.'

'OK, Tell 'em we have him in sight and ask them for the surface wind...'

And so it went on and on and on. It was frustrating to hear the controller and then having to respond through the signaller. Of course, the argument for having signallers in the crew was to pass position reports on HF when off-airways, and to knock out the odd message using the Morse key, but it seemed odd that civil airliners flying the same routes with fare-paying passengers had not employed signallers (Radio Officers) for a number of years.

Ex-fighter pilots sitting in the co-pilot seat of Transport Command aircraft were considered to be highly suspect by some of the established captains. One got the impression that the sole reason for having a co-pilot on board was to fill the other seat! But, unlike their civil counterparts, RAF co-pilots were highly experienced. They tended to be in their late twenties or early thirties, and were not shy in coming forward. Invariably both pilots would be of the same rank, usually Flight Lieutenants, and it was the norm for the flying to be shared equally between them.

Most of the trips were on our bread-and-butter route to Singapore - called the 'Changi Slip'. This began by taking an aircraft from Lyneham to El Adem in Libya, refuel, then down the side of Egypt to 'Nasser's Corner' which consisted of three hills 5,500 ft high sticking up out of the desert, then across Ethiopia into Aden.

At Aden there would be a crew change. The incoming crew would be taken down town to the Rock Hotel or, if very lucky, into the Crescent Hotel for a two or three-day rest whilst awaiting the next aircraft to come out. The outbound crew would then fly it across the Indian Ocean to Gan, the southernmost island in the Maldives, inhabited only by the RAF. A two-hour turnround for refuelling, before carrying on to RAF Changi in Singapore, with another crew waiting to start the process in reverse, back to the UK. We were accommodated in the old Japanese Officers' Mess in Changi Village close to the infamous Changi Jail. On the odd occasion, the slip would extend up to Hong Kong. We were 'limited' to a duty day of 19 hrs, which then had to be followed by 15 hrs rest.

The two legs between Aden and Changi were a problem, because the Proteus engines on the Brit generated ice like a refrigerator. In moist air conditions with an outside air temperature (OAT) between +2C and +12C ice would quickly form in the engine intakes. Lumps of ice would then break away and cause 'engine bumping' as they passed through the engine. As the lumps got bigger, the bumps got louder and could be heard by the passengers. If ignored, the engine would flameout. This was of even greater concern to the passengers, because they would witness a long tongue of flame from the jetpipe as the engine attempted automatically to relight. The problem for us was that our best cruising level on these two sectors happened to be around the FL150 mark, where the OAT was usually slap in the middle of the +2C to +12 range!

The solution was to fit heaters to the intakes, which were switched on when flying in cloud within the critical temperature range. You had to watch it like a hawk, especially at night when sometimes it was possible to be flying through very thin layers of wispy cloud without being aware of it. The answer was for pilots to take it in turns to shine a torch through the windscreen to look for traces of cloud flashing past the windscreen, or for particles of ice seen to be forming on the wiper blades. Needless to say, we were all bright eyed and bushy tailed when crossing the Indian Ocean!

Whilst climbing out of Aden, home bound in the early hours on my second trip on the slip, the tranquillity of the night was shattered by bells ringing and lights flashing.

"Fire on Number One!" shouted Paddy, our flight engineer.

I glanced quickly to double check that it was indeed Number One, as Frank Baker ordered

"Fire action Number One," where upon Paddy feathered the propeller and hit the engine fire extinguisher. We then got the check lists out, and ran through the drills.

Was it a fire and, if so, is it now out?

"Ask the loadmaster down the back if he can see any flames" said Frank,

"And Sig, send out a Pan call to Khormaksar and tell them we have a fire warning and that we are jettisoning fuel and returning."

And I only came into Transport Command for a quiet life! I took little part in this real-life drama, except to check that all those flashing hands around the cockpit were going to the right knobs and tits. But I joined the action when it came to fuel jettisoning: there was no other option, the fuel panel with the jettison switchery was on a panel down the side of my seat. We ran through the check list and shortly afterwards the loadmaster came up front to confirm that he could see no sign of fire, and that both jettison tubes were out and discharging fuel. We then stooged around the bottom end of the Red Sea for an hour before landing back at Khormaksar on three engines. It had been a false warning, but as the extinguisher had been activated it meant an engine change. Two days later we were on our way again.

On my return Mansell Childs-Villiers, our aristocratic squadron adjutant, had a message for me:

"You're going to see your old mate King Hussein again next week!"

"Am I?";

"Yes, you are a special guest along with the Secretary of State for Air, Julian Amery, and members of the Air Council at a dinner in the Mess at RAF Wattisham, being held in the King's honour."

It was a memorable evening, and when I was introduced to His Majesty we exchanged a few words and he thanked me for helping the RJAF through a difficult period. Returning to Wattisham also brought back happy memories of my time with No.257 Squadron.

At a later date, I was also invited to have dinner with the King, the Jordanian Prime Minister and Erik Bennett whilst they were staying at the Dorchester Hotel in London.

Then, in July 1961, Frank Baker and I did flights into Kuwait carrying British troops, following Iraq's threat to invade the country. We had positioned into Nairobi to pick up troops already in Kenya, and then we took them direct to Kuwait by over-flying the eastern corner of Saudi Arabia at night, without lights. We landed as daylight broke at what was to become the new international airport, but which at the time was just a runway in the desert. The only approach aid was a solitary, short range NDB (Non-directional Beacon). Six Hunters from No.208 Squadron had already arrived, together with an RAF ground party.

Who should be sitting in one of the Hunters at 'readiness' was 'Slash' Slaney, who had been with me on No.257 Squadron at Wattisham. There was a continuous stream of transport aircraft arriving, both RAF and civil, with troops and equipment. The next aircraft to us on the apron was a British Eagle Britannia, with the troops being seen off the aircraft by a couple of stewardesses at the top of the steps!

Sadly, the RAF had a fatality without a shot being fired, when one of the ground crew walked into a propeller half an hour before our arrival. It brought home to us the reality of being in a war zone.

No sooner were the troops off the aircraft than we were on our way back to Khormaksar. Flight time limitations went out of the window, as we set off a second time with more troops and equipment. Then, with the deployment complete, and after a well-earned rest, we set off back to the UK.

On many of my stopovers in Nairobi, I met Vernon and Veronica Heaver who came from Maidenhead but who had moved to Kenya just after the Second World War. On one such occasion Vernon, who knew my mother, asked if she would like an African Grey parrot.

Mum said "Yes please", so the next time I was homeward bound through Nairobi I rang them, and the parrot complete with a large cage was duly delivered to the aircraft at Embakasi Airport. Then when we were carrying out our pre-flight checks someone came out and said that our schedule had been changed. Instead of flying back to the UK we were to position the aircraft to Aden and await further instructions. Vernon and Veronica had long since departed, so we had no alternative but to take the parrot with us. On arrival in Aden the parrot accompanied us in the crew coach to the Rock Hotel. Frank Baker said there was no way he was going to share a room with me and that bloody parrot, so in desperation I looked to George Dobson our navigator. Sympathetic to my problem he agreed, and the three of us got in the lift and went up to our room on the third floor. The first two days passed peacefully enough, because someone told us to put a blanket over the cage at night, but then its feathers started to fall out, so we consulted an Arab vet on the phone.

"I don't do home visits - bring the bird to me and I'll see what I can do".

Down in the lift we went and into the open boot of a taxi went the parrot, squawking like hell as we drove at speed downtown.

The vet had a close look at the bare flesh around its neck and said it was only temporary, and sold me a spray to treat it. Back in the taxi to the hotel and up in the lift again to our room. George was sorry to see it back, but I did promise to seek another room if we had not moved out within a few days.

To everyone's relief, we received a signal that said we were to fly a freighter back to the UK the next day. By now, practically everyone in Transport Command knew about "Nick Carter's parrot", so it was no surprise to be met by a 'reception committee' when we got back to Lyneham, not least the customs chaps, with their little books open at the page referring to the importation of tropical birds. Unbeknown to them, I had previously written to the Board of Trade and obtained an import licence, so I was in the clear. The parrot then went on show in the Officers' Mess until the following day when it completed the final stage of its journey, in the boot of my Ford Cortina with the lid up, for 70 miles along the A4 to Maidenhead. Miraculously, it was still alive on arrival, and continued to live a happy and cosseted life for a further 15 years!

At my bachelor-night party I 'talked shop' with Johnny Collins, my mate from FTS days (who was later tragically killed in a BEA Trident which crashed at Staines after the leading edge slats had been inadvertently retracted). He told me that on one occasion, when flying as a first officer with BEA, he had taken control from a captain whom he thought was about to hit the undershoot whilst landing at Athens. I had a similar occurrence of my own some time later. Whilst turning downwind in the circuit at El Adem, the aircraft failed to straighten out on the downwind leg, so I looked across to the captain whose leg it was and asked "You alright?"

"Negative. You have control."

I continued with the approach and landing. Probably something he had eaten, because a couple of hours later he was fine...

It can happen to co-pilots as well! Once, when flying with Bill Dobson on an empty positioning flight from Seletar to Changi, and it was my leg. Just after V1 was called I was violently sick all over my instrument panel.

"You have control!" I blurted.

At the same time the Nav called 'rotate', and Bill eased back on the pole and we were airborne. Teamwork at its best! When I got to the Transit Mess at Changi, the doctor was called, and he diagnosed food poisoning. Bill borrowed a co-pilot from another crew that was in transit to take part in an air display the following day, whilst I was confined to bed.

The high point of my time as a transport pilot came in early 1962 when the Western Allies got a bit edgy about Soviet MiGs buzzing civil airliners whilst they were flying into and out of Berlin along the corridors. The Berlin Wall had been erected the previous year, and now the Russians had threatened to close the corridors and to shoot down any aircraft which failed to comply. So it was decided that RAF pilots would stand by to fly BEA Viscounts empty in and out of Berlin, should the need arise to call the Russian bluff. Air Ministry having conceded that we could fly these aircraft without a navigator, flight engineer or a signaller!

I teamed up with Mo Moorhouse, and we were sent to the BEA Ground School at Heston for a couple of weeks. After attending the technical lectures, and doing a few hours on the simulator, we flew with Captain Gaine to Stansted for flying training on the Viscount 800. I use the term training loosely as, when we arrived at Stansted, we discovered that Mo as captain was to get one hour's dual in the circuit, and me as his co-pilot was to get nothing, nor even an invitation to sit in the co-pilot's seat! We both said this was unacceptable, and not the way we operated in Transport Command. After a bit of 'argy-bargy' it was agreed I could do two circuits – big deal!

A few days later we flew out as supernumerary crew on a scheduled service to Tempelhof Airport in Berlin, where we were given rooms in the Kempinski Hotel along with the BEA pilots. Each morning we would potter off down to the airport to collect our BEA daily allowances and to be briefed on the latest situation. Were we going today or not? But nothing happened – perhaps the Russians knew we were there! Most of our time was spent eating, drinking and frequenting night clubs for three weeks. A great life!

After returning to Lyneham my next trip was with Bill Eglington to Uganda. We were to take part in their Independence Day celebrations. We landed at Entebbe, and were booked into the Lake Victoria Hotel. The group captain in charge of the detachment said we had two days to rehearse a low-flypast over 20 towns and villages.

The low flying was a piece of cake – to me anyway, but the rest of the crew were not so enthusiastic. On the first practice, we encountered severe turbulence, and poor old 'Squire' More-combe, our navigator, was sick all over his charts and spent the rest of the trip in the loo. It was nearly all pilot navigation anyway, although that was not so easy as it was mainly over jungle, with no roads, railway lines and little in the way of townships. Plus we had another difficulty – it was almost impossible to see the ground over the nose of the Britannia. There were also other factors to consider. The fly-past was to finish overhead a large stadium in Kampala at a predetermined time, in company with a Vulcan bomber and four Hunters. Although it had the makings of a gigantic cock-up, it did go off quite well, despite the fact that we had to fly balls-out at 250 kts in order to make life as easy as possible for our friends.

The next month we were 'gun running' to the Indians in support of their border conflict with the Chinese, refuelling at Nicosia, routing over southern Turkey and Iran, and then running down the Gulf to Sharjah where we slipped crews and had a 12-hour daylight kip before picking up the following aircraft and taking it into Delhi at night. Then a quick turnround and back to Sharjah for another stopover before returning the same way to the UK.

When the crewing schedules went up for December 1962 I discovered that I had been rostered for the Changi Slip over Christmas, with a trip up to Hong Kong on Boxing Day. This came as a bit of a surprise as I had only been married three months. I stuck my head in the boss's office and, before I had time to open my mouth, he said

"I know what you are going to say, but I'm sorry I can't change it. But you can, if you wish, take your wife with you if you pay for her accommodation and food."

That seemed a fair deal, so off we went.

As it happened, the winter of 1962\63 was particularly severe, and homeward bound on the slip on New Year's Eve we got as far as El Adem, but were unable to fly the last leg because heavy snowfalls in the UK had closed most airfields including Lyneham. We savoured the delights of El Adem for four days before getting a signal say 'all was clear – come on home lads.'

Off we went but, as we crossed the Channel, we were told by the airways controller that Lyneham had more snow, and we were to divert to Heathrow, which we did, spending the night in a hotel at Stanwell. Lyneham was on the phone the next morning to say the runway was now clear again, so we set off once more and flew off-airways with London Radar until passing Reading, when we were able to contact Lynham Approach. We were told the weather had deteriorated again and they now had a cloud base of 400 ft with moderate to heavy snow showers, and a visibility of 500yds. To add to our problems, we were told that we would be the first aircraft to land at Lyneham for five days, and to take care on landing as they had four-foot high banks of snow on each side of the runway. They also said the runway was snow-covered, and the braking action was poor!

It was the captain's leg (fortunately) and we were cleared for a GCA approach on runway 07. The standard procedure was for the pilot flying the aircraft to stay on instruments, obeying the instructions from the GCA talkdown, and then to look ahead and land after the monitoring pilot had called that the runway lights were in sight. We proceeded down a rather turbulent glide-path and, as the runway lights came into view at 300 ft I called

"Runway ahead",

Whereupon the captain said, "You have control!"

This came as something of a surprise to me, but as it was not the time for a discussion I acknowledged, "I have control," as I grabbed the control column and popped the aircraft down. No question of touching the brakes, but the engineer got the props into reverse pretty pronto, and we came to a safe stop. The captain looked relieved… and he'll be even more relieved that his name is safe with me!

The distinction between civil first officers and military co-pilots was graphically illustrated by the length of time each had to wait for a command. A co-pilot on RAF Britannias could be a captain (but still a Flight Lieutenant) after three years. With state airlines it could be a soul-destroying ten-year wait.

At the end of my third year on the squadron, my boss, John Lewis, called me in for my annual appraisal. He said I would be eligible for a command in three months, but to be put on the course I would need to extend my engagement for a further four years. The RAF were not prepared to incur the cost of my command training if they were only to get one year's further service from me, and I could see the logic in their thinking.

I was beginning to like the flying, because it was so easy, but I was also keen to seek other opportunities outside the RAF. There was another factor; to extend my engagement by four years I would need to change to a Branch Commission, which meant I would get a pension but loose my £4,000 gratuity. I gave it very careful thought, and decided that now was perhaps the time to 'call it a day' and have a normal family life. So I accepted that I would remain a co-pilot in the right-hand seat, all fat dumb and happy, until my time was up.

Some of the chaps on the squadron always seemed to get the best trips, usually those going West-about. They were known as the 'country club', others never seemed to be off the Changi Slip. I never quite made it into the 'club', but on becoming the longest serving co-pilot on the squadron, I did manage a few specials. In April 1963 I was crewed up with Squadron Leader 'Chick' Chamberlain to take cadets from the RAF College Cranwell on a tour of the USA.

We flew up to Cranwell the night before, and it brought back memories of my time as a sprog officer cadet 11 years previously. The next day we flew to Gander in Newfoundland to refuel, and then continued to Andrews Air Force Base just outside Washington, the home of the President's aircraft – Air Force One. There was a reception for us at the British Embassy and we stayed in Washington for three days.

The next leg took us to Offutt AFB in Nebraska, to be shown around a very deep hole in the ground which was the headquarters and control centre of the Strategic Air Command. Four hours later, we continued onto Peterson AFB at Colorado Springs, where we were the guests of the United States Air Force Academy for four days. We then flew back to McGuire AFB near New York for a three-day stopover. On this leg we experience some pretty severe turbulence which seemed to get worse the nearer we got the destination. Then two things happened. We lost an engine, and my nav bag was hurled across the flight deck, smashing a bottle of Jack Daniels which I was taking home. We told air traffic of our predicament and were cleared for a priority landing at McGuire. As we approached the runway, we could see a bevy of fire engines and ambulances positioned on either side of the runway. On touchdown 130 budding Air Rank cadets in the back all burst into spontaneous applause. Sadly, though, they were whisked off to some function or other before being able to buy the beers!

We stayed in New York for three days whilst somehow the RAF managed to get a new engine out to us. On the last leg we flew direct from McGuire to Waddington in just under 11 hours.

About this time the RAF was getting rather concerned about the number of refusals we were getting to requests to over-fly some countries, especially in the Middle East, so it was decided that we should have some practice at polar navigation. This had little or no effect on the pilots, as in most cases we blindly followed instructions from the navigator, but we did take a bit more than a passing interest in this exercise. We were scheduled to fly from Lynham direct to overhead the North Pole, and then come back down to the US Air Force Base at Thule in Greenland for a night stop. Nine hours of flying over some pretty inhospitable territory with little or no diversions should an emergency arise. We seemed to be flying for hours in white-out conditions with no clear horizon until the nav said

"Five minutes to the Pole!"

Thank God for that we thought, now let's head for Thule and a stiff drink.

Then, as from nowhere, a voice came over the RT;

"Rafair 2301 confirm your position"

"Roger we're over the Pole at this time"

"OK Sir, we have you contact, and you're clear to Thule, as planned – good day"

Where was he, down a hole in the ice? We never knew.

Not long after that, Frank Baker and myself, with George Dobson as navigator, put this training to good use by flying a great-circle route from Edmonton in Canada direct to Lyneham. We saw the Sun set over the polar region, and ten minutes later saw the Sun rise again on another day. The total flight time was 12 hrs 15 min. This was achieved only by flight planning to Prestwick and nominating Lyneham as an alternate. When approaching Prestwick at 30,000 ft and, after checking our fuel state and the weather, we 'diverted' to Lyneham. This enabled us to do the last part of the flight using the fuel reserves earmarked for diversion purposes, a procedure often adopted by civilian airlines at the time.

My ever increasing seniority as a co-pilot meant I was rostered to fly with the boss, John Lewis on numerous occasions when he went out on route, as well as with the Station Commander, Group Captain Steedman. I also became a popular choice with my contemporaries, who had just completed the conversion to captain and who wanted someone with experience in the right-hand seat whilst getting to grips with their new command status. Finally I did route trainers to Hong Kong with the Air Training Squadron teach new co-pilots the tricks of the trade.

My last flight in the RAF was on February 21st 1964 when, with Jim Cresswell, I did a trip to Akrotiri in Cyprus. We night-stopped and returned to Lyneham the next day. For old time's sake, Jim let me fly both legs.

I got my clearance chit signed, picked up my £4,000 and walked out of the gate. It had been better than doing National Service down the mines!

APPENDIX A

Gloster Meteor Fatal Crashes

890 Meteors crashed, killing 434 pilots and 10 navigators. The following details relating to these fatalities have been compiled from the Accident Record Cards at the RAF Museum, Hendon, and from squadron ORB's at the Public Records Office, Kew.

Pre-production aircraft (F9/40) and test flights by manufacturers and sub contractors, although small in number, have been included as they contribute to the overall pattern of the crashes.

Serial	Mk	Sqn/Unit	Date	Cause
EE226	1	616 Sqn	15/07/44	Stalled on approach
EE273	3	616 Sqn	29/04/45	Collided in formation in cloud
EE252	3	616 Sqn	29/04/45	Collided in formation in cloud
EE238	3	RAE	18/05/45	Crashed doing low level aerobatics
EE288	3	504 Sqn	08/06/45	Lost control and spun in
EE308	3	74 Sqn	24/07/45	Flew into trees while low flying
EE280	3	504 Sqn	23/08/45	Mid air collision
EE302	3	245 Sqn	08/10/45	Lost control and spun in
EE316	3	1335 Flt	20/11/45	Pilot lost on unauthorised night flight
EE313	3	1335 Flt	28/11/45	Lost control and spun in
EE335	3	74 Sqn	02/01/46	Hit ground during low level beat up
EE390	3	124 Sqn	15/01/46	Mid air collision with EE392
EE392	3	124 Sqn	15/01/46	Mid air collision with EE390
EE448	3	222 Sqn	01/02/46	Lost control and spun in
EE456	3	EFS	12/02/46	Lost control and spun in
EE344	3	74 Sqn	08/03/46	Crashed during unauthorised beat up
EE293	3	245 Sqn	23/04/46	Crashed on s/e approach
EE518	4	MU	05/05/46	Aircraft broke up in flight

EE295	3	222 Sqn	01/06/46	Hit high ground in fog
EE312	3	222 Sqn	02/07/46	Lost control and spun in
EE334	3	74 Sqn	10/07/46	Mid air collision
EE538	4	MU	13/09/46	Lost control and spun in
EE490	3	CGS	13/09/46	Aircraft broke up in flight
EE338	3	PRDU	10/10/46	Lost control and spun in
EE343	3	263 Sqn	11/11/46	Missing over North Sea
EE422	3	222 Sqn	17/03/47	Lost control and spun in
EE394	3	GAC	22/04/47	Crashed on approach
EE411	3	266 Sqn	16/06/47	Lost control and spun in
EE353	3	74 Sqn	24/09/47	Crashed on s/e approach
EE385	3	56 Sqn	23/10/47	Aircraft broke up doing beat up
RA482	4	38 MU	16/03/48	Lost control and spun in
EE453	3	92 Sqn	19/03/48	Target fixation during ground attack
VT108	4	RAE	29/04/48	Ran out of fuel and crashed
VT126	4	245 Sqn	04/05/48	Flew into high ground
RA477	4	CFE	04/06/48	Lost control and spun in
RA450	4	222 Sqn	26/08/48	Lost control and spun in
EE461	3	1 Sqn	24/09/48	Mid air collision with Tiger Moth
VT123	4	245 Sqn	05/01/49	Ran out of fuel and crashed
VW782	4	CFS	27/01/49	Crashed during overshoot
VW789	4	CFE	24/02/49	Crashed during overshoot
VT140	4	1 Sqn	28/02/49	Lost control and spun in
RA382	4	AAEE	05/03/49	Lost control and spun in
VT347	4	GAC	15/06/49	Broke up during first flight
VT247	4	222 Sqn	02/09/49	Crashed doing low level aerobatics
VW434	7	56 Sqn	14/10/49	Flew into high ground – two pilots killed
VW448	7	226 OCU	15/11/49	Lost control in cloud after t/o
VT320	4	257 Sqn	21/11/49	Target fixation during ground attack
VW476	7	226 OCU	23/11/49	Stalled on approach
VT124	4	245 Sqn	23/11/49	Mid air collision with Proctor
VT238	4	43 Sqn	25/11/49	Crashed into high ground with VT276
VT276	4	43 Sqn	25/11/49	Crashed into high ground with VT238
VW788	4	203 AFS	02/02/50	Stalled on approach
VT267	4	226 OCU	21/03/50	Mid air collision with RA374
RA374	4	226 OCU	21/03/50	Mid air collision with VT267
VW277	4	56 Sqn	29/03/50	Crashed doing low level formation aerobatics
VW481	7	CFS	05/04/50	Crashed doing s/e approach

RA372	4	226 OCU	12/04/50	Lost control doing s/e circuit
VZ410	4	245 Sqn	13/04/50	Lost control and spun in
VT243	4	1 Sqn	19/04/50	Collided with VT146 doing formation aerobatics
VT146	4	1 Sqn	19/04/50	Collided with VT243 doing formation aerobatics
VW287	4	226 OCU	24/04/50	Lost control in cloud and broke up
VT185	4	Comms	24/04/50	Grp Capt lost control and spun in
VW440	7	226 OCU	26/04/50	Stalled on approach
WA616	7	MEAF	28/04/50	Lost control and spun in – two pilots killed
VT234	4	CFE	09/05/50	Hit sea while in formation
VW267	4	92 Sqn	14/05/50	Ran out of fuel and baled out but hit tail
VT173	4	1 Sqn	26/05/50	Crashed doing s/e approach
VT213	4	63 Sqn	04/07/50	Stalled on GCA approach
VW484	7	245 Sqn	06/07/50	Lost control and spun in – two pilots killed
RA422	4	203 AFS	17/08/50	Overshooting s/e with airbrakes out
VT198	4	63 Sqn	28/08/50	Stalled on approach
VW431	7	ITF	14/09/50	Collided with F84D USAF
WA614	7	203 AFS	27/09/50	Ran out of fuel over sea – two pilots killed
VW292	4	203 AFS	28/09/50	Overshooting s/e with airbrakes out
EE290	3	500 Sqn	14/10/50	Mid air collision
WA673	7	CFS	30/10/50	Lost control and spun in – two pilots killed
EE599	4	205 AFS	30/11/50	Ran out of fuel on second solo
VZ558	8	74 Sqn	07/12/50	Lost control on approach at night
VT342	4	TFU	21/12/50	Lost control and spun in
VZ449	8	74 Sqn	05/01/51	Lost control and spun in
EE550	4	615 Sqn	06/01/51	Lost control and spun in
VZ469	8	43 Sqn	19/01/51	Hit sea low flying
VW255	4	205 AFS	25/01/51	Lost control and spun in
VW474	7	203 AFS	14/02/51	Lost control and spun in – two pilots killed
VZ498	8	245 Sqn	16/02/51	Ran out of fuel and crashed in sea
VW289	4	226 OCU	23/02/51	Crashed after t/o
WA677	7	205 AFS	27/02/51	Lost control and spun in – two pilots killed
VZ404	4	504 Sqn	18/03/51	Lost control and spun in

WA791	8	66 Sqn	12/04/51	Flew into ground in formation
VZ518	8	66 Sqn	12/04/51	Flew into ground in formation
VZ527	8	66 Sqn	17/04/51	Broke up during low beat up
VT102	4	615 Sqn	30/04/51	Lost control on GCA approach
WE933	8	64 Sqn	06/05/51	Lost control and spun in
WA827	8	245 Sqn	19/05/51	Lost control after engine failure
VT189	4	226 OCU	28/05/51	Target fixation during ground attack
VT281	4	600 Sqn	18/06/51	Mid air collision on break for landing
VT275	4	600 Sqn	18/06/51	Mid air collision on break for landing
WB110	8	41 Sqn	18/06/51	Lost control after t/o
VT239	4	205 AFS	19/06/51	Lost control and spun in
VZ509	8	74 Sqn	19/06/51	Lost control and spun in
WA877	8	66 Sqn	20/06/51	Broke up in flight
VW438	7	602 Sqn	23/06/51	Ran out of fuel on first solo
WA771	8	56 Sqn	24/06/51	Crashed on approach
VT246	4	226 OCU	27/06/51	Target fixation during ground attack
WA953	8	56 Sqn	27/06/51	Sqn CO doing low level beat up
VZ569	8	65 Sqn	03/07/51	Mid air collision – pilot ejected too late
EE584	4	504 Sqn	07/07/51	Ran out of fuel
VZ418	4	205 AFS	10/07/51	Lost control and spun in
VT121	4	611 Sqn	22/07/51	Flew into high ground
WF790	7	4 Sqn	19/08/51	Low level aeros – pilot and airman killed
WA843	8	92 Sqn	23/08/51	Spun in after oxygen problem
VZ510	8	263 Sqn	10/09/51	Broke up on test flight
WE869	8	63 Sqn	15/09/51	Mid air collision – pilot ejected too late
WF842	7	612 Sqn	17/09/51	Lost control and spun in – two pilots killed
VZ581	9	208 Sqn	17/09/51	Lost control and spun in
VT324	4	205 AFS	25/09/51	Lost control and spun in
VT307	4	203 AFS	05/10/51	Flew into cliffs in formation
VW301	4	203 AFS	05/10/51	Flew into cliffs in formation
WA787	8	263 Sqn	10/10/51	Crashed shortly after t/o
VT278	4	226 OCU	25/10/51	Lost control and spun in
VZ497	8	56 Sqn	01/11/51	Collision on runway with WA940
WA940	8	63 Sqn	01/11/51	Collision on runway with VZ497
WF767	7	203 AFS	30/11/51	Crashed during night t/o – two pilots killed
VZ587	9	2 Sqn	04/12/51	Hit ground low flying
VT339	4	226 OCU	07/12/51	Broke up low flying

VW304	4	203 AFS	20/12/51	Tail knocked off in circuit
EE332	3	206 AFS	04/01/52	Broke up doing low level high speed run
WA759	8	92 Sqn	07/01/52	Mid air collision in circuit
WE868	8	19 Sqn	20/01/52	Mid air collision
WA882	8	222 Sqn	12/02/52	Flew into high ground
WH232	7	Stn Flt	21/02/52	Lost control on s/e approach
WA726	7	500 Sqn	24/02/52	Crashed in circuit
WE937	8	64 Sqn	29/02/52	Lost control and spun in
WH342	8	66 Sqn	29/02/52	Mid air collision
VT326	4	203 AFS	04/03/52	Flew into high ground
WE888	8	56 Sqn	04/03/52	Crashed doing low level aerobatics
VT283	4	203 AFS	14/03/52	Hit trees on approach
VZ411	4	226 OCU	01/04/52	Lost control and spun in
VW269	4	203 AFS	24/04/52	Lost control and spun in over sea
WA665	7	205 AFS	24/04/52	Broke up in cloud
EE417	3	206 AFS	29/04/52	Unauthorised aerobatics over home
VW298	4	205 AFS	29/04/52	Collided with RA480 in circuit at night
RA480	4	205 AFS	29/04/52	Collided with VW298 in circuit at night
VZ643	7	607 Sqn	05/05/52	Lost control – pilot baled out but was drowned
WB119	9	79 Sqn	05/05/52	Target fixation during ground attack
WH167	7	207 AFS	13/05/52	Crashed on approach
WA679	7	RAFFC	16/05/52	Crashed overshooting – two pilots killed
WD607	11	141 Sqn	20/05/52	Mid air collision – navigator drowned
VT176	4	203 AFS	21/05/52	Crashed on night t/o
WF745	8	CGS	21/05/52	Lost control and spun in
WF854	7	65 Sqn	28/05/52	Lost control and spun in – two pilots killed
WB158	10	231 OCU	28/05/52	Crashed during overshoot
VT336	4	207 AFS	06/06/52	Lost control and spun in
WB161	10	13 Sqn	07/06/52	Air Marshall Atcherley missing off Cyprus
VT344	4	203 AFS	17/06/52	Crashed on night t/o
EE414	3	206 AFS	24/06/52	Broke up in flight
WE861	8	226 OCU	26/06/52	Lost control and spun in
WH130	7	203 AFS	16/07/52	Mid air collision
WD716	11	228 OCU	19/07/52	Ran out of fuel – pilot and Navigator drowned

WD608	11	141 Sqn	24/07/52	Lost control and spun in – air to air on flag
RA369	4	215 AFS	24/07/52	Lost control and spun in
WA821	8	222 Sqn	25/07/52	Flew into high ground
RA376	4	215 AFS	11/08/52	Lost control in formation and spun in
EE491	3	206 AFS	13/08/52	Lost control at night and spun in
WK657	8	92 Sqn	14/08/52	Sqn CO crashed doing aerobatics
WD714	11	228 OCU	19/08/52	Mid air collision – pilot and navigator killed
RA429	4	205 AFS	20/08/52	Lost control doing aerobatics
VZ542	8	Stn Flt	09/09/52	Crashed practising for aerobatic display
WA822	8	66 Sqn	09/09/52	Lost leader in cloud and spun in
EE401	3	206 AFS	09/09/52	Mid air collision
VT127	4	203 AFS	16/09/52	Crashed doing low level aerobatics
WL454	7	20 MU	17/09/52	Hit ground during formation flypast
WL409	7	Stn Flt	24/09/52	Hit high ground with no R/T
EE528	4	205 AFS	26/09/52	Lost control and spun in over sea
WH472	8	263 Sqn	29/09/52	Flew into high ground
WK749	8	72 Sqn	17/10/52	Mid air collision with WK690
WK690	8	72 Sqn	17/10/52	Mid air collision with WK749
VZ461	8	43 Sqn	22/10/52	Lost leader in cloud and spun in
VZ563	8	63 Sqn	22/10/52	Lost control and spun in doing PI's
VW268	4	205 AFS	27/10/52	Lost control and spun in
WH362	8	226 OCU	04/11/52	Mid air collision with leader after t/o
WL433	7	209 AFS	07/11/52	Lost control and spun in – two pilots killed
WF823	7	CFE	07/11/52	Hood came off – two pilots killed
WE914	8	245 Sqn	17/11/52	Crashed practising s/e landing
WD723	11	228 OCU	17/11/52	Broke up in flight near Sunderland
VZ428	4	215 AFS	21/11/52	Lost control and spun into mud flats
WL402	7	211 AFS	04/12/52	Lost control s/e flying – two pilots killed
WH473	8	616 Sqn	11/12/52	Mid air collision at night with WH455
WH455	8	616 Sqn	11/12/52	Mid air collision at night with WH463
WF774	7	66 Sqn	12/12/52	Practice engine failure on t/o – two pilots killed
WG978	7	206 AFS	18/12/52	Collided with leader during t/o
WH442	8	247 Sqn	18/12/52	Mid air collision
VW365	9	2 Sqn	18/12/52	Crashed in circuit

WF852	7	CFS	31/12/52	Crashed during CFS Aerobatic Competition
WL365	7	205 AFS	02/01/53	Lost control and spun in
WG981	7	206 AFS	03/01/53	Hood came off – two pilots killed
VW283	4	207 AFS	02/02/53	Missing over sea
VT265	4	206 AFS	02/02/53	Lost control and spun in on first solo
VW282	4	203 AFS	02/02/53	Missing off Flamborough Head
WK924	8	211 AFS	04/02/53	Lost control and spun in
WL455	7	209 AFS	09/02/53	Lost control and spun in – two pilots killed
VS983	10	541 Sqn	11/02/53	Crashed on GCA approach
WA839	8	43 Sqn	22/02/53	Lost control and spun in at night
WH311	8	226 OCU	25/02/53	Lost control and ejected but was too late
WL381	7	CFS	25/02/53	Crashed doing low level aero's – two pilots killed
VT304	4	209 AFS	11/03/53	Missing over sea
WH351	8	19 Sqn	18/03/53	Mid air collision on flypast for Marshall Tito
WK858	8	19 Sqn	18/03/53	Mid air collision on flypast for Marshall Tito
WD676	11	68 Sqn	19/03/53	Lost control – navigator baled out – pilot killed
WH358	8	CFE	24/03/53	Missing over North Sea
WF760	8	615 Sqn	29/03/53	Lost control in cloud and spun in
WG972	7	231 OCU	07/04/53	Crashed during overshoot at night
WH347	8	CGS	13/04/53	Broke up in flight
VZ501	8	72 Sqn	17/04/53	Lost control and spun in
WG989	7	206 OCU	20/04/53	Lost control and crashed in circuit
WF747	8	600 Sqn	25/04/53	Lost control and spun in without hood
WH246	7	205 AFS	04/05/53	Crashed into radio mast – two pilots killed
VZ446	8	74 Sqn	05/05/53	Target fixation during ground attack
WF821	7	64 Sqn	16/05/53	Crashed in North Sea – two pilots missing
WK929	8	211 Sqn	19/05/53	Crashed shortly after t/o
WM258	11	264 Sqn	13/06/53	Hit high ground – Sqn CO and navigator killed
WG971	7	206 OCU	17/06/53	Crashed night flying
VW483	7	215 OCU	19/06/53	Crashed on s/e approach – two pilots killed

WF775	7	500 Sqn	29/06/53	Crashed on s/e approach – two pilots killed
WE862	8	616 Sqn	03/07/53	Lost control and spun in off Malta
VZ560	8	257 Sqn	08/07/53	Mid air collision with WE862
VZ556	8	257 Sqn	08/07/53	Mid air collision with VZ560
WA735	7	Stn Flt	08/07/53	Stn Cdr at Leuchars killed after hood came off
WX973	9	79 Sqn	16/07/53	Hit trees on approach
VT138	4	215 AFS	21/07/53	Flew into high ground
WK978	8	64 Sqn	22/07/53	Lost control and spun in
WB113	9	79 Sqn	24/07/53	Ran out of fuel
WM222	11	68 Sqn	28/07/53	Crashed into trees
WM146	11	256 Sqn	29/07/53	Mid air collision F86 – navigator killed
WA724	7	141 Sqn	10/08/53	Crashed on GCA approach – two pilots killed
WA856	8	1 Sqn	16/08/53	Mid air collision with WA868
WA868	8	1 Sqn	16/08/53	Mid air collision WA856
VT290	4	JCU	17/08/53	Lost control and spun in
WA758	8	19 Sqn	18/08/53	Flew into high ground
WE964	8	66 Sqn	18/08/53	Broke up in flight
WM177	11	85 Sqn	19/08/53	Lost control and spun in – pilot and nav killed
WK861	8	222 Sqn	22/08/53	Crashed on house formating on leader
WH189	7	87 Sqn	31/08/53	Hit high tension wires – two pilots killed
WE917	8	211 OCU	02/09/53	Lost control and spun in
RA475	4	206 AFS	03/09/53	Lost control and spun in
WF648	8	257 Sqn	04/09/53	Broke up in dive
WA778	8	66 Sqn	04/09/53	Broke up in flight – ejected but too low
WA712	7	209 AFS	08/09/53	Broke up after catching fire at night
WD621	11	256 Sqn	08/09/53	Hit high ground – pilot and navigator killed
WF695	8	Stn Flt	11/09/53	Mid air collision
WA836	8	74 Sqn	19/09/53	Broke up doing aerobatics – ejected too late
WA927	8	56 Sqn	19/09/53	Broke up doing high speed beat up
WF792	7	Stn Flt	25/09/53	Crashed on s/e approach – two pilots killed
WE912	8	616 Sqn	27/09/53	Aircraft on fire – unsuccessful ejection
WH407	8	226 OCU	28/09/53	Crashed doing low level aerobatics
WE856	8	19 Sqn	02/10/53	Broke up during aerobatic display

EE462	3	210 AFS	04/10/53	Crashed doing aerobatics over mums' house
VT303	4	209 AFS	14/10/53	Lost control and spun in
WH467	8	263 Sqn	26/10/53	Spun in after doing PI on bomber
WB118	9	79 Sqn	31/10/53	Hit high ground in cloud
WK886	8	245 Sqn	04/11/53	Sqn CO spun in doing air to air on flag
WK805	8	500 Sqn	07/11/53	Unsuccessful ejection after mid air collision
WL458	7	500 Sqn	09/11/53	Lost control on s/e approach – two pilots killed
WH384	8	610 Sqn	14/11/53	Flew into hill in formation with WH383
WH383	8	610 Sqn	14/11/53	Flew into hill in formation with WH384
WH197	7	215 AFS	09/12/53	Crashed on approach
WA654	7	RAFFC	31/12/53	Aircraft fire – pilot died after baling out
WH288	8	226 OCU	19/01/54	Lost control and spun in
WA632	7	207 AFS	19/01/54	Crashed in circuit on first solo
WM175	11	85 Sqn	21/01/54	Ran out of fuel – pilot and navigator killed
WH298	8	257 Sqn	24/01/54	Lost control and spun in
WH244	7	209 AFS	12/02/54	Hit high ground after being diverted at night
VW430	7	209 AFS	12/02/54	Hit high ground after being diverted at night
WF754	8	600 Sqn	13/02/54	Lost control and spun in
WL430	7	26 Sqn	16/02/54	Lost control on s/e overshoot – two pilots killed
WK692	8	604 Sqn	20/02/54	Mid air collision over North Weald
WK 696	8	604 Sqn	20/02/54	Mid air collision over North Weald
WF815	7	207 AFS	01/03/54	Lost control and spun in – one pilot baled out
WK863	8	245 Sqn	05/03/54	Mid air collision – pilot ejected but too late
WL423	7	209 AFS	12/03/54	Lost control and spun in – two pilots killed
WM248	11	87 Sqn	18/03/54	Lost control and spun in – pilot and nav killed
WD778	11	228 OCU	24/03/54	Ran out of fuel on approach – pilot and nav killed
WL462	7	604 Sqn	03/04/54	Mid air collision with WL462 from 111 Sqn
WB143	9	2 Sqn	08/04/54	Hit ground on army co-op exercise

EE525	4	207 AFS	12/04/54	Lost control – baled out but drowned
WS746	14	85 Sqn	26/04/54	Ran out of fuel – pilot killed
WH278	8	616 Sqn	22/05/54	Lost control and spun in
WH422	8	226 OCU	27/05/54	Lost control after hood shattered
WK906	8	211 AFS	08/06/54	Flew into high ground at night
WH239	7	228 OCU	28/06/54	Lost hood – baled out but too low
WS600	12	85 Sqn	29/06/54	Ran out of fuel – pilot and navigator killed
WE897	8	43 Sqn	24/07/54	Mid air collision
WL374	7	CFS	28/07/54	Mid air collision with WL457 – two pilots killed
WL457	7	CFS	28/07/54	Mid air collision with WL374 – two pilots killed
WK936	8	245 Sqn	09/08/54	Crashed into hanger on ground attack
WA966	8	CFE	16/08/54	Lost control in cloud and spun in
WH458	8	RAFFC	27/08/54	Lost control and spun in
WH190	7	206 AFS	27/08/54	Lost control and spun in
WL343	7	4 FTS	11/09/54	Crashed doing aerobatic display
WH287	8	263 Sqn	13/09/54	Broke up flying low level in battle formation
WH302	8	610 Sqn	18/09/54	Crashed doing aerobatic display
RA365	4	203 Sqn	20/09/54	Lost control doing s/e circuit with airbrakes out
WG973	7	112 Sqn	26/09/54	Crashed during overshoot – two pilots killed
WS691	12	152 Sqn	04/10/54	Mid air collision with F86 – pilot and nav killed
WK679	8	72 Sqn	15/10/54	Crashed after controls jammed in circuit
WM179	11	Stn Flt	21/10/54	Crashed on GCA approach – pilot and nav killed
VT232	4	4 FTS	15/11/54	Engine failure on night t/o
VW302	4	12 FTS	19/11/54	Ran out of fuel
WX974	9	2 Sqn	03/12/54	Lost control and spun in doing PI's
WL363	7	IAM	09/12/54	Lost control and spun in
VW419	7	206 AFS	15/12/54	Hit trees with instrument failure – two pilots killed
WK723	8	CGS	21/12/54	Lost control and spun in
WB108	8	211 AFS	21/12/54	Flew into high ground
WA666	7	12 FTS	10/01/55	Lost control and spun in – two pilots killed

WL342	7	FTU	10/01/55	Crashed shortly after t/o
WF783	7	72 Sqn	11/01/55	Crashed on s/e circuit – two pilots killed
VT115	4	4 FTS	01/02/55	Crashed doing night circuit
WL408	7	12 FTS	02/02/55	Crashed doing low level aeros – two pilots killed
WM169	11	87 Sqn	22/02/55	Crashed on approach – pilot and navigator killed
WE963	8	34 Sqn	03/03/55	Mid air collision with DH Vampire
WH200	7	CFS	09/03/55	Crashed on t/o – two pilots killed
WL354	7	211 AFS	16/03/55	Crashed doing aerobatics – two pilots killed
WL474	7	211 AFS	01/04/55	Crashed during s/e overshoot – two pilots killed
WD754	11	256 Sqn	21/04/55	Crashed on t/o – pilot and navigator killed
WM268	11	141 Sqn	09/05/55	Lost control and spun in – pilot and nav killed
WE904	8	211 AFS	12/05/55	Lost control and spun in
WD605	11	29 Sqn	20/05/55	Lost control and spun in – pilot and nav killed
WE916	8	211 AFS	26/05/55	Lost control at night and spun in
VT263	4	206 AFS	15/06/55	Lost control and spun in
WL265	9	79 Sqn	24/06/55	Ejected but parachute not fastened
WS662	12	153 Sqn	30/06/55	Failed to get airborne – pilot and nav killed
WA891	8	63 Sqn	07/07/55	Flew into cliffs
WK982	8	FWS	15/08/55	Mid air collision with WH395
WH395	8	FWS	15/08/55	Mid air collision with WK982
WH249	8	19 Sqn	27/08/55	Flew into high ground in cloud
WB122	9	79 Sqn	05/09/55	Crashed on approach
WK820	8	245 Sqn	15/09/55	Crashed doing low level aerobatics
WS683	12	AWOCU	21/09/55	Mid air collision with WS621
WS621	12	AWOCU	21/09/55	Mid air collision with WS683
WG947	7	231 OCU	04/11/55	Engine failure on t/o
WS727	12	153 Sqn	09/01/56	Crashed during air display – pilot and nav killed
WS661	12	AWOCU	20/01/56	Aero's over parents home – pilot and nav killed
WS694	12	152 Sqn	16/04/56	Crashed over sea – pilot and navigator missing

WE895	8	609 Sqn	22/04/56	Lost control and ejected but too late
WH355	8	FWS	28/06/56	Lost control and spun in
WH280	8	615 Sqn	26/08/56	Mid air collision
WE853	8	615 Sqn	26/08/56	Mid air collision
WK985	8	608 Sqn	27/08/56	Ran out of fuel – died after ejecting through hood
WK 787	8	Stn Flt	11/09/56	Crashed during Battle of Britain display
WL137	8	41 Sqn	05/10/56	Lost control and spun in
WA855	8	41 Sqn	13/10/56	Lost control and ejected too late
WM314	13	39 Sqn	06/12/56	Crashed on approach
WF848	7	FECS	21/12/56	AVM Braithwaite crashed in bad weather
WE974	8	74 Sqn	03/01/57	Mid air collision – killed ejecting through hood
WA879	8	74 Sqn	03/01/57	Failed ejection following mid air collision
WK681	8	65 Sqn	04/01/57	Crashed after hitting tree
WE887	8	233 OCU	14/01/57	Mid air collision with WH457
WH457	8	233 OCU	14/01/57	Mid air collision – killed ejecting through hood
WS753	14	25 Sqn	04/02/57	Flew into high ground – pilot and navigator killed
VW370	9	208 Sqn	27/03/57	Ejected whilst on fire but too late
VW432	7	208 Sqn	05/04/57	Crashed in circuit
WL410	7	FWS	12/04/57	Crashed on s/e approach
WG961	7	Stn Flt	27/06/57	Crashed on s/e approach – two pilots killed
VW488	7	Comms	08/08/57	Crashed on t/o – two pilots killed
WA794	8	CAACU	11/10/57	Flew into hill in bad weather
WL368	7	CFE	18/10/57	Pax had suitcase on lap – pilot and pax killed
WH204	7	Comms	21/11/57	Crashed on s/e approach
WS782	14	85 Sqn	04/03/58	Mid air collision – pilot and navigator killed
WS700	12	72 Sqn	04/03/58	Mid air collision – pilot and navigator killed
WL359	7	4 FTS	21/04/58	Crashed performing low level aerobatics
WH206	7	Stn Flt	20/01/59	Ran out of fuel – one pilot baled out – one killed
WL478	7	RAFFC	19/02/59	Crashed on s/e approach

WL480	7	Comms	15/07/59	AVM Embling stalled overshooting with flaps up
WF835	7	228 OCU	02/10/59	Lost control – one pilot baled out – one killed
WF766	7	AAEE	11/11/60	Broke up and crashed after t/o
WF771	7	RAFFC	29/01/62	Crashed after t/o – both pilots killed
WG962	7	CFS	26/06/62	Engine failure on t/o – two pilots killed
WH231	7	ETPS	11/03/65	Lost control on s/e approach
XF274	7	RAE	14/02/75	Crashed attempting s/e roller! – two pilots killed
N/K	7	BoB Flt	25/05/86	Mid air collision with DH Vampire at display

Fighter Pilot Slang & RAF Terminology

Air Box	Air Ministry
Angels	Altitude in 1,000's ft
Avgas	Aviation petrol
Avtag	Jet Fuel
Avtur	Jet fuel
Balbo	Large formation of aircraft
Balls-out	Max speed
Bandit	Enemy aircraft
Bang-out	Eject
Big chop	Killed
Bingo	Fuel check
Blood Waggon	Ambulance
Bogy	Unidentified target
Bought-it	Killed
Brahma	Good looking woman
Break	Hard turn to avoid attacker
Brown job	Army officer
Buster Buster	Full throttle
Chicks	A number of fighters in a formation
Chiefy	Flight Sergeant
Chopped	Taken off a course
Clag	Bad weather
Clampers	Bad weather – no flying
Close hanger doors	Stop talking shop
CRDF	Cathode Ray Direction Finding

Deck	The ground
Ditch	Crash in sea
Dock	Sick Quarters
Driver airframe	Pilot
Duff gen	Incorrect information
Erk	Airman
ETA	Estimated Time of Arrival
ETD	Estimated Time of Departure
Fish head	Officer RN
Fly a desk	Desk bound job
Gash	Spare
GCA	Ground Controlled Approach
GCI	Ground Controlled Interception
Gear	Undercarriage
Gone for a Burton	Killed or disappeared
Goolie chit	Carried by aircrew in the Middle East
Got the chop	Suspended or killed
Gremlin	Bug in system
Griff	Information
Hairy	NCO aircrew
Hit the silk	Bale out
Irons	Khife fork and spoon
Jet Jockey	Jet pilot
Line shoot	Boasting
Loiter	Standing patrol
Mae West	Life jacket
NDB	Non Directional Beacon
Nylon let down	Parachute descent
PI	Practice Interception
Pigeons	Heading and distance to base
Pit	Bed
Plumbers	Ground crew
Pongo	Army officer
Prang	Crash
QDM	Magnetic bearing to a station
QDR	Magnetic bearing from a station
QFE	Altimeter setting height above airfield

QNH	Altimeter setting height above sea level
Queen Bee	Senior WRAF officer
RMI	Radio Magnetic Indicator
Rock Apes	RAF Regiment
Roger	Acknowledgement
Rubarb	Low level strike
Scramble	Get airborne quickly
Scrambled Egg	Gold braid on senior officers hat
Scraper	Sqn Ldr's thin ring
Scrub round	Leave alone
Scrubbed	Stopped or taken off course
Sit Rep	Situation Report
Slope off	Quietly disappear
SOP	Standard Operating Proceedure
Sprog	New boy
Station Master	Station Commander
Tally Ho	Contact with target
Tit	Push button
Trade	Target to be intercepted
Trapper	Examiner from CFS
Trolley acc	Ground start battery
Vector	Heading to steer
Wad	Roll or sandwich
Wilco	Will comply
Wizard	Very good

APPENDIX C

Bibliography

Archives Department, Royal Air Force Museum, Heston

Public Records Office, Kew. AIR 27. Squadron ORB's

The Royal Air Force, Air Chief Marshall Sir Michael Armitage. Arms & Armour Press

RAF Fighter Command 1936-1968, Norman Franks. Patrick Stephens Ltd 1992

Meteor, Bryan Philpott. Patrick Stephens Ltd 1986.

Meteor, Steven Bond. Midland Counties Publications Ltd 1985.

Sir James Martin, Sarah Sharman. Patrick Stevens Ltd 1996.

RAF Fighter Command Instrument Rating Sqn Examiners Questions and Answers.

Hussein of Jordan, James Lunt. Macmillan London Ltd 1989

The Luftwaffe War Diaries, Cajus Beckker. MacDonald & Co 1967

Uneasy Lies The Head, King Hussein of Jordan. William Heinemann Ltd.

Testing Early Jets. Wing Commander R P Beamont, CBE, DSO, DFC, FRAeS

Fighter Test Pilot. Wing Commander R P Beamont CBE, DSO, DFC, FRAeS Patrick Stevens Ltd 1986.

Epilogue

After leaving the Royal Air Force the author became the landlord of the Bear Inn at Henley-onThames. But he soon missed the world of aviation and after having his application for a civil pilots licence turned down on medical grounds he looked at other opportunities. Eventually he joined BOAC, as it was then, as a simulated flight instructor, working on the VC 10 and B707 flight simulators, then after the merger with BEA he took on the Trident 3. He also conducted refresher courses on instrument rating renewal proceedures, for BA captains prior to them attending the CAA instrument rating examiners course with the Civil Aviation Flying Unit at Stansted.

Leaving BA in 1980 he became a freelance air charter broker for BBC TV News where he was instrumental in the coverage of such incidents as the Manchester prison riots, the Hillsborough football disaster, the Hungerford massacre, the Zeebrugge ferry

Nick Carter, in 2000.

sinking, the Pan Am B747 crashing on Lockerbie, the British Midland aircraft crashing on the Ml and Richard Branson's balloon sinking off the coast of Scotland. to name but a few. Later he went on to act in a similar capacity for Sky News and a number of foreign news gathering organisations. He also had an office supplies business until his eventual retirement in 1995.

Then last year, after 40 years, he was invited back to Jordan as a guest of the Royal Jordanian Air Force where he met Princess Muna, mother of the present king of Jordan, King Abdullah, and her second son, Prince Feisal, who commands one of the RJAF squadrons. At a cocktail party at the home of the British Air Attaché he was reunited with three of the Jordanian pilots who had been with him on No. 1 Squadron RJAF flying Hawker Hunters, and who he had not seen for forty years. Saleh Kurdi having retired as the Commander-in-chief of the RJAF, Nasri Jimiean just about to retire as Vice President Royal Jordanian Airlines and personal pilot to HM King Hussein and Fakhri Abuhmaidan ex Royal Jordanian Airlines and now resident in the USA.

Nick Carter now lives in retirement in the riverside town of Maidenhead in Berkshire where he is an active member of the local Rotary Club.

Meteors of 257 Squadron.

Photo courtesy of MoD.